CAVALIERS

CAVALIERS

*The Royalist Army
at War 1642–1646*

JOHN BARRATT

SUTTON PUBLISHING

First published in 2000 by
Sutton Publishing Limited · Phoenix Mill
Thrupp · Stroud · Gloucestershire · GL5 2BU

This paperback edition first published in 2004

British Library Cataloguing in Publication Data
A catalogue record for this book is available from the British
Library

ISBN 0 7509 3525 1

Typeset in 10/12 pt Photina.
Typesetting and origination by
Sutton Publishing Limited.
Printed and bound in England by
J.H. Haynes & Co. Ltd, Sparkford.

CONTENTS

ACKNOWLEDGEMENTS

It is a pleasant task to record my thanks to the many individuals and institutions who have in their various ways assisted in this project – perhaps beginning with the producer and cast of a 1950s television version of 'Children of the New Forest', who between them kindled the spark of what was to become a lifetime interest!

Librarians are generally a long-suffering, patient yet resourceful species, and I have sorely tried the endurance and abilities of the staff of, among others, the Bodleian Library, the British Library, the Sydney Jones Library University of Liverpool, Liverpool Record Office, Wirral Libraries and Cheshire County Record Office. They have never failed me. Thanks are also due to all at Sutton Publishing, especially Jane Crompton and Clare Bishop.

The proceedings, over more than ten years, of the Partizan Press English Civil Conferences and, perhaps even more, the convivial and lively discussion sessions that accompany them (and often extend into the wee small hours), have been a rich source of inspiration, stimulation and information. Thanks are due to all of the participants, who must now total hundreds, but especially to Ivor Carr, Les Prince, Stuart Reid, Keith Roberts, Dave Ryan, John Tincey and Alan Turton. Many of their researches and theories have found their way into these pages; the errors and omissions remain my own.

John Barratt
July 2000

CHRONOLOGY

1639
First Bishops' War ends in reverse for Charles I

1640
13 April–5 May   First 'Short Parliament'

Second Bishops' War

20 August	Scottish Covenanting army crosses River Tweed
28 August	Battle of Newburn: Covenanting victory
16–26 October	Treaties of Ripon effectively end war
1 November	'Long Parliament' meets
11 November	Earl of Strafford impeached

1641

15 February	Triennial Parliament Bill calls for a Parliament to be held at least every three years
12 May	Strafford executed
24 June	'Ten Propositions' of Parliament propose curbs in royal powers
22 October	Outbreak of rebellion in Ulster
11 November	Earl of Ormonde made Lieutenant General of government forces in Ireland
1 December	'Grand Remonstrance' of Parliament presented to King

1642

January	Attempt by King to arrest 'Five Members' fails; Charles leaves London

February	Queen Henrietta Maria goes to Holland
5 March	Parliament passes Militia Ordinance to take control of militia from King
18 March	King establishes Court at York
1 June	King presented with Parliament's 'Nineteen Propositions' proposing further drastic curbs on royal powers
18 June	King rejects 'Nineteen Propositions'
June	Confederate Supreme Council nominated in Ireland
June	First arms and officers from Continent arrive for Royalists
2–3 July	Fleet declares for Parliament
15–27 July	First siege of Hull ends in Royalist failure
2 August	Goring surrenders Portsmouth to Parliament
22 August	King Charles raises his Standard at Nottingham signalling official start to war
23 September	Prince Rupert wins cavalry action at Powick Bridge
23 October	Battle of Edgehill ends in marginal Royalist victory; King occupies Oxford
12 November	Rupert storms Brentford; advance on London halted at Turnham Green, Royalists retreat to Reading

1643

19 January	Hopton repulses Parliamentarian invasion of Cornwall at Braddock Down
February	Queen and arms convoy land at Bridlington
2 February	Rupert takes Cirencester, clearing communications between Oxford and the West
19 March	Royalist victory at Hopton Heath
3 April	Rupert storms Birmingham
7–21 April	Rupert takes Lichfield. First mine to be used in England is exploded
25 April	Earl of Essex takes Reading
21 May	Goring captured at Wakefield
May	Cornish Royalist victory at Stratton
June	Newcastle defeats Fairfaxes at Adwalton Moor

14 June	Rupert's Chalgrove Raid disrupts Parliamentarian operations in Thames Valley
4 July	Battle of Lansdown; Hopton fails to defeat Waller in inconclusive action
13 July	Wilmot and Byron defeat Waller at Roundway Down, giving Royalists supremacy in West
26 July	Rupert storms Bristol
6 August–4 September	Royalists fail to capture Gloucester
1 September	'Cessation' agreed between Ormonde and Irish Confederates. English troops in Ireland released to fight for Royalists in England
2 September	Earl of Newcastle lays siege to Hull
4 September	Prince Maurice takes Exeter
20 September	First Battle of Newbury; King fails to destroy army of Earl of Essex
25 September	Solemn League and Covenant signed between Covenanting regime in Scotland and English Parliament
October	Prince Maurice takes Dartmouth
11 October	Royalist defeat at Winceby
12 October	Newcastle abandons siege of Hull
13 November	Contingent of English troops from Ireland lands in North Wales
13 December	Royalists take Beeston Castle
26 December	Lord Byron lays siege to Nantwich

1644

19 January	Scots army invades England in support of Parliament
25 January	Sir Thomas Fairfax defeats Byron at Nantwich
3 February	Scots reach but fail to take Newcastle upon Tyne
19 February	Scots cavalry defeated by Langdale at Corbridge
February	Rupert appointed President of Wales and Royalist Commander-in-Chief in Wales and the Marches
27 February	Parliamentarians lay siege to Lathom House in Lancashire

29 February	Parliamentarians under Sir John Meldrum lay siege to Newark
March–April	First Scottish Royalist uprising on Deeside
7–8 March	Indecisive action between Newcastle and Scots at Bolden Hills
21 March	Prince Rupert relieves Newark
23 March	Indecisive action between Newcastle and Scots at Hilton
29 March	Hopton and Forth defeated by Waller at Cheriton ending Royalist offensive plans in South
11 April	Belasyse defeated at Selby
22 April	Allied armies lay siege to York
25 May	Rupert storms Stockport
28 May	Rupert storms Bolton
11 June	Rupert takes Liverpool
29 June	Oxford Army defeats Waller at Cropredy Bridge
1 July	Rupert relieves York
2 July	Allies defeat Rupert and Newcastle at Marston Moor
16 July	York surrenders
21 August	Oxford Army defeats Essex at Beacon Hill (Lostwithiel campaign)
31 August	Oxford Army defeats Essex at Castle Dor (Lostwithiel campaign)
1 September	Montrose defeats Covenanters at Tippermuir
3 September	Skippon surrenders Essex's infantry and guns at Lostwithiel
13 September	Montrose defeats Covenanters at Aberdeen
18 September	Lord Byron defeated at Montgomery
20 October	Newcastle upon Tyne falls to Scots
27 October	Parliamentarians fail to destroy Oxford Army at Second Battle of Newbury
6 November	Prince Rupert appointed Lieutenant General of Royalist armies
9 November	'Third Battle of Newbury': Oxford Army relieves Donnington Castle
19 December	House of Commons passes Self-Denying Ordinance to create New Model Army

1645

2 February	Montrose defeats Argyll at Inverlochy
19 February	Maurice relieves Chester
22 February	Parliamentarians take Shrewsbury
2 March	Langdale relieves Pontefract
4 April	New Model Army formed
22 April	Rupert defeats Massey at Ledbury
24 April	Cromwell defeats Northampton at Islip
29 April	Cromwell repulsed at Faringdon
9 May	Montrose defeats Covenanters at Auldearn
10 May	Royalist Council of War at Stow-on-the-Wold decides to divide forces
30 May	Rupert storms Leicester
14 June	Oxford Army defeated at Naseby
18 June	New Model Army under Fairfax retakes Leicester
2 July	Montrose defeats Covenanters at Alford
10 July	Royalist Western Army under Goring defeated at Langport
23 July	Fairfax takes Bridgwater
15 August	Montrose defeats Covenanters at Kilsyth
10 September	Rupert surrenders Bristol; dismissed by King
13 September	Montrose defeated at Philliphaugh
24 September	Royalist Horse defeated at Rowton Heath
October	Northern Horse defeated at Shirburn
14 October	Cromwell storms Basing House

1646

3 February	Byron surrenders Chester
16 February	Hopton defeated at Torrington
12 March	Royalist Western Army surrenders to Fairfax at Truro
21 March	Last Royalist field army under Astley destroyed at Stow-on-the-Wold
5 May	King Charles surrenders to Scots at Newark
24 June	Surrender of Oxford
19 August	Surrender of Raglan

1647

16 March — Surrender of Harlech Castle, the last Royalist garrison in mainland England and Wales

1648

23 March — Royalist uprising in South Wales

28 April — Langdale takes Berwick

21 May — Royalist rising in Kent

1 June — Fairfax defeats Kent Royalists at Maidstone

14 June — Fairfax begins siege of Colchester

8 July — Scots army under Hamilton invades England in support of King

11 July — Cromwell takes Pembroke

17–19 August — Scots army destroyed at Preston and Winwick Pass

28 August — Surrender of Colchester

1649

30 January — King Charles I executed

5 February — Charles II proclaimed in Edinburgh

2 August — Michael Jones defeats Ormonde and Irish Confederates at Rathmines

15 August — Cromwell arrives in Dublin

12 September — Cromwell storms Drogheda

16 October — Cromwell storms Wexford

1650

27 April — Montrose defeated at Carbisdale; captured, tried and executed

July — Cromwell invades Scotland

3 September — Cromwell defeats Scots under David Leslie at Dunbar

1651

20 July — Lambert defeats Scots at Inverkeithing

6 August — Charles II and Scots army invade England

22 August — Charles occupies Worcester

25 August — English Royalists under Earl of Derby defeated at Wigan

| 3 September | Charles II and Scots defeated by Cromwell at Worcester |
| 13 October | Charles II escapes to France |

1655

| March | Failed Royalist rising under Penruddock |

1658

| 14 June | Battle of the Dunes; Charles II's troops fight in defeated Spanish army, Cromwell's with victorious French |
| 3 September | Death of Oliver Cromwell |

1659

| 19 August | Booth's Royalist rising defeated by Lambert at Winnington Bridge |

1660

| 1 January | George Monck and English army in Scotland cross Border and ultimately support Charles II |
| 29 May | Charles II is restored to throne |

INTRODUCTION

It is often said that history is written by the victors, and for a long time this maxim could be applied to the English Civil War. Following the first serious, if considerably romanticised study of the Royalists, that of Eliot Warburton in his frequently inaccurate transcription of part of Prince Rupert's correspondence entitled *Memoirs of Prince Rupert and the Cavaliers*, published in 1849, over a century passed before any further major research was undertaken purely into the Royalist armies.

The received image of the patriotic and moral motivations of the Parliamentarian party, personified in Oliver Cromwell, had much greater appeal to the ideals of Victorian England than did their supposedly morally, politically and religiously suspect opponents, however 'wrong but romantic' the Cavaliers might be. The result was that while leading scholars such as Charles Firth and Godfrey Davies explored primarily the nature of the Cromwellian forces, no corresponding work was done on their opponents. It was not until the 1950s and '60s that the pioneering work of Brigadier Peter Young sparked the growth of interest in the King's armies. It is a tribute to Young's knowledge and diligent mining of hitherto neglected sources that, despite the modification by modern research of some of his interpretations, his work remains an invaluable source for any researcher into the military aspects of the Civil Wars.

Young's work signalled the start of an upsurge of interest into the Royalist war effort. During the next two decades, able historians such as Ian Roy, Peter Newman and Ronald Hutton cast much light on King Charles' armies. At the same time, the growth in interest in the historical 're-enactment' movement, itself begun by Peter Young with his foundation of the 'Sealed Knot', not only provided thousands of people of all ages and walks of life with a hitherto unsuspected and engrossing hobby, but also germinated a new 'wave' of interest in the Civil War. Researchers such as Les Prince, Keith Roberts, Stuart Reid, John Tincey and Philipp Eliot-Wright have uncovered a wealth of new information on all aspects of the war, their work brought to the attention of a wider interested audience by David Ryan through the medium of his Partizan Press and its invaluable series of English Civil War Conferences.

There were also a number of publications on the military aspects of the war, including major studies of the Parliamentarian New Model Army and the Army of the Eastern Association. But there was still no detailed account, incorporating the fruits of modern research, readily available on the army which for almost four years upheld the cause of King Charles I in the First Civil War. This book, the product of an interest – some might say 'obsession' – in the 'Cavaliers' that dates back over thirty years, attempts to fill the gap.

Part One provides a general portrait of the King's armies of 1642 to 1646, discussing how they were raised, armed, equipped, supported and commanded, and the tactics they employed.

In Part Two, I examine in more detail a number of different aspects and episodes of the history of the Royalist armies and the men (and women) who, willingly or otherwise, with devotion, resignation or reluctance, found themselves caught up in King Charles' war. I look at some of the differing characteristics of the major regional forces in a cosmopolitan army that had in its ranks men from every part of the British Isles as well as much of Europe. Also examined are some key episodes in the story of the King's war, which illustrate aspects of the nature of the men who fought it. My only regret is that limitations of space have prevented detailed coverage of everything worthy of record. I have, for example (partly because of availability of material), chosen to concentrate on the principal Royalist field force – the so-called 'Oxford Army' – and the main regional armies in the North and West, whose input into the war was arguably the greatest, rather than the equally interesting, but militarily less influential forces in, for example, Lancashire and the East Midlands.

PART ONE

ONE

BACKGROUND TO WAR

'If they [English soldiers] be well ordered, and kept in by the
rules of good discipline, they fear not the face or the force of
the stoutest foe.'

Edward Lupton, *Warlike Treatise of the Pike*,
1642, p. 1

The opening years of the English Civil Wars have frequently
been portrayed as a clash between largely amateur armies
who gained their knowledge of war through the harsh school of
trial and error in battle. Even the eminent authority Sir Charles
Firth claimed: 'The history of the Civil War is the history of the
evolution of an efficient army out of a chaos.'[1]

Firth is supported by some contemporary writers, who
bemoaned the decline of English military prowess in the years
following the death of Elizabeth I.[2] By 1642 England had enjoyed
almost a century of largely unbroken internal peace, as a result
of which there were visible signs of obvious neglect in the
country's military preparedness; the fortifications of many of her
towns, for example, had fallen into disrepair (apart from those
such as at Berwick, where continuing tensions with Scotland
had ensured their maintenance). Unlike many of her European
contemporaries, England maintained virtually no standing army,
and the effectiveness of her militia forces was regarded with
justifiable doubts.

However, though peace might reign at home, men from England
and Wales were constantly involved in conflict overseas during the
first part of the seventeenth century. The end of the long war in

Ireland in 1604 was followed within a few years by the outbreak of conflict in Europe, as Protestant and Catholic powers collided in what became known as the Thirty Years' War. Though England avoided direct involvement, and was spared the horrors suffered by some of her Continental neighbours, large numbers of men from England, Wales and especially Scotland saw action in that war, mainly, though not exclusively, in the service of the Protestant cause. English volunteers serving in the Palatinate gained a number of tributes, while the Swedish forces of Gustavus Adolphus also employed many professional soldiers from the British Isles, especially Scots, thousands of whom saw service abroad during this time.[3]

English troops had fought alongside the Dutch since the early days of the latters' long conflict with Spain, and this tradition continued, service with the English Brigade in the Low Countries becoming an accepted part of the education of many a young English gentleman. The names of the English officers in Dutch service in the 1620s and '30s read almost like a roll-call of many of the leading figures of the Civil War: Royalist commanders such as Jacob Astley, George Goring, Charles Lucas, Ralph Hopton, George Lisle, Henry Wilmot and hundreds of others gained their first military experience on the Continent. In many cases, they were career or professional soldiers, who demonstrated their calling by returning to foreign service at the end of the Civil War.

This involvement in Continental military affairs meant that British military thinking was directly influenced by developments in Europe. The early seventeenth century was a time of considerable evolution in tactics, although this built more on existing practices than has sometimes been suggested. Contemporary military theorists were impressed by the military organisation of classical times, which they sought to adapt to modern conditions, or at least used to validate their ideas. Their success was limited, partly because of a lack of clear understanding and, more significantly, partly because of the inherent problems when providing the kind of well-trained, disciplined and equipped regular forces that such tactics required.

Although the Spanish armies, among others, had been making gradual innovations for some time, the major new developments came in the Low Countries, where the 'Dutch system' was developed from the 1590s onwards by Prince Maurice of Nassau and his cousins. Their theories were widely propagated by military writers, among them Jacob de Gehyn, whose *Wapen Handlingen* was first published in 1607 and speedily translated into a number of languages, including English, and John Cruso, whose *Militarie Instructions for the Cavall'rie*, published in 1632, would be a widely used text in the early stages of the Civil War.

The Dutch system was the first to adapt classical theories successfully by establishing a long-serving professional force that put into practice the ideas of Maurice and his adherents. They introduced an intensive and complex drill system, as well as reforming the organisation of their forces to produce a new tactical unit known as the 'battalion', much smaller and more manoeuvrable than the massive and unwieldy 'tertia', which had been the basic formation of the previous century. The battalion built on the increasing effectiveness of firearms.[4] Instead of the fifty ranks or more that formed the 'tertia', the battalion had ten or less, and made maximum use of firepower by training its musketeers to fire successively by rank; with well-disciplined and confident troops, this strategy could result in an almost continuous barrage, ranks wheeling to the rear to reload and then moving forward to take their place in the firing line again.

These tactics were built upon and refined by Sweden's Gustavus Adolphus, who reduced the battalion to six ranks, or even three when firing a 'salvee', in which all the musketeers discharged their pieces simultaneously. Gustavus also supported his infantry with light three-pounder guns, which could be manoeuvred relatively easily, as well as introducing 'shock' tactics for his cavalry, developed further during the English Civil War.

As the bulk of English volunteers served with the Dutch, it was natural that their system became dominant in England rather than the Swedish refinements, which were better known, if not necessarily followed, in Scotland. A number of English veterans wrote military manuals based on what they had observed abroad. Among the most influential was Captain John Bingham, whose *Tactiks of Aelian* . . . formed the basis of the official militia instructions of 1623 and 1638, themselves virtually copied in the regulations produced for the Royalist Oxford Army in 1642 and 1643. Other English writers without actual service abroad drew their information from veterans, among them William Barriffe, whose *Militarie Discipline: or the young artillerieman*, first published in 1635, went through numerous editions and was one of the most widely used manuals of the Civil War.

The growing interest in military matters demonstrated itself more practically in a concern for the effectiveness of the local defence forces and the appearance, mainly in London, of several military 'societies', such as the 'Society of the Artillery Garden'. These were made up of wealthier citizens, who met regularly to train, hiring veterans of the Dutch war as tutors, including such later influential military figures as Phillip Skippon and Henry Tillier. It was partly the influence of these societies that helped increase the effectiveness of the London trained bands.

THE TRAINED BANDS

There were two categories of local defence forces in England and Wales, known collectively, and sometimes imprecisely, as the 'militia'. The wider and militarily less effective category consisted of the entire capable male population aged between sixteen and sixty, the 'posse comitatus', which could be summoned by a county sheriff in times of major emergency such as foreign invasion or insurrection.

More militarily significant, at least in theory, were the trained bands. They had their origins in Tudor times, when the increased costs of military equipment made it impracticable to arm and train adequately the entire male population. There was also a desire on the part of the government to have available a socially and politically reliable force in case of rebellion or invasion. Because of their internal security role, it was emphasised that recruits should be 'men sufficient, of able and active bodies; none of the meaner sort or servants; but only such as be of the Gentrie, Free-holders, and good Farmers, or their sonnes, that are like to be resident'. They were to 'meet to be sorted in bands, and to be trained and exercised in such sort as may reasonably be borne by a common charge of the whole county'. Each county was required to provide an agreed number of men, at its expense, and its Lord Lieutenant and his Deputies were responsible for setting the quota for individual areas.

Such a system, particularly the grounds for assessing the eligibility or financial contribution of a particular individual, was open to abuse, and the whole procedure lent itself to inefficiency. Command was usually given to men of local prestige, who frequently lacked military experience. In most cases, they were members of the local gentry rather than the nobility, drawn from the class increasingly regarded as the natural leaders of their communities. One result, of particular significance in 1642, was that in practice they grew to have more authority over the trained bands than did the central government. Neither King nor Parliament could automatically rely upon their support.

Equally unclear was precisely where and how the trained bands could be employed. They were intended for 'home' defence, which, as a rule, most interpreted as meaning within their own county. But there had been cases in the 1590s of their being employed, whether legally or not, abroad. The deciding factor, in practice, would prove to be the attitudes of the bandsmen themselves and their leaders.

Numerically the trained bands represented a significant force. In 1638 it was estimated that in England and Wales they totalled 93,718 foot and 5,239 horse.[5] Their effectiveness was more questionable. In an attempt to remedy the inexperience of most of the officers of the bands, the government appointed muster-masters for each county with the task of organising training. But the results varied according to the degree of cooperation and financial support that each muster-master received within his county. As a result, training was frequently sketchy. The Trained Band Company of the City of Chester, for example, totalled about 100 men including, in 1613, 1 carpenter, 3 malsters, 7 tanners, 7 bakers, 6 hatmakers, 6 butchers, 3 drapers, 13 shoemakers, 5 glovers and 7 tailors.[6] The company had its headquarters in the 'Pentice', a wooden building in the centre of the town where its equipment and arms were stored. Though in theory trained bands met regularly for exercises, including every three years a General Muster of the entire trained bands of a county, the effectiveness of such gatherings was doubtful. In 1639 the military commentator Robert Ward complained that the training sessions were treated as 'matters of disport and things of no moment',[7] social occasions to eat and drink with friends rather than carry out serious military practice. As they had to be purchased by the local community, the arms of the trained bands were replaced as infrequently as possible, and were often obsolete and in disrepair.

The authorities were aware of these deficiencies, and no monarch since medieval times did more than Charles I in trying to remedy them. From the early 1620s onwards he embarked on a series of attempted reforms, including the publication of training regulations. None of these had more than limited success. In 1639, for example, although the Chester Trained Band now employed a professional soldier, William Maxey, as its lieutenant, on a salary of £5 a year, it remained under the captaincy of a city alderman, Francis Gamull, and the continuing essentially social nature of its gatherings may be glimpsed in an entry in the City Treasurer's Accounts: 'A quart of sack and cakes in the Pentice when Mr Mayor and Sir Thomas Smith came from vewinge of the Citty souldiers.'[8] With the partial exception of the London trained bands, influenced as they were by the military 'societies', standards as a whole remained low.

THE SCOTS WARS AND REBELLION IN IRELAND

The earlier years of the reign of Charles I saw generally disastrous military intervention in Continental affairs. The expeditions to Cadiz (1625) and La Rochelle (1627) both failed despite the considerable numbers of men involved. Volunteers proved insufficient to fill the ranks, and conscription had to be enforced. Ironically, one reason for the poor showing of the English troops in these expeditions was the inferior quality of those conscripts brought in to make up numbers. Local authorities followed the usual practice of meeting their quotas by offloading gaolbirds and other undesirable members of their communities, while considerably more men were lost through disease than in action.

The growing tensions between the King and his Scottish subjects culminated in the First Bishops' War of 1639. The government met this crisis with a mixture of improvisation and traditional methods. But, however disappointing the performance of the troops, the experience gained in raising the armies of 1639 and 1640 proved invaluable two years later.

The King appointed colonels and commissioned officers for the units that were raised, but individual counties were responsible for recruiting and clothing their quotas of other ranks, who were then armed and equipped by the Crown. The process proved far from easy. Enthusiasm for the war was lacking, and desertions, indiscipline, and even violence against their officers were common among the unwilling conscripts. Thomas Lunsford, commanding a regiment raised in Somerset, wrote on 22 June 1639: 'I find my regiment in the greatest disorder; divers of them in troops daily returned home . . . we are daily assaulted by sometimes 500 of them together, have hurt and killed some in our own defence, and are driven to keep together on our guard.'[9]

While the counties attempted to provide uniforms, arms and equipment were the responsibility of central government. Once again, particularly in the development of a network of contacts for purchases abroad, the experience of the Bishops' Wars proved invaluable for the later Royalist armies. In January 1639 the Council of War ordered the purchase in Flanders of 7,000 muskets, with rests and bandoliers, together with a large amount of other equipment. However, possibly because the inspectors employed were English gunsmiths with a vested interest, problems of the Civil War were foreshadowed when much of the imported material was reported defective.[10] The demands of the Scots Wars also led to an expansion of England's own munitions industry, although because the bulk of manufacturers were located in London, the main benefits would later accrue to Parliament. The brief duration of both wars, with little actual fighting, meant that participants gained minimal combat experience. But, even if in a negative way, the officers of the English forces learnt a good deal about the problems of raising, equipping, training and maintaining an army.[11]

The troops raised to fight the Scots had scarcely been disbanded when news arrived in the summer of 1641 that rebellion had broken out in Ireland. To meet the crisis, Parliament reluctantly authorised the raising of men, eventually to total 2,000 horse and 10,000 foot, in England and Wales, with another 10,000 foot from Scotland. More would be recruited later, both in England and from the loyalist population in Ireland, until about 40,000 men in all would be fielded.

Thanks to the continuing expansion of the arms industry, particularly around London, it proved possible to arm all of these troops adequately, although clothing and feeding them proved more difficult, partly because of widespread corruption. Opinions differ on whether King or Parliament ultimately gained the most from the military expansion. On balance, however, Charles' opponents seem to have benefited more. Although the arsenals of munitions in Hull and the Tower of London (remaining from the Scots Wars) were depleted by the new demands, Parliament began the war in possession of most of England's expanded armaments manufacturing capability, as well as four regiments of foot still awaiting transport to Ireland, which formed a valuable cadre for the field army forming under the Earl of Essex. The King, however, had to begin raising an army from scratch, and encountered serious difficulties.

RAISING AN ARMY

A major factor pushing King and Parliament over the brink and into civil war in the spring of 1642 had been the question of who should control the militia. Parliament, by means of the Militia Ordnance, managed to create confusion and uncertainty, and the King was forced to seek other methods to exert what he deemed to be his right to raise troops. He utilised what was essentially a medieval institution, the Commission of Array, first introduced in 1324 but not used since 1557, and intended originally to meet the threat of invasion. Commissioners appointed by the King were empowered to call out all the men in a county able to carry arms. Those unfit to serve would be required to make a contribution towards the equipping and support of the remainder until they left their native county, when they would become the responsibility of the monarch.

The reality was much less clear-cut. Parliament, as might be expected, declared the King's tactic illegal, and the judiciary tended to be ambivalent in its verdict; the outcome therefore depended upon the degree of support enjoyed by each party in a particular area. Although the details of the mechanics involved are now unclear, there is no doubt that the King's supporters carried out a good deal of prior canvassing of opinion before Commissioners were appointed, as it was essential that the posts be occupied by active Royalist sympathisers.[12]

But the Commissions of Array were not the King's preferred method of raising an army. Originally he hoped to enlist in their entirety the trained bands in counties where his support appeared strong, if necessary by replacing officers of suspect loyalties by known Royalist supporters. This policy was followed in reverse by Parliament, but both sides, with a few exceptions, met with mixed success. Attempts to replace their existing officers caused considerable resentment among the men of the trained bands. Although the Royalists did succeed in retaining at least some of a few units where they were able to preserve the existing command structure intact (such as Conyers Darcy's Yorkshire Regiment), these were very much the exception. The reluctance of the trained band units to become actively involved in the contest was an important factor in the King's failure to occupy Hull in July 1642, and this in turn helped convince him of the need to raise 'volunteer' regiments, which would not be influenced by the conflicting views of their existing officers and which would, in theory, be more willing to serve outside their own localities.

The machinery of the Commission of Array provided the authority to raise the men for these regiments, although individual units were actually formed by virtue of commissions issued by the King to prominent supporters, who in turn appointed their officers. The use of the Commission of Array, together with the practice of colonels recruiting officers from among their own relatives, neighbours and retainers, who then raised their companies locally, meant that the original regiments of the King's army had a strong 'county' basis, although this rapidly became diluted as the war went on, and men were obtained from wherever they were currently serving or by impressment.

Initially, the response to the King's appeals for support proved disappointing. When he raised his Standard at Nottingham on 22 August, Charles had no more than 800 horse and 500 foot under his command, and it was not until September, when he moved his headquarters to Shrewsbury, that he began to build up an army of any respectable size. Part of the reason for the slow response may have been because it was harvest time, a factor that might have been expected to affect more rurally based Royalist recruiting to a greater extent than the Parliamentarians, who had the populations of London and other large towns to draw upon. But, in fact, Parliament encountered similar problems, and it is unwise to make too many assumptions about the relative popularity of the opposing sides from their success in raising troops.[13] Although there were sufficient active partisans to form the armies that met at Edgehill in October, together with slowly growing regional forces, many supporters of both King and Parliament were unwilling to make a commitment until Edgehill had proved not only that the war was likely to be prolonged, but also that their side had a realistic prospect of surviving beyond the first encounter.

A key role in raising the large numbers of recruits from Lancashire, Cheshire and North Wales, who filled out the ranks of the King's army at Shrewsbury, was played by Lord Strange, shortly to become 7th Earl of Derby. Derby had claimed that he could provide 10,000 men in three days,[14] and, although this boast was inflated, two regiments of foot, perhaps 2,000 men, came from Lancashire, and possibly another 4,000 men from Cheshire.[15] Derby's influence on recruiting in North Wales was also significant. Coercion and threats played a role, and some trained band companies were probably forcibly enlisted, but in other areas, such as the strongly Catholic Hundred of Amounderness in Lancashire, recruits seem to been obtained relatively easily.[16] However, this success was achieved at a price, for, as the war spread and intensified during the winter and spring of 1642/3, local Royalists found themselves seriously weakened by the numbers of men drawn off in the previous summer.

Arming the new recruits presented another serious challenge.[17] The resources of the trained bands were an obvious target. Though most county committees were unwilling voluntarily to hand over their weapons, as early as August the King began to requisition the contents of the trained band magazines. He probably obtained about 2,000 arms from Nottinghamshire, Derbyshire and Leicestershire, while Derby gained control of about three-quarters of the trained band equipment in Lancashire.[18] The poor condition of many of the troops he later raised for the war in Lancashire suggests that most of the available arms were sent to equip the field army at Shrewsbury.

It was a considerable achievement for the Royalists and their powers of improvisation that by September 1642 they had succeeded in raising, and at least adequately equipping, a field army totalling some 14,000 men, which at Edgehill on 23 October proved capable of fighting the Earl of Essex to a standstill.

TWO

THE OFFICERS

'. . . they are not a little mistaken, which think their birth a sufficient pretence to places of honour, without any qualification or merit, there being other things more reall and essentiall required in an officer, namely, Knowledge, experience, valour, dexteritie etc. . . .'

John Cruso, *Militarie Instructions for the Cavall'rie*, 1632, p. 2

The enduring image of King Charles' armies is of rural tenantry led into battle by the gentry who were their masters. While there is some truth in this, especially in the earlier stages of the war and in some of the regional armies, notably the Cornish and the Earl of Derby's Lancashire forces, it is not an entirely accurate picture as the Royalist forces rapidly changed and evolved under the pressures of conflict.

GENTLEMEN AND PROFESSIONALS: THE ROYALIST OFFICER CORPS, 1642–3

It is sometimes claimed, inaccurately, that the rival forces in 1642 were mainly officered by amateurs, who learnt their profession, if they lived long enough, in the hard school of practical experience. As discussed in Chapter 1, there was a considerable reservoir of military knowledge available in the British Isles, as well as from Europe, which both King and Parliament were quick to tap. As early as July 1642, Parliament offered half pay as a 'retainer' to unemployed professional soldiers on the pretext of obtaining their

14

services for the war in Ireland, though actually to deny them to the King.[1] This ploy was not particularly successful, and the Royalists had already begun their own attempts to recruit from the same source.

As well as purchasing arms, Queen Henrietta Maria and her agents abroad were scouring Europe for career soldiers who were willing to serve the King. When Prince Rupert arrived in August 1642, he brought with him about forty professionals of various nationalities, and others, for example George Goring and some Scots, who joined the Earl of Newcastle's Northern forces in February 1643, arrived in significant numbers over the next few months.

The nature of English society and King Charles' need to raise an army from scratch were inevitably reflected in the Royalist officer corps of 1642. It was a constant theme of Royalist propagandists that the English gentry were the backbone of the King's cause. Sir John Oglander went so far as to claim that the King's side 'were almost all gentlemen, and of the Parliament's few'.[2] The latter part of his claim was a considerable exaggeration resulting from the need to highlight the legitimacy of the King's cause by claiming that virtually all of the 'gentry' – the natural leaders of English society – were Royalist. In fact, there is overwhelming evidence that Parliament had an almost equal proportion of 'gentry' among its officers.[3]

It was only cooperation, and indeed active involvement, by the gentry that enabled either side to field an army in 1642. Many were influenced in their decision to support the King by their belief in a hierarchical society, with the monarch as its ordained head under God. Most Royalists would have agreed with Dudley Digges that 'disloyalty to their King is disloyalty to God'.[4] In this respect Royalism may be seen as the reaction of an older patriarchal order to what was perceived as a threat to the social structure represented by the ambitions of the King's opponents. The result was an almost feudal loyalty to the King (a significant number of his officers throughout the war were members of the extensive pre-war royal household or their families), and a lack of the self-doubts that at times afflicted some of their opponents.

The King's need to raise an army by means of the Commissions of Array and by using individual supporters to raise units were other factors that made the support and active involvement of the gentry essential. It was natural to issue commissions to the middle and lesser gentry, as the accepted leaders of the community, particularly in the more rural areas from which the King drew a large part of his support. Nor is it particularly surprising that many who had had little involvement with pre-war public affairs felt their position so threatened by the political events of 1641–2 that they took an active military role at least in the opening phases of what was confidently expected to be a short war.

The usual practice was for a leading local figure, whether gentry or 'grandee', to be commissioned to raise a regiment.[5] He in turn would call upon his network of relatives and gentry neighbours to raise companies or troops from among their families, retainers and tenants, and to use their influence in 'beating the drum' for volunteers. Hence it was natural that some of the regiments forming the armies of 1642 had a distinct regional and in some cases family feel.[6]

The previous military experience of the new officers varied. Although it may occasionally have some basis in reality, the popular picture of the country gentleman, copy of Barriffe or Cruso in hand, attempting to keep one page ahead while instructing his motley band in the rudiments of warfare, was rare. The need to utilise all available sources of military expertise and experience in forming the Royalist officer corps was rapidly acknowledged, and although the colonels of the first regiments raised were normally of 'grandee' or middle gentry status, the value of professional soldiers as 'advisers' was also recognised.

The exact definition of a 'professional' soldier can cause confusion, and the distinction needs to be drawn between the large numbers of gentry who, at some stage, had been involved in military activity on the Continent as part of their education, and those individuals, often though not exclusively from the same social background, who had sufficient military involvement and experience to be termed 'career' soldiers.[7] These merge at the far end of the scale into those, both from the British Isles and further afield, for whom soldiering was a full-time and permanent livelihood, and whose choice of allegiance in the Civil War might be from conviction or literally 'mercenary'.[8] For the sake of simplicity, for all except some foreign 'mercenaries' the term 'professional' is employed here when describing both the latter two categories.

The pattern is clearly illustrated by examples from the units in the Royalist Army at Edgehill. Some regiments had a distinctly 'aristocratic' feel to them, for example the Prince of Wales' Regiment of Horse, with the Earls of Northampton and Westmorland each commanding a troop, and the officers of Northampton's Troop consisting of two of his sons and Lieutenant Robert Arden, 'a Gentleman of one of the most ancient Families in Warwickshire'.[9] Yet even in this regiment one troop was commanded by Captain Davison, 'an old experienced Low Country Soldier, who was recommended for that Empoly, by the old Earl of Northampton'.[10] The desire to employ professionals wherever possible was more marked in other units, not surprisingly including Prince Rupert's Regiment of Horse, which had at least five.[11]

The same trend was apparent among the foot, especially in regiments raised by men sufficiently wealthy to hire professional soldiers, for whom such considerations were more important than they initially were to the 'gentleman' officers. The unit raised by the wealthy Ralph Dutton, following a common pattern, had veterans of the Bishops' Wars, Stephen Hawkins (who probably had European experience as well) and Degory Collins as lieutenant colonel and major respectively. It also included at least three other officers who had served in the same regiment as Hawkins during the Bishops' Wars, and who were probably recruited by him in 1642.[12] Richard Fielding's regiment included five professional officers, both Fielding and his lieutenant colonel were veterans of European service.[13] Thomas Lunsford based the core of his Somerset regiment largely on the unit that he raised for service in 1640, and so not only his officers but also a useful proportion of the rank and file had some previous experience.[14]

Other units, such as Sir Edward Stradling's South Wales foot, had few in their ranks, possibly because their commanders had fewer funds, or because the immediately available supply of professional officers had been taken up by other commanders, and their performance seems to have suffered accordingly.[15] In all, the Royalist Army at Edgehill had at least fifty officers with prior military experience, and the numbers would steadily increase.

The winter of 1642, with the prospect of a prolonged conflict, saw the beginning of significant changes in the Royalist officer corps. The vast majority of colonels (about 90 per cent) continued to be of 'grandee' or gentry status, partly from social and political considerations, and also because they initially had the wealth to equip the units they had raised.[16] However, overall there was less active military involvement by the higher ranks of society. Colonel Sir Thomas Salusbury cannot have been the only 'amateur' soldier who apparently found the reality of war not to his taste,[17] and other leading figures departed after Edgehill, either to raise troops in their areas of influence, or to run the machinery of government there, or simply to resume the management of their own estates. As well as these vacancies there was an ongoing need to replace losses from other causes.

One result was that the established regiments of the Oxford Army quite rapidly lost much of their original regional identity. They received replacements, both of officers and men, from any available source, and, although the Northern and Cornish armies retained a strong local connection, the degree of kinship among officers was increasingly diluted. There are numerous examples of regiments serving widely in different parts of the country, recruiting officers and men wherever they were stationed. John Byron's Regiment of Horse included officers not only from Nottinghamshire, where it was originally raised, but also from Cheshire, Lancashire, Cumberland, Flintshire and Shropshire.[18] Charismatic leaders such as Prince Rupert could generally attract recruits wherever they went, and the list of his officers is still more cosmopolitan, with representatives from Durham, Yorkshire, Oxfordshire, Surrey, Dorset, Stafford, Kent, Hampshire, Carmarthen, Brecon, Shropshire, Herefordshire, Wiltshire and Suffolk.[19] The eventual result would be a truly 'national' Royalist Army so far as representation from territory controlled by the King was concerned.[20]

The same factors grew to influence the social background of the Royalist officer corps. Even in the higher ranks there were examples of colonels from non-grandee or gentry backgrounds, such as the lawyer William Mason, the Newcastle merchant Francis Anderson, and the remarkable Sigismund Beeton, son of a cobbler.[21] Though such individuals represented no more than 10 per cent of the total, there is persuasive evidence that over half of the Royalist officer corps as a whole came from the ranks of the lesser gentry or had more obscure origins. There are sufficient references to occupations such as 'play actors', 'choristers', and even a 'rope dancer', to suggest that the background from which the King's officers were drawn was much wider than often implied.[22]

THE RISE OF THE 'SWORDSMEN', 1644–6

Prince Rupert's influence was a significant factor in the decline of 'grandee' participation in Royalist military affairs. The 'aristocratic' commanders of 1643, Derby, Capel, Carbery, Hertford and Newcastle, were all eventually removed or resigned. Others of lower rank, such as Lord Chandos, departed in discontent when they were passed over in favour of men of lesser social standing. This process quickened from the beginning of 1644, when Rupert took up command on the Welsh Borders and began replacing the 'gentlemen', such as Sir Francis Ottley, Governor of Shrewsbury, and Lord Capel, commanding in Cheshire, Shropshire and North Wales, with 'swordsmen' like Sir Michael Earnley and Lord Byron.[23]

Although the 'swordsmen' were regarded by many of the King's more traditionalist supporters as upstarts threatening the integrity of the social structure, their importance to the Royalist military machine assured them of advancement. Richard Page, a professional soldier of obscure social origins, and Matthew Appleyard, from the army in Ireland, with Joseph Wagstaffe, Major General of Foot in Maurice's Western Army, were among those knighted for their services. Significantly, King Charles seems to have endeavoured to limit the impact on the traditional social fabric by awarding knighthoods (most commonly for gallantry in the field) rather than hereditary honours. Comparatively few of the latter titles (eighteen in all) were granted, among others to Jacob Astley, the veteran Major General of the Oxford Army foot, Charles Gerrard, who was granted a peerage towards the end of the war as compensation for the loss of his command in South Wales, and John Byron, apparently in acknowledgement of his role at Roundway Down and First Newbury, and of the remarkable loyalty of the Byron family as a whole. At a time when the King's material resources were so strained, such rewards, with the implication of more tangible gratitude later, were usually all that he could offer.

The rise of the 'swordsmen' had considerable implications for the conduct of the war. To commanders like Byron, Sir Marmaduke Langdale, and Gerrard, military considerations took precedence over the feelings and well-being of the civilian population. This led to rising discontent among local communities. It is thus difficult to assess how far the Royalist war effort benefited from the impact of the 'swordsmen'. If they had won a quick military victory their failings would not have mattered, but in the long term their activities and civilian reaction probably cost the King more than he gained.

THE MERCENARIES

The mercenary, or 'soldier of fortune', had a long and honourable tradition. Medieval English kings, and the Tudors, had made considerable use of them, and so there was ample precedent for their employment in the Civil War. Both King and Parliament recruited them, which did not prevent each from condemning the other for doing so. As well as 'technical' experts such as Bernard De Gomme and Bartholomew La Roche, non-English officers were employed in a wide variety of other roles. Most important were the Scottish professional soldiers who took up employment with both sides. They were sometimes regarded with suspicion by the King's grandee supporters. Lord Herbert of Raglan described Patrick Ruthven, Earl of Forth, that most underrated of Royalist generals, as a mere 'soldier of fortune', with the implication that he served the King primarily from considerations of gain. This is unfair both in the case of Ruthven and a large number, perhaps the majority, of his fellow-countrymen who chose to follow the King from personal belief and often at considerable sacrifice, resisting offers and persuasions to change sides, particularly after Scotland's alliance with Parliament.

Their impact was considerable. Ruthven is discussed elsewhere, as is that other leading Scottish Royalist soldier, James King, Earl of Eythin. But there were many other Scottish officers of note in the King's armies, ranging from relatively senior commanders like Sir James Henderson, Governor of Newark in 1643, and the cavalry commander Lord Crawford,[24] to numerous majors and captains, such as William Farmer who acted as the Countess of Derby's adviser and effective garrison commander in the defence of

Lathom House. Especially in the earlier part of the war, they provided the Royalists with much necessary expertise while the 'amateur' officers learnt their business.

Many other nationalities also served the King, although their numbers are impossible to estimate. Unlike the Scots, who were at least Charles' subjects, their motives for participation were more varied. A significant factor was the winding down of the conflict in Europe, creating a pool of professional soldiers in search of new employment. Few were (at least openly) as cynical in their motivation as the notorious Croat Captain Carlos Fantom, who told his first employers (the Parliamentarians – he later changed sides), 'I care not for your cause, I come to fight for your half-crown and your handsome women'.[25] The Irish involvement is examined in Chapter 14, and the next most numerically important were the French. Sympathies in France were generally pro-Royalist. This was partly the influence of Queen Henrietta Maria, who induced a surprisingly large number of mainly young men, often searching for adventure and honourable exploits, to enlist in the Royalist cause. Many of them served in the Queen's Regiment of Horse, formed in 1643, which included in its ranks at least four French officers and a number of other volunteers.[26] There was also at least one largely French regiment of horse, under a professional soldier, Bertrand Rosin La Plane, serving in the West Country in the latter stages of the war.[27]

Apart from these units, individual Frenchmen were to be found in the Royalist forces. Among them were Arnold De Lisle, a lieutenant colonel of the Prince of Wales' Regiment of Horse, Major Jean Barre, probably a professional soldier who in 1660 was to petition Charles II for funds, and Major Jamot, who served 'though a soldier of fortune, with great integrity and honour' throughout the First Civil War and at the siege of Colchester in 1648.

Other nationalities are also encountered, though in smaller numbers. Among them is the enigmatic Nicholas, Comte de St Pol,[28] evidently a Lorrainer, who first appears at Newark in 1644, and, by way of Marston Moor and the Oxford Army, eventually fetched up as Byron's Major General of Horse in Chester in 1645. A couple of Florentines, the ruthless Colonel John Devalier, operating on the Welsh Border, and Bernardino Gascoigne, lieutenant colonel to Richard Neville, a capable soldier who only escaped execution after the siege of Colchester because of his foreign nationality, are known together with a sprinkling of others. Johann Phelip Heitter, Dutch or German, was a colonel of horse, again on the Welsh Border, where Rupert and Maurice made particular use of foreign mercenaries. Another German or Dutchman, Major Cornelius De Wit, served with distinction in Robert Werden's regiment in the Chester area.[29]

Despite the unsavoury reputation that they often enjoyed, the majority of King Charles' mercenaries stayed remarkably loyal. The most glaring exception was the Scots professional John Urrey, who transformed the well-timed switch of allegiance into something approaching an art form. Beginning the war in the army of the Earl of Essex, Urrey went over to the Royalists in June 1643, bringing with him useful information on enemy movements. After leading a successful cavalry raid on High Wycombe, Urrey rose in Rupert's favour, gaining a knighthood and becoming his Major General of Horse at Marston Moor. It may be that Urrey shared the distaste of some other Scots in the King's service at the prospect of fighting against their fellow countrymen, for his behaviour at Marston Moor was criticised, and on the eve of the Second Battle of Newbury Urrey switched back to the Parliamentarians. Possibly finding his welcome somewhat tepid, Urrey returned to Scotland and a command in the forces fighting Montrose. He suffered a severe defeat at Auldearn in May 1645, and eventually turned Royalist again. Presumably even Urrey's permutations of loyalty had their limits. In 1650, when fighting with Montrose in his last forlorn attempt to rekindle rebellion in Scotland, Urrey was captured and executed for treason. Perhaps more surprising than Urrey's flexible loyalties is the apparent readiness of his various employers to continue to accept the services of one who displayed no discernibly outstanding talent other than self-interest.[30]

THE CAVALIER LEGEND

The description 'Cavalier', given to the supporters of King Charles by their Parliamentarian opponents, was, so the Royalist chaplain Edward Simmons told them, a term of approbation – 'Your enemies call you Cavaliers, a name as they take it of great reproach else you may be sure they would not call you by it' –

whereas in reality, he claimed, 'A Compleat Cavalier is a Child of Honour, a Gentleman well borne and bred, that loves his King for conscience sake, of a clearer countenance, and bolder looke than other men, because of a more loyall Heart.'[31]

Nevertheless, the image of the 'Cavalier' as an undisciplined, roistering, licentious debauchee has always captured the popular imagination. There were, of course, many individuals who matched the description. George Goring is perhaps the best known. Though 'generally esteemed a good commander . . . [he was] exceedingly facetious and pleasant company . . . very tall and very handsome . . . His expenses were what he could gett, and his debauchery beyond all presidents . . .'.[32] Lord Wilmot's love of good company was well known, while Sir Joseph Wagstaffe, Major General of Foot in the Western Army, was noted for enjoyment of 'mirth and jollity'. Sir Thomas Lunsford, a colonel of foot, was described in 1637 as 'a young outlaw who neither fears God nor man . . . a swaggering ruffian'.

Some, such as the colourful Henry Washington, ferocious Governor of Worcester in the closing stages of the war, and Goring's boon companion and brief successor as Commander-in-Chief in the West, Thomas Lord Wentworth, seem almost deliberately to have cultivated the image of the licentious 'Cavalier'. Yet the 'wild boys', however colourful and striking their antics, were a minority. A typical Royalist field officer was in his early thirties, an established family man with estates and responsibilities in the community. For every Goring and Washington there were others like Sir Bevil Grenville, dutifully writing home to his wife about the cares of family, his estates and tenants, or that deeply honourable and devout man of principle, Sir Henry Slingsby. Colonel Sir Henry Gage, the Roman Catholic English veteran from the Spanish Army of Flanders, who enjoyed a brief but dazzling career with the Oxford Army before his premature death in January 1645, was noted both for his piety and ability – 'a compleat Soulgier and a wise man'.[33] The same characteristics may be found in the junior ranks. Richard Atkyns, serving in Prince Maurice's Regiment of Horse, was called 'the Praying Captain', while Richard Symonds of the King's Lifeguard of Horse spent much of his off-duty time studying genealogy and church monuments.

DUTY AND REWARD

The life of a Royalist officer was a dangerous one. Quite apart from disease, officers tended to suffer the highest percentage of casualties in action. Between 1642 and 1646 it has been estimated that over 20 per cent of the colonels commissioned either died or were killed in action,[34] and casualty rates among more junior officers were at least as high. Most officers, either from relatively humble origins or with their personal resources in enemy hands, existed in conditions of near poverty. Such were the Northern Horse, fighting in 'exile' in the South after the defeat at Marston Moor, and Sir John Mennes, a Kentish man, serving as General of the Ordnance to Prince Rupert on the Welsh Border in the spring of 1644. On the afternoon of 2 February he wrote gloomily to the Prince, saying that: 'I must crave your Highness's pardon if I quit the place for I have no wherewithall to subsist any longer having received but £22 nowe in eleven monthes and lived upon my own, without free quarter for horse or man, the fortune I have all in the rebbells hands or in súch tenants as have forgott to pay.'[35] Others, with their wives, children and other dependents, existed in cramped lodgings in Oxford and other garrison towns.

Despite lack of material reward, and, eventually, without hope of victory, the majority of Royalist officers remained remarkably loyal to the cause they served. Although as the tide of defeat swelled and more and more of them bowed to the inevitable, and 'compounded' (paid a fine based on their resources) in order to make their peace with Parliament, very few actually turned Roundhead. Even professional soldiers like Richard Grenville, Joseph Wagstaffe and Horatio Cary, whose original switch to the Royalists was perhaps for reasons of self-interest, never apparently attempted to turn their coats again. King Charles was fortunate in the men who formed his officer corps.

THREE

THE HORSE

'. . . a most noble and necessarie part of the militarie professsion . . .'

John Cruso, *Militarie Instructions for the Cavall'rie*,
1632, p. 1

THE THEORY

By 1642, despite greater firepower and better discipline increasing the effectiveness of the foot, the horse were still regarded by most military theorists as the ultimate battle-winning force. They generally classified cavalry under three broad categories. The first, the lancer, though employed by the Scots throughout the period with some success, were not used by English forces. The second type, the cuirassier or heavy horse, were still thought of as élite. These fully armoured horsemen, mounted on the traditional 'great horse' or charger, were ruinously expensive both to equip and maintain, as well as being horribly vulnerable to disciplined firepower. Apart from a couple of Parliamentarian units, notably Haselrigg's famous 'Lobsters' (though even these subsequently dispensed with their cuirassier equipment), only some senior officers may have retained full armour for very long.

The third category of cavalryman was the 'harquebusier'. The term was originally used to denote a type of light horse, but came to be employed to describe the standard cavalry trooper of the English Civil War, whose ideal condition is portrayed by John Vernon, himself a Parliamentarian cavalry officer:

The Harbuysers . . . arming is chiefly offensive, his defensive Arms, are only an open Caske or Head-peece, a back and brest with a buffe coate under his arms; his offensive Armes are a good Harquebus, or Carbine, hanging on his right side with a belt by a sweble, a flask and Carthareg case, spanner and two good fire-lock pistols in houlsters. At his saddle a good stiffe sword sharp pointed, and a good poll-axe in his hand, a good tall horse of fifteen handfulls high, strong and nimble, with false reins to your bridle made of an Iron Chain as the former.[1]

In theory, a cavalry regiment consisted of 500 officers and men, organised into roughly six troops. In the case of the Royalists, each of these was supposed to comprise 'sixty men compleat besides officers', but in practice both the number and individual strengths of troops in a regiment varied widely. Though ideally the colonel should be a 'souldier of extraordinary experience and valour',[2] this was rarely the case, especially in the earlier stages of the war, although most regiments attempted to include at least one professional as either lieutenant colonel or major. Each troop was commanded by a captain, who were ranked as first, second and so on according to their seniority. These officers tended to be a mixture of 'amateurs', usually of gentry status, and professionals of various backgrounds. Second in command of the troop was its lieutenant, with a cornet, as third, also responsible for its colours. Ranking fourth was the troop quartermaster, who also dealt with quartering and supply.

A troop was to have three corporals, experienced and literate soldiers, who each commanded a squadron of twenty men and led patrols, convoy escorts and the like. There were also supposed to be two trumpeters in each troop, who, as well as their main role in communicating orders, would act as emissaries in negotiations with the enemy and also as unofficial 'spies', tasked with obtaining as much information as possible at the same time. The non-commissioned officers of a troop were completed by a clerk, saddler, farrier/veterinarian, ideally a surgeon and sometimes a chaplain.

RAISING THE ROYALIST HORSE

In 1642 the Royalist horse had to be recruited from scratch. The usual practice was to issue commissions for the King's supporters to raise '500 horse volunteers', though at first most regiments were only troop-sized. Initially, a regiment was raised at its colonel's own expense; some wealthy commanders, such as the Earls of Northampton and Newcastle, had considerable success, recruiting among their relatives, dependent minor gentry and tenants. Newcastle's troop joined the King at Hull in July, riding 'fifty great horses all of a darke Bay, handsomely set out with ash-colour'd ribbins, each man gentilely acoutred and armed'.[3] Also off to a good start was Sir John Byron, whose Nottinghamshire-raised regiment was provided with £5,000 'mounting money' by the fabulously wealthy Marquis of Worcester.

The cost of maintaining a regiment of horse was considerable, amounting to about £52 per week per troop, though in the summer of 1642, at the opening of what was anticipated would be a short decisive campaign, initial costs were assured by an undertaking from the King's leading supporters to maintain 2,015 horse for three months at a cost each of 2s. 6d. a day.[4]

Though there was no initial shortage of horses, arms and equipment for the cavalry were more difficult to obtain. The King's Lifeguard of Horse, 300 strong and consisting of noblemen, between them supposedly worth £100,00 a year, and their retainers, was so relatively well equipped as to earn the derisive and deeply resented nickname of 'the Troop of Show'. But few others were so fortunate. The Earl of Clarendon was probably only slightly exaggerating when he wrote of the Royalist horse on the eve of Edgehill: 'amongst the horse, the officers had their full desire if they were able to procure old backs and breasts and pots, with pistols and carbines for their two or three first ranks, and swords for the rest. . . .'[5]

'GENTLEMEN VERSUS DECAYED SERVING MEN'? THE SOCIAL BACKGROUND

In an oft-quoted letter written in the aftermath of Edgehill, Oliver Cromwell compared the opposing horse, saying of the Parliamentarians: 'Your troopers are most of them decayed serving men, and tapsters, and such kind of fellows; and their troopers are gentlemen's sons, younger sons and persons of quality.'[6] Though Cromwell's words are often taken as an accurate description of the rival Horse, at least in the earlier stages of the war, the reality was less clear-cut. Few Royalist units, with the exceptions of the King's Lifeguard, and perhaps the particularly blue-blooded Prince of Wales' Regiment, conformed with Cromwell's stereotype. Rupert's Regiment (having at Edgehill seven troops totalling about 465 men), while it attracted many gentry recruits, also followed Cruso's advice in appointing officers of previous experience, such as Lieutenant Colonel Dan O'Neill (an Irish professional soldier), Captain Sir Richard Crane of the Lifeguard (who had been with Rupert at Lemgo), and at least three other troop commanders. Junior officers seem to have been drawn from a surprisingly wide spectrum, including three out-of-work play actors.[7] Other regiments show a similar profile.

Less information has survived on the origins of the rank and file. Later in the war, the personnel of a typical 'line' cavalry regiment might include up to one-third whose background might be termed 'gentry', and although in the opening months of the war the proportion was probably higher, many troopers were of yeoman status, or were estate servants and tenant farmers, or anyone, including townsmen, able to provide a horse. 'Maimed soldiers' petitions provide many examples of troopers from humble backgrounds who in some cases served for the duration of the war.[8]

The Parliamentarian horse were not noticeably dissimilar. The Earl of Essex's Lifeguard at Edgehill included many younger sons of Parliamentarian peers and gentry, and most other cavalry officers came from similar backgrounds to those of their opponents. Though possibly a higher proportion of the rank and file were of urban origin, none of the Parliamentarian horse were in the sorry state suggested by Cromwell. The undeniable superiority of the Royalist horse in the opening months of the war must be explained by other factors: firstly, their greater number of professional officers; secondly, that unlike their opponents at this stage, the King's horse at Edgehill were serving as complete regiments rather than independent troops; and thirdly, most importantly, the tactics they employed.

TACTICS

The success of the Royalist horse has generally been credited to Prince Rupert. While he was undoubtedly an inspirational and charismatic commander who quickly won the loyalty of the men who followed him, the exact role the Prince played in devising the tactics they followed is less clear. Aged twenty-three on the outbreak of war, Rupert had relatively limited combat experience, and had never commanded a force larger than a brigade. After his brief active military career had culminated with capture at Lemgo in 1638, Rupert had supplemented his knowledge with extensive study of the military theorists and discussions with his Imperialist captors. But there were a number of Royalist cavalry officers with considerably more experience, such as Henry, Lord Wilmot, later Lieutenant General of the Oxford Army horse, and Patrick Ruthven, that vastly experienced veteran of the Swedish service, who, significantly, played a major role in the initial training of the Royalist cavalry in the summer of 1642.

In the early months of the war, the opposing sides practised sharply differing tactics. Those of the Parliamentarians were based on Dutch doctrines emphasising the use of firepower to break up the impetus of an enemy assault before responding with a charge or countercharge. Often derided, these tactics could, in fact, work successfully if the troops employing them were sufficiently well motivated and trained. Even as early as the action at Powicke Bridge in September 1642, Nathaniel Fiennes' horse employed them with some effect, and by the following summer better trained and more experienced Parliamentarian horse were putting up a significantly stronger performance using basically similar tactics to those employed at Edgehill. But, in general, they never successfully matched the tactics of the Royalist cavalry.

These latter are usually said to have been modelled on those developed partly by the Swedish forces of Gustavus Adolphus, but there were, initially, significant differences, as comparison of two contemporary descriptions demonstrates. Before his horse went into action at Edgehill, Prince Rupert 'passed from one Wing to the other, giving positive Orders to the Horse, to march as close as was possible, keeping their Ranks with Sword in Hand, to receive the Enemy's Shot, without firing either Carbin or Pistol, till we broke in amongst the Enemy, and then to make use of our Fire-Arms as need should require, which Order was punctually observed'.[9]

Compare this with a contemporary account of Gustavus's orders: 'Only the first or at most the first two ranks, when near enough to see the whites of the enemy's eyes, were to give fire, then to reach for their swords; the last rank however was to attack without shooting but with swords drawn, and to keep both pistols (or in the front ranks, one) in reserve for the melee.'[10]

Gustavus was still making considerable use of firepower, albeit more effectively than in the older 'caracole' tactics, but the 'charge' of the Swedish horse remained a fairly ponderous affair, involving a pause while the leading ranks fired their pistols at about 10 yards' range, before closing in for the mêlée. At Edgehill, Rupert dispensed with this preliminary, and went straight into hand-to-hand combat. The Royalists were making a virtue of necessity brought about by their initial serious shortage of firearms.

The inspiration for the Royalist tactics, which have aptly been described as employing troops equipped as light horse or harquebusiers in the role of heavy cavalry or cuirassiers,[11] is unclear. Certainly, Swedish tactics played an important part, but similar techniques had been used earlier in the century by Polish horse, again because of a shortage of firearms, and both Rupert and Ruthven would have known of this.[12] The Prince may also have been influenced by the success of the improvised charge which his horse had made at Powick Bridge. But even at this stage of the war, the Royalist cavalry were not generally indulging in the wild undisciplined career of popular legend. While anxious to get to grips with the enemy before the latter could make full use of their superior firepower, the Royalists still advanced in 'close order' – which precluded a pace faster than a 'good round trot'.

At Edgehill, Royalist tactics met with general success, but the incomplete training of many of the troopers resulted in most of the reserves becoming caught up in an unrestrained pursuit. But even now, a few professional soldiers like Sir Charles Lucas were able to retain at least some control, and later writers have been unduly influenced by the inaccurate statement of the Earl of Clarendon that 'Though the King's troops prevailed in the charge and routed those they charged, they seldom rallied themselves in order, nor could be brought to make a second charge the same day. . . .'[13] As we shall see, this claim is amply contradicted by other evidence.

The tactics employed so successfully at Edgehill were generally adopted by the other Royalist forces, though as firearms became more plentiful by the summer of 1643 they more closely resembled the recognised Swedish doctrines.

But the Parliamentarians were also improving in quality, as testified in a description of the action at Chalgrove (14 June 1643), which also demonstrates that the Royalists had absorbed the lessons of Edgehill: 'To say the truth, they stood our first charge of Pistols and Swords, better than the Rebels have ever yet done . . . [while the Cavaliers] had learn'd by Edgehill, not to pursue too far: so that now contenting themselves to have routed the rebels, they were seen to rallee themselves again into action handsomely, and suddenly in their ground.'[14]

The developments in tactics are illustrated in Sir John Byron's account of the sweeping Royalist victory at Roundway Down (13 July):

> The command I gave my men was, that not a man should discharge his pistol till the enemy had spent all his shot, which was punctually observed, so that first they gave us a volley of their carbines, then of their pistols, and then we fell in with them, and gave them ours in their teeth, yet they would not quit their ground, but stood pushing for it a pretty space . . .[15]

Byron's description is amplified by another participant, Captain Richard Atkyns of Prince Maurice's Regiment: '[we] immediately charged the whole body; the charge was so sudden that I had hardly time to put on my arms, we advanced at full trot 3 deep, and kept in order . . .'.[16] However, Roundway Down was almost the last of the major Royalist cavalry successes; their margin of superiority was narrowing.

ROYALIST SUPREMACY

The Royalist cavalry arm was expanded rapidly during the winter of 1642/3. At this stage, volunteers for the horse were still relatively easy to obtain, and the old regiments maintained and indeed increased their strength, while some new units also recruited with success, although it sometimes proved difficult to retain them once raised. The experience of Richard Atkyns was probably a common one:

> within one month, I mustered 60 men besides officers, and almost all of them well armed; Master [John] Dutton [a wealthy Gloucestershire Royalist who also raised a regiment of foot] giving me 30 steel backs, breasts and head pieces, and two men and horses completely armed: and this was done upon duty, without any advance of money, or quarters assigned; wherein every fourth or fifth man was lost.
>
> My troop I paid twice out of my own purse, and about a fortnight after, at the siege of Bristol [7 March 1643], I mustered 80 men besides officers; whereof 20 of them gentlemen that bore arms.[17]

By the winter of 1642 the equipment of a Royalist cavalryman was becoming more standardised. On 14 December Captain Gerard Croker's Troop of forty-four men was issued with:

Backes	33
Breasts	33
Potts	33
Van [arm] braces	1
Pre-gauntlets	2
Holdsters	13 paire
Gorgetts	25[18]

Because of their cost, buff-coats (£10 for one of good quality, compared with £2 for a basic set of harquebusier armour) were rarely part of standard issue, although they were worn by some officers who could afford the price.

By the autumn of 1643, the improvement in munitions supplies enabled Sir Charles Lucas to re-equip his regiment after the First Battle of Newbury in more satisfactory fashion, receiving:

Pistolls furnished with Holsters and Spanners	60 paire
Carbines	40
Bandeleeres	80[19]

Cavalry firearms were imported in large numbers; a consignment that arrived from Holland in December 1643 included 1,000 carbines costing 31s. each, and 1,000 pistols at 51s. a pair. Though their quality varied, these imports were essential for the Royalist cavalry arm, for wastage was extremely high, both from battle losses and damage. Although many swords were imported from the Continent, the majority were manufactured in England. In the earlier stages of the war, the short-handled pole-axe seems to have been a popular weapon among the Royalist horse, though its use declined.

There is no evidence that regulation clothing was issued to the Royalist horse, as it was, whenever possible, to the foot. Such matters seem to have been the responsibility of the individual colonel or troop commander. On 16 November 1644 the Royalist newsletter *Mercurius Aulicus* reported a raid on Warwick by Captain John Moore of the Earl of Northampton's Regiment, in which 120 yards of red cloth was taken, 'with which the courageous Captaine intends to clothe his Souldiers'.[20] In August 1644 Sir Thomas Dallison, Colonel of Prince Rupert's Regiment of Horse, informed the Prince that he had obtained a large quantity of cloth to make cloaks for his troopers. Scarlet seems to have been particularly popular for officers, both horse and foot. As well as a cloak, or long riding coat, to protect them from the elements, most troopers also had a short jacket or cassock, breeches, and, ideally, riding boots.[21] A variety of headgear was in use, least common being the wide-brimmed hats popularly associated with the Cavaliers. More practical for horsemen were the type of cloth headgear known as 'monteros' or, apparently particularly popular, fisherman-style woollen 'Monmouth' caps.

The lack of uniformity in dress and the similarity in equipment of the opposing sides led to the need to identify allegiance and units by means of coloured scarves (often red or crimson for the Royalists) and flags or 'cornets', which in the case of the horse frequently bore political or religious slogans appropriate to the King's cause or satirising their opponents.

Essential to any cavalry trooper, if he were not to degenerate into a mere foot soldier, was his horse. Most troopers seem to have had only one mount, though an officer might have several, including both a 'riding' horse for travel, and a battle-trained mount for combat. Initially, a trooper was expected if possible to provide his own horse, with losses from disease or combat replaced by the army. The considerable demand was met by purchases from professional horse dealers, donations from sympathisers, who were sometimes promised some financial compensation, captures from the enemy or confiscations from real or pretended enemy supporters. A captain might be given funds to purchase mounts for his troop, at an average of between £7 and £10 each, or a group of troopers would establish a joint fund to replace those mounts whose loss (supposedly through an owner's negligence) was not covered by the authorities.

Horses were a constant headache to the average cavalry commander. As well as the problems encountered in providing adequate fodder and shelter, they were sometimes not helped by the actions of their own men. In June 1644, in the absence of Sir Charles Lucas from his regiment, one of his officers complained that: 'Our captaine hath left the troope and the souldiers are so without government that they sell the horses from under them and then say they lost them. . . .'[22]

By the early summer of 1643 a typical Royalist cavalry regiment consisted of four or five troops, totalling 300 to 400 men. Its officers were a mixture of gentry, frequently related to one another, and professional soldiers from a variety of backgrounds. The troopers were predominantly of rural origin, though they also included townsmen drawn from a wide range of occupations.

Conscription was not generally employed for the horse, so desertion rates were normally lower than in foot units.

Rarely mentioned, even by contemporaries, are the large number of non-combatants frequently accompanying a cavalry unit. In a Continental comparison, in 1646 one Bavarian regiment of horse included in its ranks 481 troopers, 236 servants, 102 women and children and 9 sutlers.[23] Though no detailed figures are available for the Royalists, references suggest a similar situation. In the summer of 1644 witnesses wrote disapprovingly of the large number of women camp-followers, known as 'leaguer ladies', who accompanied the Northern Horse, and in December the same troops in Salisbury looted items of clothing for women and children.[24] Cruso recommended that each trooper should have a boy to forage for him and look after his horse and equipment.[25] The Bavarian statistics suggest that this ratio was neither practical nor desired, but in November 1645, when a Royalist force under Sir William Vaughan was attempting to relieve Chester, it included a large number of horseboys or 'padees'. Those captured were released as 'not worth the keeping'.[26]

By the winter of 1642/3 the unexpectedly prolonged war was causing increasing problems for the Royalist horse. Too many commissions were being issued to raise regiments without the necessary funds to maintain them, and the King was forced to allow his existing units to maintain themselves by free quarter. Discipline was also a problem; in December Byron warned Rupert that his regiment 'had hardly been kept from . . . mutiny, and doth daily diminish',[27] while Lieutenant Colonel Dan O'Neill told the Prince of problems he was encountering with Rupert's Lifeguard: 'The officers of your own troop will obey in no kind of thing, and by their example neer a soldier in that company.'[28]

CHANGING TACTICS

The King's horse retained general superiority over their opponents for about nine months after Edgehill, but the training and tactical abilities of the Parliamentarian cavalry were gradually improving, exemplified by the tough fighting and severe casualties incurred by the Cavaliers at First Newbury

(20 September 1643). Byron, for example, lost 100 men, a third of his regiment.

By early 1644 both sides were similarly equipped and using basically the same tactics, described by Captain John Vernon:

> Those troops that are to give the first charge . . . are to be at their close order, every left-hand man's right knee must be locked under his right-hand man's left ham. . . . In this order they are to advance toward the Enemy with an easy pace, firing their Carbines at a convenient distance . . . then drawing neere the Enemy, they are to take forth one of their Pistols out of their holsters . . . firing as before. . . . Having thus fired, the troops are to charge the Enemy in full career.[29]

The Royalist cavalry were increasingly having to fight on the defensive. Following Continental developments, Rupert attempted during the last two years of the war to address the changing situation by increasing the firepower available to his cavalry by means of interspersed 50-strong squads of 'commanded' musketeers.

By the end of the war cavalry actions had become brutal slogging contests, which might last for half an hour or more, with units breaking off to re-form and then resuming the action. At Marston Moor (2 July 1644) a Parliamentarian observer noted: 'The Enemie's Horse, being many of them, if not the greatest part, Gentlemen, stood very firm a long time, coming to a close fight with the Sword, and standing like an Iron Wall, so that they were not easily broken.'[30] Contrary to accepted legend, the now experienced Royalist horse were capable of being rallied after a reverse and committed to a countercharge. Again at Marston Moor, Prince Rupert 'met his own regiment turning their backs to the enemy, which was a thing so strange and unusual he said zwounds, do you run, follow me . . .' and led them in a counter-attack.[31]

At Naseby, Rupert's horse did not, in fact, indulge in the reckless pursuit of legend. There had been no repeat of the rout inflicted at Edgehill, and the Royalists had themselves suffered severely in a close-fought engagement. While some took part in a controlled pursuit, the remainder stayed on the field to support the foot. The main problem for the Royalist horse at Naseby was that they were simply too few in number.[32] Even in the closing stages of the war, at encounters such as Rowton Heath and Shirburn, the King's cavalry could still fight with spirit and determination.

THE RISE OF THE PROFESSIONAL

The hard fighting of 1643 wore down the strength of the Oxford Army horse. Byron and others pressed unsuccessfully for the veteran regiments to be rested and recruited, but the Aldbourne Chase rendezvous of 10 April 1644 demonstrated the weakened condition of the Royalist cavalry. The twenty-six regiments present varied in number between 80 and 300 men, possibly not including officers, with an average strength of 150 troopers.[33] But the dwindling strength of a regiment did not necessarily result in a corresponding reduction in its establishment of officers, which tended to be maintained even if the number of troops was reduced. They continued to be paid at their usual rate, (an average of 10s. a day for a captain, 5s. for a lieutenant, and 4s. for a cornet, compared with an ordinary trooper's 2s.). This meant that the cost of maintaining a regiment was far more than its numerical strength might indicate, and the increasing need to brigade together several weak units on the battlefield resulted in units that often lacked experience in serving together, and which contained too many 'reformadoes' – officers without commands, who often found it difficult to serve in a subordinate capacity. Though for the moment most Parliamentarian units suffered from similar weaknesses, the reorganisation caused by the formation of the New Model Army would leave the unreconstructed Royalist horse at a fatal disadvantage.

In February 1644 Prince Rupert took up command in Wales and the Marches, and began a reorganisation of the Royalist forces there which saw a marked rise in the influence of the professional soldier. For example, Lord Capel's old Regiment of Horse was taken over by Colonel Marcus Trevor, a professional soldier from Ireland. Command of Lord Cholmondeley's largely moribund Cheshire Regiment was assumed by another career soldier, John Marrow, who revitalised it, and led it with such distinction until his death in August 1644 that he earned the reluctant accolade from the Cheshire Parliamentarians of 'a second Nimrod . . . a stout soldier and brave commander'.[34]

The rise of the professional was less striking in the Oxford Army, where units were evidently not re-recruited as successfully as in Rupert's command. The proportion of horse to foot dropped from the generally recommended ratio of 1:1 to nearer 2:1. In August 1644 the dismissal of its Lieutenant General, the usually capable Lord Wilmot, on probably exaggerated accusations of treasonable intent, caused initial upheaval and a petition to the King from the cavalry officers, but the main long-term result was Wilmot's replacement by George Goring. Goring had proved a highly effective cavalry commander in the North, and was the only senior Royalist commander to emerge with credit from the débâcle at Marston Moor. But he was also an ambitious self-seeking political intriguer, and eventually a combination of dissolute living and ill health would do much to undermine his undoubted talent. Writing of the early summer of 1645, when Goring's failings were more evident than was the case a year earlier, his brigade major, Sir Richard Bulstrode, said:

> He was a Person of extraordinary Abilities as well as Courage, and was, without any Dispute, as good an Officer as any served the King, and the most dextrous, in any sudden Emergency, that I have ever seen, and could extricate himself with the least Concern. . . . But . . . he had likewise his blind Side, for he strangely loved the Bottle, was much given to his Pleasures and a great Debauchee . . .[35]

Though scoring some striking successes in his new command, notably at the Second Battle of Newbury (20 October 1644), Goring proved unable to work amicably with Rupert after the latter was appointed as Lieutenant General. The outcome was that, with the King's connivance, Goring and 1,500 of the 'Old Horse' of the Oxford Army were given an effectively independent command, and left to operate futilely in an unsuccessful thrust towards Sussex and in deadlocked operations in the West. The situation came to a head on the eve of the Naseby campaign with the decision to send Goring and his horse back to the West, leaving the Oxford Army at Naseby with a distinctly second-rate mix of cavalry, who were too few and too lacking in cohesion to deal with the New Model horse.

The end of the Royalist horse was protracted and hard fought. After Naseby, his 3,000 to 4,000 surviving horse provided the only coherent field force left to the King outside the West of England, but, though it had considerable nuisance value, it was incapable of matching the New Model in the open field or preventing the piecemeal reduction of the Royalists' remaining territory. After defeats at Rowton Heath and Shirburn, followed by the resignation of most of its best remaining officers following Rupert's quarrel with the King, the remnants of the Oxford Army horse largely disintegrated.

In the West, under Goring's increasingly erratic leadership, and that of his acting successor, Thomas Wentworth, the indiscipline and depredations of the Royalist horse made them objects of hatred among the civilian population and local Royalist forces. Assuming command of the Western Army in the last desperate days of the war, Ralph Hopton said of his cavalry: 'Amongst them were divers gallant men, but in general I cannot say they were exact upon duty.'[36] Clarendon, unsurprisingly, was less charitable, writing of 'those horse whom only their friends feared and their enemies laughed at, being only terrible in plunder and resolute in running away'.[37]

During the closing months of the war, throughout the steadily shrinking areas under Royalist control, the King's horse increasingly turned to near banditry in order to survive. With the Royalist distribution and manufacturing system breaking down, they were frequently miserably equipped and woefully understrength. For example, Vaughan's force defeated at Denbigh Green on 1 November 1645 consisted of 1,200 men drawn from at least ten regiments, of whom it was said that 'scarce a tenth man hath a pistol',[38] while a Parliamentarian account of the Royalist surrender of Bristol in September 1645 includes a description of some troopers who may have been members of Prince Rupert's once proud Regiment of Horse:

First there came a half-dozen of carbines in their leathern coats and starved weather-beaten jades, just like so many brewers in their jerkins made of old boots, riding to fetch in old casks; and after them as many light horsemen with great saddles and scarce a sword amongst them, just like so many fiddlers with their fiddles in cases by their horses sides . . .[39]

The reasons for the ultimate failure of the Royalist horse after so promising a birth are to a great extent bound up with those for the wider Royalist defeat. The Cavalier horse were the equal of their opponents in most respects, but the seeds of eventual defeat lay in the failure to come to grips with the need for root and branch reform and reorganisation which became increasingly apparent from early 1644 onwards. The inability of the King and his generals to resolve the disputed command situation of the Oxford Army horse was a major factor in the Royalist defeat at Naseby. It is ironic that, by his inability to resolve this question, Prince Rupert, who had contributed so much to the early success of the cavalry with whom his name would for ever be associated, also bore a major responsibility for its defeat.

Four

THE FOOT

'From Gloucester Siege till Arms laid down
In Trewoe fields, I for the Crown,
Under St George Marched Up and Down . . .'
William Mercer, *The Moderate Cavalier*,
1671

THE FIRST CAMPAIGN

Though the cavalry were still regarded as the 'queen of battle', the role of the foot soldier steadily increased in importance throughout the first part of the seventeenth century, and the English Civil War confirmed this trend.

The organisation of a regiment of foot was clearly laid down by the military theorists. Following the Dutch pattern, by 1642 a standard unit consisted of between 1,000 and 1,200 rank and file, plus officers. It was composed of ten companies, the companies of the field officers varying between 140 and 160 men, and the remainder averaging 100.[1] In practice, however, this rule was honoured more in the breach than the observance.

A foot regiment was commanded by a colonel, usually of gentry or aristocratic background, who often put up most of the money to raise and equip it. His lieutenant colonel and major, who in some cases actually led it in the field, might be professional soldiers. Also on a regiment's strength were all or some of the following miscellaneous officers: a quartermaster, surgeon, provost-marshal, chaplain, wagonmaster and drum major.

Each company was led by a captain,[2] and its officers completed by a lieutenant and ensign, with three sergeants, three corporals and two drummers. Both sides in 1642 aimed at the recommended Dutch ratio of two musketeers to one pikeman, although this was not achieved in the Royalist forces for some time. In the early stages of the war, when commanders had large numbers of raw recruits, the expertise of the professional soldier was invaluable and their services were in high demand. The wealthier colonels were better able to attract professional officers, and the regiment raised by the Gloucestershire merchant Ralph Dutton included at least five veterans of the 1640 war. The King's Lifeguard was similarly well provided for; both its Colonel, Lord Willoughby d'Eresby, and Lieutenant Colonel, Sir William Vavasour, had seen service against the Scots, along with a number of their officers. Other colonels were less fortunate, counting themselves lucky if perhaps their lieutenant colonel and one or two other officers had previous experience.[3]

COMMAND

The Major General of Foot was an important part of the military hierarchy. King Charles showed wisdom in his selection of Jacob Astley, who led the Oxford Army foot throughout the war. Astley, a Norfolk man of vast experience in Dutch and Swedish service, was already sixty years of age when appointed as Sergeant Major of Foot in the Scots War of 1639. A former tutor of Prince Rupert, Astley was the natural choice as Major General, 'a command he was very equal to, and had exercised before, and executed with great approbation'.[4] A solid professional soldier, Astley was summed up by Clarendon as 'honest, brave, plain, prompt in giving orders, cheerful in any action, and as fit for the office he exercised as Christendom yielded'.[5] He was no great innovator, 'rather collected the ends of debates, and what he was himself to do, than enlarged them by his own discourse, though he forbore not to deliver his own mind'.[6]

Astley had an excellent team of brigade commanders. Outstanding among them was Colonel George Lisle. Son of a bookseller, Lisle was a highly experienced professional soldier, who came to prominence leading his brigade of musketeers at First Newbury. He distinguished himself at Cheriton and in the defence of Shaw House at Second Newbury in October 1644, when, stripped to his shirt to aid identification by his men in the gathering dusk, he led three counter-attacks. Lisle was reportedly offered a knighthood in November 1644 but declined, commenting 'he would not be tempted or receive any honour till he was sure to keep it, and then doubted not but he should as well deserve to be a Lord as many that were near his Majesty'.[7] Commanding, with distinction, a brigade at Naseby, Lisle eventually accepted his knighthood in the twilight of the Royalist cause in November 1645.

Equally characteristic were Lisle's last words. Sentenced to death by Fairfax for his part in the defence of Colchester in 1648, Lisle asked the firing squad to come closer, wryly dismissing their assurances of accuracy: 'Friends, I have been nearer you when you have missed me.'[8]

Among Astley's other senior commanders were Sir Nicholas Byron, 'a person of great affability', who led a tertia at Edgehill and First Newbury, Thomas Blagge, described by his commander as 'a notable griper', who, perhaps because of this, seems to have lost favour with the King, and Sir Jacob's son, Bernard, who was appointed to brigade command in the autumn of 1644.

Prince Rupert made few changes in the command structure of the foot after his appointment as Lieutenant General. He might, perhaps, have liked to replace Astley with Henry Tillier, the leading theoretician who had been his Major General in 1644, but Tillier had been captured at Marston Moor and was not exchanged until the summer of 1645. The only change which may be attributed to Rupert was the rather surprising appointment of Sir Henry Bard. A young man who only became a colonel in 1643, Bard, described as 'a compact body of vanity and ambitions', though with evident charm,[9] had a meteoric rise. The defeat at Cheriton was blamed in part on Bard's rashness, but he was given one of the few regiments of foot to be strengthened and reorganised in Rupert's 'new-modelling', and was a brigade commander at Naseby, receiving a peerage in July. His evident status as a protégé and friend of the Prince is perhaps underlined by his daughter becoming a mistress of Rupert in later years.

ARMS AND EQUIPMENT: THE RISE OF THE MUSKETEER

The Royalist *Military Orders and Articles* of 1642 laid down the desirable arms and equipment of the King's foot:

> The Armes of a Pike-man are, Gorget, Curats, head-piece, Sword, Girdle and Hangers.
> The Armes of a Musquetier are, Musquet, a Rest, Bandeliers, Head-piece, Sword, Girdle and Hangers.[10]

For a long time this remained a pious hope. The Royalist foot began the war severely lacking in arms. Clarendon described the condition of the King's infantry at Edgehill: 'The foot (all but three or four hundred who marched without any weapon but a cudgel) were armed with muskets, and bags for their powder, and pikes; but in the whole body there was not one pikeman had a corselet, and very few musketeers who had swords.'[11] He is supported by the Royalist Ordnance Papers. In November sufficient powder was issued to the army to supply the needs of 4,000 musketeers, only perhaps half of the total Royalist foot, so given that some firearms would have been captured at Edgehill, at that stage the proportion of musket to pike must have been under 1:1.[12]

Lack of firepower was a major factor in the King's decision not to withdraw at Turnham Green, for with only 17 tons of black powder in store, once the immediate needs of the musketeers and the twenty-seven guns of the artillery train had been met, very little was left in reserve.[13] The problem continued well into the following year.

So far as the pikeman was concerned, experience soon demonstrated, as it already had on the Continent, that the full panoply of cuirass, grieves, gorget and helmet served only to hinder and slow him down, without adding a commensurate amount of protection. The Earl of Essex, who had begun the war issuing body armour to at least some of his pikemen, soon dispensed with it, and there is no evidence that it was ever worn in the Oxford Army.[14] The shortage of muskets and ammunition was more serious. In February 1643, for example, the King's

Lifeguard of Foot had 322 of its 512 men unarmed. It took until April to supply them, and even then with twice as many 'long pikes' as muskets.[15]

Shortage of munitions crippled the Oxford Army foot during the spring of 1643. By May, with the arrival of the first major arms convoy from the North, and the Oxford munitions industry beginning to come on stream, the situation was easing slightly, and the foot regiments at Culham Camp seem to have been resupplied with arms at the approved 2:1 ratio.[16] By late summer, with the arrival at Oxford of the Queen and her great convoy from the North, the growing supplies of imported arms from the Continent brought in through West Country ports, and the capture of the arms manufacturing capabilities of the Bristol area, the situation was considerably improved. Weapon shortages were not henceforward a serious problem, although difficulties still occurred in obtaining sufficient supplies of powder, and more particularly in transporting it to where it was needed. In the spring of 1644, for example, Prince Rupert's foot on the Welsh Border were reported as being 'very poor and ragged, very many had no arms but swords'.[17]

By late 1643 a typical musketeer was equipped with a matchlock musket and rest, and a cheap sword. In the earlier stages of the war, the Oxford Army musketeers carried their ammunition either simply stuffed into their pockets or in powder bags made from 'calfe skinns tanned and oyled' by glovers and bookbinders in Oxford.[18] As supplies became more plentiful, certainly by late 1644, these had been replaced by the traditional bandolier, with twelve or more powder chargers. Pikemen carried pikes varying in length between 12 and 16 feet[19] and the same type of sword as the musketeer.

Most of the Oxford Army foot began the war wearing civilian dress, their allegiance denoted by coloured ribbons, rosettes or hat bands, usually red. Possibly only the Lifeguard of Foot and a couple of other regiments, clothed by Thomas Bushell, the great industrialist and businessman, were uniformed at Edgehill.[20] However, in November, faced by a prolonged campaign, the Royalist Council of War issued orders to the Reading tailors to prepare 4,000 suits of clothes for the army.[21]

Whenever possible, troops were issued with new clothing at

the start of the campaigning season, and in March 1643 Bushell was contracted 'to procure for the King's Souldiers Cassocks, Breeches, Stockings and Capps at reasonable rates to be delivered at Oxford'.[22] By the summer all the units then in the Royalist capital had been clothed in either red or blue suits and montero caps. Although other coat colours, mostly green or various shades of grey, are noted from time to time, these in the main belonged to troops such as the reinforcements received from the North and Ireland, and blue and red remained the colour of preference for the Oxford Army foot throughout the war.[23] Civilian clothing was still sometimes supplied, notably in the autumn of 1644, when the inhabitants of Devon and Somerset were called upon to provide for the ill-clad troops returning from the Lostwithiel campaign.[24]

As the war went on there was a tendency to increase the proportion of musketeers. They were always preferred for garrison duty, but there was increasing recognition of musketeers' mobility. Prince Rupert took a detachment of 500 'commanded' musketeers, probably mounted behind his troopers and dragoons, on the Chalgrove Raid of June 1643. Lieutenant Colonel George Lisle commanded a detachment of 1,000 musketeers, drawn from a number of regiments, designed to operate with the cavalry, and possibly themselves mounted, during the Gloucester campaign of 1643, supplemented by another 500-strong brigade under Colonel Theophilous Gilby, out of the Bristol garrison.

The increased mobility caused by dispensing with pikemen was again highlighted during the rapid marches of the King's army in the prelude to the battle of Cropredy Bridge in June 1644. All of the 2,500 foot with the King on the first stage of his 'escape' from the armies of Essex and Waller were musketeers, probably mounted.[25]

There are examples of regiments, perhaps understrength ones, previously armed on the orthodox 2:1 musket/pike ratio, apparently converting, at least for a time, to all-musketeer units.[26] Most, however (especially those regiments that maintained respectable numbers), retained the pike throughout the war.

VOLUNTEERS AND 'PRESSED MEN': RAISING THE ROYALIST FOOT

The Royalist army that fought at Edgehill theoretically consisted of volunteers. Though this was, with reservations, indeed true of the horse, the actual situation among the seventeen foot regiments is less clear. Many of the rank and file were pressured by various means into enlisting. In some units, such as Sir William Pennyman's, raised in Yorkshire early in the summer, trained bandsmen, serving under their pre-war officers, who were frequently their landlords or employers, formed the bulk of the troops.[27] The ranks of the King's Lifeguard included a large number of tenants of its Colonel, Lord Willoughby d'Eresby, and a contingent of Derbyshire leadminers despatched by their employer, Thomas Bushell.[28] Compulsion, with obvious implications in case of refusal, is highlighted in the Lancashire regiments of Lord Molyneux and the Gerrards. Molyneux's lieutenant colonel, Thomas Tyldesley, summoned his tenants together, and compelled them to enlist, while the leading Royalist magnate in the county, the Earl of Derby, ordered his to report for duty 'on pain of death', and instructed his officers to shoot any stragglers or would-be deserters.[29]

Significant though it was, compulsion was not the only means by which the Royalist foot were raised. In the early days, when it was generally expected that one battle would decide matters, many were attracted by the prospect of adventure, of seeing the world beyond the narrow confines of their own village or town, the promise of relatively generous and regular pay, and the hope of booty and glory. Although other pressures played a part, the proceedings that Richard Gough recorded at the village of Myddle in Shropshire were doubtless duplicated widely during the summer of 1642. The local Royalist Commissioner of Array, Sir Paul Harris, 'a proud imperious person', employed two recruiting agents, Robert Moore and Matthew Bagley:

> The veriest knaves in Pimhill hundred . . . Sir Paul Harris sent out warrents requiring or commanding all men, both householders with their sons, and servants and sojourners, and others within the hundred of Pimhill that were between

the age of sixteen and six score to appear on a certain day upon Myddle Hill. . . . And there I saw a multitude of men, and upon the highest bank of the hill I saw this Robert Moore standing, with a paper in his hand, and three or four soldier's pikes, stuck upright in the ground by him, and there he made a proclamation, that if any person would serve the King as a soldier in the wars, he should have 14 groats [44p] a week for his pay . . .[30]

Such an offer, when the average pay of an agricultural labourer was about 3p a day, was highly attractive, and mass recruitments of this sort, as well as 'beating the drum' in villages and towns by a regiment's officers and recruiting sergeants, met with a good response. As a result, the regional origins usually associated with the regiments that fought at Edgehill are in some cases deceptive. Wherever their officers and perhaps a small cadre of men may have hailed from, the bulk of the rank and file were often only recruited after the King's arrival at Shrewsbury, mainly from the West Midlands or Wales.

Although recruits were drawn from a wide spectrum, the majority were from labouring or similarly poor backgrounds. Among the twenty men from Myddle whom Gough lists as serving with the Royalist forces (thirteen would not return), at least seven were unemployed, with criminal records, or of no fixed abode. They included 'an idle fellow, who was a tailor and went from place to place in this parish, but had no habitation . . .' and the 'bastard son of Richard Challoner. . . . This bastard was partly maintained by the parish, and being a big lad, went to Shrewsbury, and was there listed, and went to Edgehill to fight and was never heard of afterwards in this country.'[31] From the very start of the war, parish authorities lost no opportunity to 'off-load' individuals regarded as a burden on their local community.

Others enlisted to escape from difficulties in civilian life. Thomas Ash of Myddle was 'a proper comely person with a good country education'. Heavily in debt, Ash enlisted in the Royalist foot 'to shelter himself from the fatigue of duns', but never rose higher than corporal, and 'brought nothing home but a crazy body, and many scars'.[32] Men of previous military experience were highly sought after, men such as William

Booth of Nantwich who, after the Restoration, was to petition for a pension stating that he had been 'a true and faithfull servant for His Majesty . . . in England and Ireland . . . and was wounded and maymed in fights in Ireland, first at Ross and Swords, at Finlays and Mulingar and had his head broke in pieces, and three pieces of his skull taken out, and then shott in shoulder, cutt in legg, runne into the Breast with a pike then his Matie was pleased to send for him out of Ireland to be one of his guard'.[33] The evidence of such sources as the Quarter Sessions Records suggests that recruits also tended to be drawn from men in steady if humble employment whose enlistment contained an element of compulsion.[34] They included, for example, many cobblers, malsters and leather workers of Francis Gamull's Regiment in Chester, a 'volunteer' unit raised late in 1642, supposedly solely for the defence of the city. Most of them were employees of or otherwise economically dependent upon Gamull and his officers, who were mainly from leading Chester merchant families. However, even this 'voluntary' aspect soon disappeared when all citizens of military age were compelled to enlist in its ranks.[35]

On top of the losses of the autumn campaign, during the winter of 1642/3 the foot of the Oxford Army was depleted still further by sickness and desertion. It has been estimated that the average foot company could lose up to half of its strength during the winter,[36] and although some of the deserters might, willingly or otherwise, eventually return, their tales at home of the realities of military life served to discourage other potential volunteers. By the spring, average regimental strength was only about 500 men, and the fifteen Oxford Army foot regiments at the capture of Bristol in July may have totalled only about 4,500 soldiers.[37]

As Royalist territory was poorer in manpower resources than that of Parliament, there was an ongoing and worsening shortage of foot in the Oxford Army. Conscription on a local basis was introduced from as early as the spring of 1643, and by the end of the year was in place throughout almost all Royalist-held territory.[38] Warrants were issued by the Council of War in Oxford to a county's Commissioners of Array, or an impressment committee drawn from them, to raise a specified number of men by a stipulated date. Major Royalist garrisons such as Chester,

Shrewsbury and Bristol seem to have acted as clearing houses for recruits. Here they were mustered and either formed into new regiments or sent on to the field armies. At Bristol, at least, they were often clothed and armed as well.

Enforcement of conscription was in the hands of the parish authorities and constables, backed by military support if necessary. The quota from each parish was met by a variety of methods. The *posse comitatus* might be summoned and the required numbers selected from it. An undated instruction to the Royalist Commissioners in Carmarthenshire outlines the critera used:

First for the persons you are to impresst for or same you shall make choyce – Of such as are of able bodyes – Of such as are for their quality fitt to be Common Souldiers – Of such as are fitt by the age between 20 and 60 years – Of such as being single are not housekeepers – Of such as not being housekeepers are out of service rather than such as are in – Of such as are Mechanicks rather than husbandmen . . .[39]

The reality was different. Constables came under pressure, and sometimes threats, from local communities anxious to avoid conscription. Rounding up deserters was an easier option, as was seizing unfortunate strangers or vagrants who happened to be passing through the parish. Royalist officials would have echoed the Parliamentarian High Constable in Norfolk who instructed his deputies to 'have an especiall care to take idle serving men and such other able persons as live dissolutely or without imployment'.[40] Unfortunately, the county authorities and sometimes the army were apt to object to receiving predominantly the dregs of society, and another consideration was that a constable remained responsible for his recruits until he had delivered them to a captain or conductor who was to take them to the army. If any escaped beforehand, the constable had to find a substitute.

In an effort to prevent such losses, strict penalties could be imposed. Those refusing to serve could be proceeded against by martial law, and a £1 bounty was offered for bringing in deserters, who were subject to execution if they resisted.[41] Nevertheless, renewed with fresh quotas for 6,000 men by the Parliament in Oxford in 1644, conscription never achieved its targets. Although the local Royalist authorities often met the demanded targets, many of the recruits were syphoned off into regional forces, particularly of a strong independent general such as Prince Rupert in the Welsh Marches in the spring of 1644. A great many more, despite all precautions, found means to escape en route. Typical were the 600 Hampshire men pressed into service in February 1645; 100 deserted immediately, and 200 more on the march to Winchester.[42]

The final source of recruits were enemy prisoners, though these on the whole were of limited value. Many of the prisoners taken at Cirencester in February 1643, for example, chose to join the King's forces rather than endure the horrors of Oxford Castle prison, and about 1,000 of the captured garrison of Bristol also enlisted. But such recruits were generally poorly motivated, and liable either to switch sides again, or more often simply to desert.

MANPOWER PROBLEMS

Few Royalist foot regiments ever approached full strength. Much depended on the resources, ability and reputation of individual colonels. Prince Rupert's famous regiment of Bluecoats (taken over by the Prince after the death of Colonel Henry Lunsford at the storm of Bristol in 1643) maintained respectable numbers throughout the war. At least 700-strong at Marston Moor, it recovered from that disaster by being given priority in the new drive for manpower that followed in North Wales and its borders, and could muster 500 men at Naseby in June 1645.[43] Possibly because a cadre of experienced officers and NCOs had been retained, it also maintained its formidable fighting ability.[44] Indeed, when considering the effects of 'wastage' on the Royalist foot, it should be remembered that examples such as the petitions from 'maimed' soldiers demonstrate that most units contained a significant number of men who served throughout the war and who thus provided a core around which new recruits could be absorbed in a surprisingly short time.[45]

In the field, wastage was less from battle than from other causes. During the Lostwithiel campaign of 1644, for example, the Oxford Army's original strength of 5,000 foot declined to 3,500, and Prince Maurice's Western Army from 4,500 to

2,000. The majority of losses were as a result of sickness, detachments for garrison duty and desertion.[46] Ironically, the latter was at its greatest following a military success. The Oxford Army was effectively crippled for several vital days after the capture of Leicester in May 1645, partly because hundreds of its foot had made off with their booty from the town, and the victorious New Model suffered in the same way after Naseby.

The dwindling strength of the average regiment of foot is demonstrated by some units of the Oxford Army in April 1644.

Sir James Pennyman	119 officers, 360 men (11 companies)
Sir Theophilous Gilby	107 officers, 268 men (11 companies)
Sir Stephen Hawkins	104 officers, 171 men (9 companies)
Sir George Lisle	81 officers, 189 men (8 companies)
Sir John Owen	39 officers , 106 men (4 companies)[47]

Some units were still weaker. William Eure had 32 officers and 59 men in 3 companies, and Sir Thomas Blackwell's 4 companies consisted of only 30 officers and 56 men.[48] If the 12 infantry regiments whose strengths are known had been at full establishment, they would have totalled 1,002 officers (actual figure 923) and 9,000 other ranks (actual figure 2,231).[49] This situation worsened throughout the war. It was far easier to obtain one new officer than it was to replace a large number of private soldiers, and a colonel would do so, in order to repay favours and retain the support of influential friends and associates, by employing one of their relatives. But this led to a number of serious consequences. Firstly, in theory, the weekly upkeep of a Royalist foot company was about £22, but some £13 of this total went on payments to officers and NCOs.[50] Thus the weak foot regiments cost proportionately far more to maintain than is immediately obvious. Secondly, the existence of too many understrength companies, however they were brigaded together on the battlefield, led to confusion and poor performance.

The Royalists were not alone in facing these problems.The Parliamentarian armies of 1644 were in a similar state.[51] The Oxford Parliament of 1644 failed to persuade the King to reduce the numbers of officers in his army. This led to reform attempts in the winter of 1644/5. The so-called 're-modelling' of the Parliamentarian forces is well known; much less well documented is a similar process initiated by Prince Rupert, newly appointed as Lieutenant General. The New Model Army of Sir Thomas Fairfax was largely an amalgamation of the commands of the Earl of Essex, Sir William Waller and the Eastern Association. In the Royalist army no such process occurred. Although Rupert was able to merge one or two smaller units, vested interests and opposition prevented a root and branch overhaul of the Oxford Army, with the result that at Naseby no foot regiment totalled more than 500 men, and some had fewer than 200.[52]

TACTICS

The infantry tactics of both sides were very similar. The pikes were employed mainly to hold off enemy horse, or, in what was basically a rugby scrum known as 'push of pike', to force back or knock over their opponents. But the musketeers would have claimed that the brunt of the fighting fell upon them.

Usually musketeers either fired successively by rank in the Dutch style (using formations six deep) or followed the Swedish method of doubling ranks and firing by 'salvee'. These tactics could be used in combination. At Edgehill, both sides seem to have adopted the first method, with disappointing results. As the war went on, however, the Royalist foot seem to have taken the initiative whenever possible (in four of its six major actions, the Oxford Army foot were the attackers). This was partly to utilise Royalist cavalry superiority, but, because of the recurrent Royalist shortage of powder, it was also aimed at achieving a quick decision without prolonged exchanges of fire. As a result, the Swedish tactics were popular. They are described by a participant at Breitenfeld (1632):

First giving fire unto three little field pieces that I had before me, I suffered not my musketeers to give their volleys, till I came within pistol-shot of the enemy; at which time I gave the order to the three first ranks to discharge at once; and after them the other three: which done we fell pell-mell into their ranks, knocking them down with the stock of the musket and our swords.[53]

This is echoed in Royalist accounts. At Brentford in November 1642 Captain John Gwynne relates that the King's foot 'after once firing suddenly . . . advance up to push of pikes and the butt-end of muskets . . .',[54] while Sir Edward Walker, in his eyewitness description of Naseby, gives a similar impression:

Presently our forces advanced up the Hill, the Rebels only discharging Five Pieces at them, but over shot them, and so did their Musquetiers. The Foot on either side hardly saw each other [because of the nature of the terrain] until they were within Carabine Shot, and so only made one Volley; our falling on with Sword and butt-end of the Musquet did notable Execution, so much as I saw their Colours fall, and their Foot in great disorder . . .[55]

The pattern of unearthed musket shot at Naseby confirms the picture of a ferocious Royalist onslaught pushing the numerically superior Parliamentarian foot back for a considerable distance before momentum was lost, partly because of the inability of the Royalists to commit sufficient reserves. The initial salvee and mêlée was followed by a prolonged exchange of fire, in which the greater Parliamentarian numbers had a decisive advantage.[56]

Further evidence of the popularity of Swedish tactics among Royalist commanders is indirectly provided by Colonel George Monck, from the forces in Ireland, who was captured at Nantwich in January 1644. In his *Observations upon Military and Political Affairs*, probably compiled shortly after his capture, Monck advocates that the musketeers be deployed in three ranks in front of the pikes, and deliver a salvee before falling on the enemy.

The carefully executed formations beloved of the military theorist were frequently rendered impracticable by circumstances. Many actions were fought in enclosed terrain, where hedges and ditches favoured the defence, and attacks were reduced to scrambling chaotic affairs with small parties of men who ineffectively exchanged fire with unseen opponents through the hedgerows. Foot often had little success when attacking in such conditions. At First Newbury, Royalist assaults became totally bogged down, and, according to Sir John Byron, 'our Foot play'd the Poltroon extremely',[57] taking cover behind banks and hedges and refusing to advance without cavalry and artillery support. But Byron was primarily a commander of horse, who never displayed much appreciation of infantry tactics. The Royalist foot at First Newbury were short of powder, had made a long march through foul weather and, in the graphic description of one of them, Captain John Gwynne, 'were like to drop down every step we made with want of sleep . . .'.[58] Casualties suffered, especially among officers, suggest that the King's foot in fact performed reasonably[59]

Pikemen still had a key role to play, particularly in beating off attacks by horse. The Royalists utilised tactics recommended by Henry Tillier to the pre-war volunteers of the London Artillery Garden:

> Files closing to the midst to their closest order, insomuch that there was not above half a foot intervall of ground between File and File, the pikes porting, and after closing their ranks forward so close, that they locked themselves within one another, and then charged on, which in my judgement is so secure a way from routing, that it is impossible for any body of Horse to enter therein . . .[60]

This advice was echoed when the Royalist foot at Cheriton repelled an attack by Haselrigg's horse: 'the foot keeping theire grounde in a close body, not firing till within two pikes length, and then three rancks at a time, after turning up the butt end of their musketts, charging their pikes, and standing close, preserv'd themselves and slew many of the enemy . . .'.[61]

Similar tactics were employed on other occasions, such as the celebrated last stand of Rupert's foot at Naseby: 'The Blue Regiment of the King's stood to it very stoutly, and stir'd not, like a walle of brasse, though encompassed by our Forces, so that our men were forced to knocke them downe with the Butt end of their Musquets. . . .'[62] This was combined with a simultaneous assault from two sides by Fairfax's Lifeguard of Horse, one party led by Sir Thomas himself.[63]

CONCLUSION

Naseby was a disaster for the Oxford Army foot. Upwards of 5,000 of them were taken prisoner, and either enlisted by Parliament or offered for service to interested European powers. Grave though the loss was, partial recovery might have been possible except that among the prisoners were most of the junior officers, the NCOs, and the cadre of experienced soldiers who had followed the King's banner since Edgehill. Although the Royalist Council of War hoped to recruit more men in South Wales and the Marches, the loss of officers and the growing disaffection of the local population rendered the plan largely stillborn.[64] King Charles' foot had fought their last major battle.

How good were the Royalist foot? Despite being poorly armed and equipped in the early months of the war, and generally outnumbered in its latter stages, the King's infantry compare favourably with their opponents. Only the New Model Army, with much greater resources in manpower, could overcome them, and even then, despite superior numbers, almost went down before the King's men at Naseby. Fairfax, who was in an excellent position to know, later said that some of his best troops were the old soldiers of the King.

FIVE

DRAGOONS AND FIRELOCKS: THE ROYALIST 'SPECIAL FORCES'

'Footeman on horseback.'

Gervase Markham, *The Souldier's Accidence*,
1625, p. 42

THE DRAGOONS

The Role of the Dragoon

The dragoon was an accepted part of the seventeenth-century European military scene. Usually thought to have originated in France, the name derived from the firearm carried by these troops – the 'dragon' – a long piece of full musket bore, fitted with a snaphaunce or firelock.[1]

Dragoons fought in all the major armies of the Thirty Years' War, gaining an unsavoury reputation. The Duc de Rohan felt that 'they have ruined the infantry, every man desiring to have a nag so that he might be the fitter to rob and to pillage',[2] and his disdain was shared by former Royalist captain of horse Thomas Lacy, who remarked in his play *The Old Troop*: 'Rascals, did I not know you at first to be three tattered musketeers, and by plundering a malt-mill of three blind horses, you then turned dragooners.'

Most contemporary writers accepted that dragoons were an essential part of an army, but were unclear about their exact role. Gervase Markham described them as 'a kinde of footeman on horseback'.[3] The dragoon was seen as a mounted infantryman, employed primarily in small-scale operations where mobility was required, such as seizing bridges and isolated strong-points, surprise attacks and raids, reconnaissance and foraging, and relieving the horse from the more mundane tasks of guarding convoys and supply trains. They also had the important task of supporting the cavalry in battle, as summarised by Sir James Turner:

> Dragoons go not only before to guard Passes (as some imagine) but to fight in open field, for if an Enemy recounter with a cavalry in a champaign or open Heath, the Dragoons are obliged to alight, and mix themselves with the squads of Horse, as they shall be committed, and their continuate Firing, before the Horse comes to the Charge, will, no doubt, be very hurtful to the Enemy. If the encounter be in a closed countrey, they serve well to line Hedges, and possess Enclosures; they serve for defending Passes and Bridges, whether it be in the Advance or Retreat of an Army, and for beating the Enemy from them . . .[4]

Although doubtless not emphasised to new recruits, dragoons were also regarded as expendable, sacrificed if necessary to cover a retreat. The unfortunate Northern Royalist dragoons deployed to break up with their fire the charge of Cromwell's cavalry at Winceby in October 1643 discovered this to their cost. Though they checked the first enemy attack, and unhorsed Cromwell himself, the dragoons fell victim to a flanking attack by Sir Thomas Fairfax, and most of them were cut down or trampled underfoot before they could regain their horses. On the other hand, sufficient numbers of dragoons well deployed in good defensive positions could be highly effective. The concentrated fire of dragoons under George Goring's command at Marston Moor inflicted horrendous casualties on Sir Thomas Fairfax's horse as they attempted to deploy out of a narrow lane.

Arms and Equipment

In 1635 John Cruso recommended that dragoons be equipped with both musket and pike. The latter, even if cut to half length of about 8 feet, would have been a very cumbersome weapon and it was not widely used in the Civil War, except for certain specific duties.[5] Dragoons were armed with the same type of basic sword as the foot and with a matchlock musket, though by 1644 the latter had generally been replaced with a firelock of rather wider bore than the infantry variety, and, at 3 feet in length, rather shorter.[6]

In June 1643 it was ordered that Prince Rupert's Dragoons be issued with 'forty muskets that are fixed and fitt for service, with bandoliers',[7] while in October the troop of dragoons attached to Sir Charles Lucas' newly raised Regiment of Horse was supplied with 'forty carabynes with belts and swivels' and eighty bandoliers.[8] Powder bags, more manageable for horsemen, sometimes replaced the bandoliers. The dragoon carbine, slightly shorter than the infantry musket at between 36 and 42 inches, was generally carried on the right, butt down.[9]

Dragoons did not wear body armour, except for the occasional pot helmet. Generally their dress was identical to that of the foot soldier, riding boots often rejected in favour of shoes for ease of movement when fighting on foot.

Organisation

In theory, a dragoon regiment consisted of ten companies, each 100-strong plus officers. But in practice there was considerable variation, five or six companies of greatly varying strength being more common. If, as seems likely, a Royalist dragoon company was organised along the same lines as its Parliamentarian counterpart, its establishment consisted of one captain, one lieutenant, one ensign, two sergeants, three corporals and 100 soldiers. Each company was further subdivided into sections of ten, and in action one man from each section was deputed to act as horseholder. In some cases a dragoon company had two drummers. The company colours might be smaller versions of the infantry flag, or guidon-type standards.

George Monck recommended that an army should have one

company or troop of dragoons for every regiment of horse (leading to the common practice, particularly it would seem in Northern Royalist regiments, of having a dragoon troop on the regimental establishment). However, this seldom happened. In 1643, for example, possibly because of difficulties in finding adequate mounts for cavalry and the enclosed nature of much of the area in which they were fighting, Hopton's Western forces had a 1:1 dragoon/cavalry ratio, while at Edgehill in 1642 both sides had approximately one dragoon to every three horse.

A Royalist Fighting Elite

The outbreak of war saw the King (in common with his opponents) raising dragoons in large numbers. At Edgehill, the four Royalist dragoon regiments were still considerably below establishment, totalling in the region of 1,500 men. Significantly, they contained many more professional and career soldiers among their officers than was the case with the horse and foot.[10]

It is unclear if this concentration of military experience, often combined with relatively humble social origins, was deliberate or if it came about because amateur and more well-to-do volunteers preferred the more prestigious horse and foot.[11] The outcome were units that, in the early stages of the war, were better trained and disciplined than the rest of the army. At Edgehill, the Royalist dragoons were noted as clearing the hedges of their opponents 'with great courage and dexterity'.[12]

During the winter of 1642 and the following spring the dragoons of the Oxford Army acted as its main assault troops, especially in the operations undertaken to clear communications between Oxford, Wales and the West by capturing Parliamentarian garrisons in the Cotswolds and West Midlands. At this stage in the war, town defences were frequently fairly minimal, making an immediate storm, rather than a prolonged siege, a feasible option. Dragoons were used to spearhead such attacks, as, for example, at Marlborough in December, where 'Sir William Pennyman, with a Regiment of Foot and some Dragoons, attempted the North-West side'. The defenders held out for about three hours, 'till at length some Granadoes having fired an Old thatcht Barn that stood near them, they were inforced to quit that post, and the King's forces having afterwards fired a Dwelling House broke through a great Inn, into the midst of the Town, shouting and crying out "A Town! A Town! for King Charles!" '[13]

The dragoons of Lieutenant Colonel Lunsford, the Earl of Northampton, Edward Grey, James Ussher and Lord Wentworth were all present on 3 February 1643 at the storming of Cirencester, and in March Ussher's men spearheaded Rupert's assault on Lichfield Cathedral Close, which was repulsed, Ussher being killed in the process.[14]

Constant exposure in the forefront of battle led to heavy casualties, especially as dragoons did not have a high priority in replacements. An example from the Parliamentarian side, which is equally applicable to the Royalists, is that of John Lilburne's dragoon regiment in the army of the Eastern Association, raised in 1643. By the following March, one company had only twenty men with horses and eighteen without. The regiment was then consolidated into five companies, each presumably reasonably up to strength, but which, by January 1645, totalled only 263 men, the result, as its colonel said, of constant hard service without respite.[15]

By the late spring of 1643, the dragoon regiments of the Oxford Army were already noticeably weaker in numbers, which may be one reason that the post of colonel general of dragoons was not filled after Sir Arthur Aston's appointment as Governor of Reading. At Chalgrove on 18 June Rupert had with him a total of 350 dragoons, but these were drawn from a number of regiments and brigaded together under Lord Wentworth.

An order of 9 July 1643 from the King to the General of the Ordnance, Lord Percy, illustrates the variety of tasks that might fall to the dragoons. With the Western Royalist forces under the Marquis of Hertford and Hopton besieged in Devizes, and critically short of ammunition, Charles instructed that 1,500 lb weight of match, powder and bullets should be despatched to them 'on horseback by Dragonners in baggs behinde them for the more speedy expedicion, for that it much imputes for the safety of that our Army to hasten it with all possible dilligence'.[16]

The last major exploit of the Oxford Army dragoons came at Bristol on 26 July 1643. Rupert's Regiment was probably present, along with five companies (perhaps 500 men) of Henry Washington's Regiment, and the two companies of Robert

Howard's. The dragoons played an important role in piercing the Parliamentarian defences (at 'Washington's Breach') as well as in the street fighting that followed.

Royalist losses at Bristol were horrendous, and the dragoons probably suffered severely. Henceforward, the dragoon regiments of the Oxford Army receive scant mention. Although both Rupert's and Washington's Regiments were almost certainly present at the First Battle of Newbury in September, no record of their actions there has survived. Washington's Regiment left the area in 1644, when it accompanied Prince Rupert to the Welsh Border, and probably the only complete dragoon regiment left with the Oxford Army was Rupert's own, now commanded by Sir Thomas Hooper, 'a man of mean Education and small Extraction',[17] probably another professional soldier. The unit fought ineffectively at Cropredy Bridge but did rather better in the defence of Shaw House in the Second Battle of Newbury in October. In November 1644 Hooper is noted as receiving thirty snaphaunce muskets towards the equipping of his regiment,[18] which may have been among the squads of 'commanded' musketeers serving with the Royalist horse at Naseby. Hooper's men ended up in the West of England, where their commander and forty remaining men surrendered at Truro in March 1646.[19]

There were a number of other reasons for the demise of the Oxford Army dragoon regiments. It has been said that the ambition of every dragoon was to become a cavalry trooper. More important, however, were the constant demands of the cavalry for all available horses. Lack of horses was to lead to the downgrading of Henry Washington's Regiment. Having played a leading part in Rupert's operations on the Welsh Border and Lancashire in the summer of 1644, Washington's men lost most of their horses in the Royalist defeats at Marston Moor and Montgomery. Apart from one mounted company, the remainder of the unit was turned into a foot regiment, and spent most of the rest of the war in the garrison of Worcester. As for weapons, the limited numbers of muskets available in the spring and early summer of 1643 tended to go to the foot. Finally, most of the dragoon officers were men of relatively small means, who were unable to subsidise their units in the way some of the cavalry colonels, for example, could. Sir Edward Duncombe disbanded his dragoon regiment in the summer of 1643 and attempted to raise a cavalry regiment, but lacked the money to sustain it.[20]

During the last two years of the war, the only dragoons attached to the Oxford Army, apart from Rupert's Regiment, were probably a few troops with cavalry regiments. It was not until the autumn of 1645 that a new dragoon force briefly appeared. After the surrender of Carlisle in July, about 150 foot from its garrison joined the King on the Welsh Border. Virtually all of the troops with him were horse, and so the Carlisle foot were mounted as dragoons and were added to the Lifeguard, fighting in this capacity at Rowton Heath in September.

Another major factor in the decline of the dragoon in the Oxford Army was the increasing use made, for specific operations, of parties of 'commanded' musketeers, from a number of foot regiments, mounted behind cavalry troopers or on their temporarily requisitioned mounts. They were employed to good effect by Prince Rupert in his relief of Newark in March 1644,[21] and were commonly adopted by both sides in the later years of the war. The Royalists, at least, seem to have experimented with a more permanent force of musketeers. During the summer of 1643, Colonel George Lisle, perhaps significantly formerly a lieutenant colonel in Sir Edward Duncombe's Dragoon Regiment, led a force of about 1,200 musketeers, formed out of parties of 'commanded' troops from regiments in the Bristol garrison, which saw action at the siege of Gloucester and First Newbury. A similar force under Colonel Matthew Appleyard served at Cheriton, and may have continued as a separate force during the Lostwithiel campaign of August 1644.

The dragoon suffered a similar fate in the main Parliamentarian armies. In August 1644, out of a total of about 3,000 horse with the Earl of Essex, there was only 1 troop of dragoons, with 9 officers and 65 men.[22]

Regional Forces

Much of the fighting in the regions, particularly between neighbouring opposing garrisons, consisted of small-scale raids, skirmishes and foraging expeditions. For such activities, often carried out in enclosed country, the dragoon was ideal. Though the majority of garrisons included at least one troop of dragoons, they were particularly widely used by the Royalist forces operating along the Welsh Border and West Midlands. In 1642, for example, the Shropshire Royalist gentry subscribed for the cost of raising a regiment of dragoons, which, under the command of Sir Vincent Corbett, was active in most of the earlier engagements in Shropshire and Cheshire. Dragoons were also common in the Northern Royalist forces. Here, the practice advocated by George Monck was adopted, with a number of regiments of horse having a troop of dragoons attached.[23]

A typical example of the use of dragoons as the Civil War equivalent of twenty-first century 'special forces' occurred in November 1643 in an attack on Parliamentarian-held Chillington House in Staffordshire. Arriving without being detected,

> Lieutenant Carter with his 16 dragoons went to the gate, and knocked till a souldier came and opened it, on whom the Lieutenant seized, and with a pistol set to his breast, commanded him to be silent till his dragoons were all come up, and then forced the souldier to shew them the direct way through the back quarters, which the souldier promised, but when he came near the Hall doore, he broke loose, and ran in crying 'Arme Arme We are all betray'd', which caused the Lieutenant to shoote the souldier that he fell dead in the Hall, where 110 Souldiers were sate at Dinner, whom the Lieutenant and his Dragoons suddenly assaulted, and with discharging two of his Muskets made them all fly in to the upper rooms, theire armes being at the other end of the House . . .[24]

Sir Thomas Leveson's horse then arrived to complete the victory.

THE FIRELOCKS

Developed at about the same time as the dragoons was another new variety of soldier, known by the outbreak of the Civil War as the 'firelock'. These soldiers took their name from their weapon, the firearm more generally, if inaccurately, known in England as the 'snaphaunce'. By 1642, the firelock had developed into a recognisable flintlock musket, of which there were three variants. It is often regarded as being superior to the matchlock, but this view is an over-simplification. The matchlock was in fact more robust and better suited to the rigours and accidents of campaigning, while the range and overall performance of the two weapons was virtually identical. Although it is claimed that the flintlock was adopted because of its greater resistance to damp, and the lack of the betraying glow of lighted match in night-time operations, these were probably not the main reasons. More significant were the safety factors – its use reduced the danger of accidental powder explosions and it was also much more economical, avoiding the need for large quantities of match.[25]

Because of the safety aspect, firelocks were often used to guard artillery trains. Richard Elton explains: 'Those who are ordained for their guard [are] to be firelocks or [are] to have snaphaunces for the avoiding of the danger that might happen by the coal of the match.'[26] This was how Captain Will Legge's firelocks were employed at Edgehill. Legge's company originally served in the Earl of Newport's Regiment of Foot during the Bishops' Wars, and was retained afterwards to guard the magazines at Hull and the Tower of London. Soon after Edgehill it was incorporated in the King's Lifeguard of Foot.

Firelocks had many other uses. The English forces serving in Ireland had employed 'snaphaunces' as early as the 1580s, and in the Rebellion of 1641, with its covert warfare of ambushes and raids, the firelock again proved his worth. The senior English unit serving there, the Lord Lieutenant's Regiment, had 400 firelocks, and there were also a number of independent companies. Two of these, commanded by Captains Francis Langley and Thomas Sandford, were among the units from the Irish Army brought over to England to serve the King; Sandford and his men had a colourful career that provides an excellent example of the value and versatility of the firelock.

Thomas Sandford was a typical professional soldier. Of minor Shropshire gentry stock, Sandford, like many younger sons, sought to better himself by military service. He was a quartermaster in the Bishop's War of 1640, and then joined the forces being raised for Ireland, enlisting a company of firelocks,

200-strong, probably mostly raised in Cheshire and North Shropshire. Sandford and his men quickly established a reputation for ruthlessness, notable even by the bloody standards of the war in Ireland. On 15 April 1642 Sandford's firelocks played a major role in the English victory at Blackhole Heath, near Athy, where the Irish forces broke in panic before his advance.[27]

In November 1643 Sandford and his fifty surviving firelocks returned to England. Arriving before Hawarden Castle, Sandford, described by his opponents as 'a man lavish in ink, and long words', threatened the Parliamentarian garrison in lurid terms:

> I presume you very well know, or have heard of my condition and disposition, and that I neither give nor take quarter. I am now with my firelocks (who never yet neglected opportunity to correct rebels) ready to use you as I have done the Irish . . . if you put me to the least trouble or loss of blood to force you, expect no quarter for Man, Woman or Child.[28]

A few weeks later, in the early hours of 13 December 1643, in one of the most remarkable operations of the war, Sandford captured the supposedly impregnable stronghold of Beeston Castle. While other troops mounted a diversion outside the main entrance to the castle, Sandford and eight of his firelocks scaled the sandstone crag on which Beeston stood, and secured its inner ward. Sandford terrorised Beeston's inexperienced governor into surrender, an act for which (as well as perhaps for entertaining Sandford to dinner afterwards, and supplying his men with beer), the unfortunate Parliamentarian was later executed by his own side.[29]

Shortly afterwards, Sandford and his firelocks were part of the army under John, Lord Byron that laid siege to the Cheshire Parliamentarian headquarters of Nantwich. Once again Sandford tried terror tactics, warning the defenders: 'Sirrah, behold the messenger of death, Sandford and his firelocks, who neither use to give, nor take quarter.' On 19 January 1644 the Royalists made a full-scale assault on the town, and the orders issued by their Major General of Foot, Richard Gibson, typify the way in which firelocks were employed:

Major Harwar with the regiment under his command and the Firelocks, with the scaling ladders, that and all the Dragoons, armed with Fire-locks or snapaunces to fall on first so neer unto the fall of the river, on this side of the water as may be; on the left hand of the bulwarks; then to be seconded with a hundred musketters; then a body of pikes; then a reserve of musketters; and let the soldiers carry as many faggots as they can; this to be at five o'clock in the morning, upon discharge of a piece of ordnance, and to fall on the wall, at discharge of some piece of ordnance.[30]

The attack was repulsed, and among those killed were the fire-eating Sandford and his lieutenant. However, this was not the end of Sandford's fearsome firelocks. Probably captured in the Royalist defeat at Nantwich on 25 January, the firelocks seem to have enlisted with the Cheshire Parliamentarian forces under Sir William Brereton, and were now serving as dragoons, described by Brereton as 'Firelocks which were soldiers in Ireland, lately mounted',[31] were regarded as the élite of his forces. Added to Brereton's existing dragoons, the firelocks were responsible for a number of exploits during the remainder of the war, notably the surprise of Chester suburbs in September 1645.[32]

The Royalists raised a number of other firelock units in the later years of the war. Notable among them was Prince Rupert's Regiment of Firelocks, probably commissioned late in 1643 and formed around a core of soldiers raised by contract in Holland.[33] Stationed at Shrewsbury in the spring of 1644, it was reinforced by troops from Ireland, including some 'native' Irish. In an unsuccessful attack on Abingdon in January 1645, five of its men who were captured were hanged under the terms of Parliament's Ordinance ordering the execution of any Irish found in England in arms for the King.[34]

Rupert's Firelocks took part in the storm of Leicester on 28 May 1645, when one of their officers, Major Bunnington, was killed. At the surrender of Bristol in September, the unit was carrying out another common duty of firelocks, that of acting as a Lifeguard for a senior officer. When Rupert marched out to surrender 'his lifeguard of firelocks came forth, all in red coats before him . . .'.[35]

By the end of the war, firelocks were widely used in the Royalist forces. Prince Maurice's small regiment operated along the Welsh Border in 1645, and among other units recorded is Sir John Watt's, or the Chirk Firelocks, probably formed from the remnants of several former firelock and dragoon units and which, 150-strong, fought at the Battle of Denbigh Green on 1 November 1645 and was destroyed in the following February in a fierce encounter in Churchstoke Church near Montgomery. A number of other units, including several operating on the Welsh Border, and Sir Henry Bard's Regiment with the Oxford Army, seem to have had a company of firelocks attached.[36]

By 1646 the specialist firelock companies, with their proven record of versatility and effectiveness, were a firmly established part of the Royalist military machine.

SIX

ORDNANCE AND MUNITIONS

'The train of artillery, which is commonly a sponge that can never be filled or satisfied . . .'
Edward, Earl of Clarendon, *History of the Great Rebellion*, 1888, VI, p. 62

THE ARTILLERY

Although artillery had been a feature of European warfare for some three centuries, its role on the eve of the Civil War was still ill-defined. For most of the sixteenth century, guns, though of increasing importance in siege warfare, were regarded as having little significance on the battlefield. This attitude was modified by the reforms of Maurice of Nassau and Gustavus Adolphus, with the latter's use of leather guns – and more significantly of 3-pounder 'regimental' pieces, especially at Breitenfeld in 1632 – certainly having an impact on observers, if less so on the enemy. Robert Ward described these pieces as 'of great service in time of fight, for two or three men could wield one of them as they pleased, both in advancing it forwards, and drawing it back, as occasion served'.[1]

Similar light pieces, including the famous 'frame' guns,[2] were employed by the Scots at Newburn in 1640, and were present at most of the major actions of the war, though on the whole with less than the hoped-for effect. They are passed over lightly in contemporary descriptions, perhaps because no accounts by artillerymen survive.

The main use of artillery was still in siege operations, and there was a bewildering variety of guns, with an array of exotic names. While there was considerable disagreement among the theorists as to the exact specifications of contemporary ordnance, generally accepted classifications include:

Name	Weight of shot	Size	Weight of Gun	Crew	Horses
Cannon Royal	63 lb	8 inch	8,000 lb	16	90
Whole Cannon	47 lb	7 inch	7,000 lb	12	70
Demi-cannon	27 lb	6 inch	6,000 lb	10	60
Culverin	15 lb	5 inch	4,000 lb	8	50
Demi-culverin	9 lb	4½ inch	3,600 lb	7	36
Saker	5½ lb	3½ inch	2,500 lb	6	24
Minion	4 lb	3 inch	1,500 lb	4	20
Falcon	2⅗ lb	2½ inch	700 lb	2	16
Falconet	1¼ lb	2 inch	210 lb	2	10
Robinet	¾ lb	1½ inch	120 lb	2	8
Base	½ lb	1 inch	90 lb	2	6[3]

The gun crews consisted of gunners and assistants, known as 'mattrosses'. A demi-cannon, for example, required four gunners and six matrosses, a demi-culverin three gunners and four matrosses and a saker two gunners and four matrossses. They were dressed in a similar style to the foot, and armed with swords and sometimes pole-axes.

A culverin had an effective range of about 2,600 yards, a demi-culverin 2,400 yards and a saker – the standard field piece – just over 2,100 yards. These were the three types of gun in most common use. Although heavier ordnance, for example the two Royalist demi-cannon known as the 'Queen's Pocket Pistols' – imported from Holland – were sometimes used, they were extraordinarily difficult to transport, except by water, and used up prodigious quantities of scarce and costly gunpowder. Provided they were positioned advantageously, culverins and even demi-culverins could be surprisingly effective against brittle medieval stone defences, though they proved much less destructive to earth fortifications.

Mortars were sometimes used against enemy garrisons, as

much for their effect on morale as for their destructive qualities (their accuracy was minimal). With a bore ranging from 8 to 15 inches, they were intended to drop incendiaries or explosive shells into the interior of the besieged garrison.

Given the enormous amounts of money and materials required to furnish and support an adequate artillery train, the Royalists began the war at a considerable disadvantage. The King's artillery train at Edgehill was put together from a variety of sources. Clarendon said it was 'destitute of all things which were necessary for motion, nor was there any hope that it could march until a good sum of money was assigned to it. Some carriage-horses and waggons which were prepared for the service of Ireland, and lay ready at Chester . . . were brought to Shrewsbury by his Majesty's order for his own train. . . .'[4]

At Edgehill the train totalled twenty guns, the heavier pieces forming the basis of the Oxford Army Train for much of the war. They included:

2 Demi-cannon
2 Culverin
2 Demi-culverin
6 Falcons
6 Falconets
2 Rabonetts (¾-pounders)[5]

These guns had been assembled from a variety of sources. Seven or eight were part of the cargo of munitions from Holland aboard the *Providence*, which was slipped ashore near Bridlington on 2 July, while others came from the private armouries of leading Royalist noblemen. Among them were two little brass drakes, belonging to Lord Paulet, which, after seeing action at Sherborne Castle, were shipped across the Bristol Channel to South Wales and joined the main field army in time for Edgehill.

Much of the credit for the formation of an adequate train of artillery in the face of considerable difficulties must go to one of the unsung heroes of the Royalist war effort. The King was fortunate that a number of the senior officials of the pre-war Ordnance and Armoury remained loyal and were able eventually to establish an excellent Ordnance Office in Oxford. Among them was the Lieutenant of Ordnance, Sir John Heydon. A Norfolk man born in 1588, Heydon, who had been a professional soldier since his youth, succeeded his brother as lieutenant in 1627, and remained in post throughout the First Civil War. Though rarely mentioned in accounts of the war, and indeed, nominally at least, acting under the orders of the General of the Ordnance, it is clear that Heydon's competence and expertise were invaluable. In 1645 Knelem Digby described him as 'that generous and knowing Gentleman; and consumate souldier both in theory and practice',[6] while another correspondent said of him, 'I have erred if there be three in Europe greater masters of the art of war for a General Commander.'[7]

Although the Royalist artillery did not distinguish itself at Edgehill, the establishment of proper headquarters and supply facilities in Oxford during the winter of 1642/3 enabled the train to be put on a firmer footing. Guns continued to be obtained from a variety of sources. Parliament had a distinct advantage both in available resources and their accessibility. For example, it controlled the furnaces and forges of the Weald, and its command of the sea made importation of weapons and equipment from abroad more secure than for the Royalists. While obtaining growing supplies of munitions, including ordnance, from the iron manufacturing areas of the West Midlands and South Wales, as well as foreign imports, the Oxford Army then had to transport them across country to where they were needed, often under the threat of enemy interception.

Both sides made considerable use of captured guns. A large quantity of ordnance fell into Royalist hands in 1643 at Bristol and Weymouth, while at the Second Battle of Newbury in October 1644 Skippon's Parliamentarian foot captured from Prince Maurice's Western Army nine 'good brass pieces' – six of them their own guns taken at Lostwithiel in September.

Both sides, initially at least, lacked experienced gunners, and considerable use was made of foreign 'experts'. The Oxford Army Train included a number of Frenchmen, among them Monsieur La Riviere, Monsieur St Martin, and Captain Montgarnier.[8] Attached, if rather loosely, to the artillery train was the King's Master Fireworker, Bartholomew La Roche. La Roche, also of French origin, was among the officers who had accompanied Prince Rupert to England in

September 1642. He was responsible for the somewhat esoteric art of manufacturing 'fireworks' – incendiary and explosive devices of various kinds, mainly for the Oxford Army – and frequently for employing them in action. La Roche appears to have concentrated mainly on mortar shells, and on producing 'firepikes' – shortened pikes or other pole-type weapons, which, tipped with inflammable material of various kinds, were employed mainly in assaults on enemy positions. At the storming of Bristol in July 1643 they caused a good deal of panic among the defenders.[9]

There are numerous references in the Royalist Ordnance Papers to La Roche being supplied with a variety of exotic materials for the practice of his 'black art', though he was frequently discontented over what he saw as neglect of his needs as well as by constant pay arrears. Evidently of a somewhat excitable temperament, La Roche on at least one occasion threatened to resign because of, as he put it, 'No Money! No Money!',[10] but he was evidently sufficiently mollified by a knighthood to remain in the King's service until the end of the war.

By the start of the campaigning season of 1643 the Oxford Army artillery train was taking on the organisation which it would retain in broad outline for the remainder of the war. At its head was the General of the Ordnance. From the spring of 1643 this post was occupied by Henry, Lord Percy, categorised as both incompetent and (perhaps fortunately in view of that) inactive. In practice, although Percy commonly signed orders and authorised issues of equipment, most of the day-to-day work continued to be performed by Sir John Heydon, and this was also the case under Percy's successor from the summer of 1644, Lord Hopton.

Operating under Heydon's instructions were several officials who had served in the pre-war Ordnance Office. Among them was Captain Henry Younger, one of the senior officers of the train, who was paid 10s. a day. Younger was a professional soldier who had been Comptroller of Artillery in 1640.[11] Edward Stephens, Clerk to Sir John Heydon, had served in the Ordnance Office for a number of years after being a professional soldier in the Low Countries. He joined the King in 1642, but received little reward for his loyalty. In 1645 he was forced to petition for relief after his pay had been seven years in arrears.[12] Edward Sherburne, a Lancashire Catholic, had been a Clerk to the Ordnance at the Tower in 1642 when he was imprisoned by the Parliamentarians. In November he escaped to Oxford. His brother, Henry, became Chief Engineer of the Oxford Army towards the end of the war, but was killed by 'tumultating souldiers' just before the close of the siege of Oxford.[13] Another notable figure was Richard March, Keeper of the Stores in the Ordnance Office since 1635, who took an increasing role in the organisation of arms manufacture, particularly after the capture of Bristol in July 1643.[14]

Although a number of foreign officers remained with the train for the duration of the war, most of the rank and file, equivalent in strength to a regiment of foot, were English. Their duties varied. As well as providing the artillery for the main Oxford Army, the train furnished guns and equipment for other forces. Small artillery trains were frequently made up for specific operations, as, for example, the one that accompanied the Marquis of Hertford and Prince Maurice to the West Country in May 1643. Consisting of one demi-culverin and one mortar, it required 10 wagons and 67 horses. This small train was manned by 4 conductors, 3 gunners, 10 matrosses, 1 carpenter, 1 wheelwright, and 1 smith. Accompanying it, probably to supervise the mortar and other explosive devices, was 'Mr Henrick the Petardier'.[15]

The artillery train that accompanied the main field army was a much more elaborate affair. A note survives in the Ordnance Papers listing the components of a 'marching train' of nineteen guns which was to be kept ready at all times. This train, remarkably similar to the one that accompanied the Oxford Army on most of its campaigns, included 2 demi-cannon, 2 culverins, 2 12-pounders, 1 'cut' demi-culverin, 1 saker, 4 6-pounders, 5 3-pounders, 2 robinets and 1 mortar. Also included were 50 rounds of ammunition per gun, La Roche and his equipment, and 100 barrels of powder with match and shot.

The guns required 144 horses to move them, and 11 wagons for their ammunition. Also needed was transport for the wealth of other equipment which accompanied the train, including 'Shovells, Pickaxes, Poleaxes, Gabions, Mitches, Lynchpins, Smeering Tubs, Lockeyes etc' as well as the 'necessaries of the personell'. This totalled a further 76 carts drawn by 524 horses.

The personnel of the train included 1 comptroller, 2

commissaries, 4 clerks, 1 chaplain, 8 Gentlemen of the Ordnance, an engineer, a master gunner and gunner's mate. The rank and file comprised 53 gunners, 21 conductors, 95 matrosses, 50 pioneers, and 196 carters and drivers. Also marching with the train were various specialist technicians, including a smith, carpenter, wheelwright, farrier, cooper, collarmaker, ladlemaker, tentmaker, and their staffs, and, to preserve discipline, a provost marshal and six men.[16]

Maintaining an adequate train of artillery was a complex and costly business, and grew more so as the train gradually expanded during the course of the war. In a muster taken in February 1644, its personnel had increased by 15 per cent since the previous reckoning, and by the spring the Oxford Parliament was expressing concern over the cost.[17] In January 1645 Prince Rupert pressed Hopton to reorganise the train, sending surplus guns to outlying garrisons, but its actual composition seems to have been little altered.[18]

It is difficult to assess how effective the Royalist artillery actually was. The King's forces never succeeded in capturing a first-class enemy fortress except by storming or a loss of will to resist. The siege train sent to Bristol in July 1643 consisted of only eight guns. This totally inadequate force was made still more ineffective by a continuing lack of ammunition. But their opponents, with generally greater material resources, did little better. Most of their successes, apart from Bristol whose capture in 1645 was in many ways a re-run of its fall in 1643, came from starving garrisons into submission, as at Chester and to some extent York, after the defeat of enemy field armies had rendered their relief impossible. The only major example of the Oxford Army attempting to reduce a major garrison by regular siege operations, at Gloucester in 1643, failed, although Clarendon is probably accurate when he said that the King had 'neither money nor materials requisite for a siege'.[19] Even so, if Essex's relief force had not arrived, the defenders would have been forced to yield within a few days.[20] At Leicester in 1645, Royalist demi-cannon were employed with good effect to breach the town's medieval defences. Until the New Model Army achieved supremacy in the field in the summer of 1645, and was consequently able to employ its own massive siege train without interference, there was probably little to choose between the effectiveness of the opposing artillery forces.

Loosely attached to the train were the engineers. Once again, general lack of English expertise in this field was reflected by the use of foreign experts. Best known among those serving the King was Bernard de Gomme, a Walloon, who accompanied Rupert to England in 1642, and later became Engineer General, playing a leading role in the storm of Bristol and improving the defences of a number of Royalist garrisons, including Chester, Liverpool and Lathom House.

Also in the King's employ was a Swede or German, Henrick Beckmann, described by Lord Digby as 'our excellent engineer', though use was made increasingly of British officers. Notable among them was Charles Lloyd, the Montgomeryshire professional soldier who had been an engineer in Dutch service and became Engineer-in-Chief and Quartermaster General to the King. It was Lloyd who was responsible for commencing the large-scale fortification of Oxford in May 1643, which were constantly refined and developed throughout the war.[21]

MUNITIONS

The Royalist armies went to war in 1642 poorly equipped in almost every respect, and the failure to reach a military decision by the end of that year led to a major equipment crisis. Although some of the regional forces seem to have been better off, the Oxford Army was effectively crippled, so far as major operations were concerned, until well into the spring of 1643. It took at least six months to organise adequate foreign imports and to put munitions manufacture in Royalist-held areas into operation. With possession of the magazines at Hull and the Tower, and soon afterwards Portsmouth, Parliament began the war in a considerably stronger position.

The main Royalist iron-producing areas, essential for the manufacture of arms, armour and shot, lay in the outlying areas of the Forest of Dean, South Wales and the West Midlands. By the spring of 1643, such manufacturers as Sir John Wintour at Lydney and Francis Walker, a major West Midlands iron manufacturer with foundries around Dudley and Stourbridge, were producing both field artillery and ammunition. The Shropshire ironworks on the Severn south-east of Shrewsbury provided Rupert with three new guns and ammunition during his operations against Lichfield, supplied the garrison of Chester, and had sent some 51 tons of iron to Oxford by May 1644.[22]

Although the Royalists were better able to provide munitions for their forces than is sometimes suggested, a major problem was caused by the geographical location of the headquarters of the main field army at Oxford. Every pikehead, musket barrel and cannon shot manufactured in Wales and the West Midlands had to be carried there before it could be used. Worcester became the great clearing house for supplies of all kinds en route to Oxford. Equipment manufactured in the forges of the Severn Valley first made its way to Worcester along the river by barge, and was then loaded aboard great convoys of wagons and pack animals for the frequently perilous four-day journey across the Cotswolds. Always liable to interruption by enemy raiding parties, this route was effectively closed in May 1645 when Parliamentarians captured Evesham.

Oxford grew to occupy an increasingly important role in the Royalist war effort. As well as being the home of the Court and quarters for many of the King's troops, the Royalist capital had a vital logistical function. It became the headquarters of the Ordnance Office, the successor to the pre-war office in the Tower of London, which continued to employ six of the nine principal original officers, giving the Royalists an advantage over its Parliamentarian counterpart. The Ordnance Office set up its headquarters in New College, where much of the day-to-day running of the department fell to Sir John Heydon and the other principal officers, including the Surveyor General, the Clerk of the Ordnance, the Storekeeper, the Clerk of Deliveries and the Treasurer.

Extensive records of the Royalist Ordnance Office survive, providing a clear picture of the work of the department in receiving supplies of arms and munitions of all kinds from importers and manufacturers, issuing them to troops in and around Oxford, and organising convoys to carry materials further afield.[23] There were local magazines in a number of places, including Bristol, Reading, Weymouth and Worcester, while the Northern Army of the Earl of Newcastle evidently had its own Ordnance Office under Sir William Davenant.

Nominal head of the Ordnance Office from May 1643 was Henry, Lord Percy. Even the Queen, to whose favour Percy was indebted for his appointment, admitted that he 'has his weak points',[24] while Clarendon said of him that 'he was generally unloved, as a proud and supercilious person'.[25] More influential than Percy, particularly in the development of Oxford as a manufacturing centre for arms and military supplies, were the two most important of the Ordnance Commissioners, the businessman Sir George Strode and John Wandesford, an MP and Yorkshire gentleman.

The King had been attracted to Oxford as his headquarters not only because of its strategic significance but also because the buildings of the university offered accommodation for his Court and some troops, and storage depots for munitions. During the winter of 1642/3 the main artillery park was established in Magdalen Grove, while the Ordnance Office took over New College Tower and Cloisters for its administration and magazine. The Law and Logic Schools were used as granaries, the Music and Astronomy Schools to store cloth and coats, and the Rhetoric School was utilised for making drawbridges. By January 1643 the Mint, originally established in Shrewsbury by Thomas Bushell, had, 'with a good store of silver ore', been transferred to New Inn Hall.[26]

As well as a store house, Oxford was also developed as a centre of arms manufacture. Use was made of a network of smiths and other craftsmen in and around the Royalist capital, advised by artificers from the Tower who had joined the King to manufacture and assemble arms and equipment, using materials transported from elsewhere. Gunpowder production also got under way. The watermills of the Thames and Isis were converted to military use and, on 8 January 1643, the first recorded consignment of four barrels of powder was received from the gunpowder maker William Baber. By May his production had totalled 55 barrels, not exceeded by Strode and Wandesford, who then took over control, until the end of the year.

An increasing quantity of other munitions was produced in Oxford. Though Strode and Wandesford were accused of putting their own commercial interests first, and no doubt lost no opportunity to line their pockets, by the end of 1643 Oxford had indeed become what the Earl of Essex described as 'the Mother Seat to hold up the spirit of the Enemy'. Swords, 4,000 in 1644, were manufactured at Wolvercote, muskets and pikes were assembled in a number of locations, and attempts were made, though only with limited success, to cast cannon using metal obtained from a wide variety of sources, including pots, kettles and pans requisitioned from the unwilling citizens of Oxford. Match and musket shot were also produced; in an eighteen-month period the Oxford manufacturers provided the Ordnance Office with 39 to 40 cwt of the former and 36 to 37 cwt of the latter.[27]

The importance of Oxford to the Royalist cause was reflected in the increasingly complex system of fortifications with which the King's engineers surrounded it, using the forced labour of troops and unwilling citizens, and the significance that both sides attached to its possession.

Oxford was not the only source of munitions for the King's forces. Throughout Royalist-held territory, and especially in areas with a manufacturing tradition such as the West Midlands and Sheffield, smiths and other small craftsmen, previously 'illegal' gunpowder manufacturers, and ironfounders were put to work making cannon, muskets, pikeheads, swords, 'granadoes', match and ammunition for the Royalist forces, and although the totals produced can never be known, they were vital for the maintenance of the regional forces.

From the summer of 1643, England's second city of Bristol became increasingly significant for the Royalist war effort. Relatively secure from enemy attack, and in an important strategic location, Bristol was in fact more suitable than Oxford to act as the Royalist 'capital'. Though often mooted, such a transfer of headquarters was regarded as politically unacceptable, but Bristol's importance grew steadily. A mint and printing press were established there. The customs dues of the port and other local taxation were used not only to finance the garrison, but also to pay for foreign arms imports into Bristol, and the town became an important Royalist administrative centre.

As well as providing a landing point for munitions imports, Bristol also acted as a reception and distribution centre for arms landed elsewhere in the South-west. Even Rupert's forces operating in the North of England in the summer of 1644 relied on munitions supplies from Bristol, a serious disadvantage because of long and insecure lines of communication.

Bristol's importance as an arms manufacturing centre increased gradually. There were at least six gunsmiths in the town in 1642 and, soon after its capture by the Royalists, Hopton was promised 2,000 muskets a week. By the following January, the highly efficient Richard March was also producing 6 to 8 barrels of gunpowder a week. Rupert wanted to transfer the bulk of munitions production from Oxford to Bristol, and though this never formally occurred, by May 1645 March was promising 15,000 muskets and 5,000 pikes a year.

The main difficulty in achieving these targets was finding the money to pay for them. Though March was supposed to receive £350 a week, in theory an ample sum for the promised weapons as well as the necessary powder and ammunition, he seems on average to have been paid less than £90. Nevertheless, partly because employment in the munitions industry exempted them from conscription, Bristol manufacturers produced a considerable, if unquantifiable, amount of munitions on credit. Bristol's role in the Royalist war effort was indeed vital, and Clarendon admitted that the loss of the city in September 1645 was as great a blow to the Royalist cause as the defeat at Naseby.[28]

Though by 1644 home production was meeting many of the Royalists' needs, arms imports from abroad were of vital importance to them for much of the war. Despite foreign rulers tending to sympathise more with the King than with Parliament, this view did not necessarily reflect those of all of their subjects, and most merchants were first and foremost businessmen who would trade with both sides. Originally only the port of Newcastle was available to land munitions from the Continent, and this, together with Parliament's supremacy at sea, severely hindered efforts. Even so, a considerable quantity of arms and other military supplies arrived in 1642/3. One cargo from Denmark, intercepted by the Parliamentarians in 1643, consisted of 2,977 muskets, 3,000 musket rests, 493 pairs of pistols, 1,500 pikes, 3,040 swords, 3,000 helmets, 476 barrels of powder and 900 bundles of match.[29] The massive cargo that Queen Henrietta Maria brought with her to north-east England in February 1643, including 32 cannon, perhaps 10,000 small arms and 78 barrels of powder, not only played an important part in outfitting the Earl of Newcastle's forces, but also carried the Oxford Army through the operations against Bristol and Gloucester until supplies from Oxford and imports across the Channel came on stream.

By the autumn of 1643, the Royalist successes in the West of England had opened for arms imports a number of shorter and more strategically convenient routes than the ports of the North-east. As early as 15 August the Dunkirk privateer *Lady of Assistance* arrived at Bristol with a cargo of 6,000 muskets, 2,000 to 3,000 'granadoes' and 'many thousands' of other arms.[30] Falmouth, Dartmouth and, increasingly, Weymouth were the main arrival points for supplies, especially from France. The King had a network of agents organising the purchase of arms on the Continent, headed by William Boswell in the Hague, Lord Goring in Paris and William Sandys at Dunkirk, and aided by a number of English merchants living abroad.[31] Attracted by potentially large profits, many foreign merchants, such as the Flemish entrepreneur Johannes van Haaesdonck, quickly become involved. Weymouth, in particular, was noted as a base of operations for French and Flemish merchants, bringing in cargoes of munitions in exchange for money or, more commonly, raw materials such as tin, wool, cloth and hides.

The quantity of munitions obtained for the Royalist forces from abroad is impossible to calculate, but was certainly enormous. Although perhaps less than half were destined for the King, between 1642 and the end of 1646 at least 74,580 firearms, 40,454 swords and blades, 13,700 pikeheads and 12,332 pieces of armour are recorded as leaving Amsterdam bound for the British Isles,[32] and this takes no account of imports from Flanders, France, Denmark and elsewhere. However, though vast in quantity, the quality of some of the cargoes was poor. In February 1644 Lord Percy's long-suffering agent at Weymouth, Captain John Strachen, reported the arrival from France of 4,917 muskets, 4,202 bandoliers, 322 pikes and 314 barrels of powder. But he added that it included 'old common powder that hath lyen in some magazines these 4 and 5 years . . . musketts of 3 or 4 score sundry bores . . . and all the old trash that could be rapt together'.[33]

As the King's cause declined, and the Parliamentary navy tightened its blockade, the attractions of supplying the Royalists dwindled. Yet cargoes continued to arrive in the West Country as long as any of its ports remained in Royalist hands. In 1645 a Flemish cargo reaching Falmouth included 6,040 muskets, 2,000 pairs of pistols 1,200 carbines, 150 swords as well as match and ammunition.[34]

It is often inaccurately claimed that the Royalist forces remained for most of the war inadequately armed and equipped compared with their opponents. Qualitatively, and in terms of arms and equipment, there was little to choose between the Oxford Army and the New Model Army on the field of Naseby. But Royalist operations were frequently hindered by logistical difficulties. The best-known example is the shortage of powder for his musketeers that played a key part in the King's decision to abandon his attempt to destroy Essex's army at the First Battle of Newbury, and the similar lack of ammunition that delayed Rupert's march to relieve York in June 1644. But these were problems of distribution rather than availability. From the early summer of 1643 onwards, the King's magazines generally contained sufficient supplies of arms and ammunition. The difficulties lay in their location. To transport required materials from Oxford or Bristol to armies often operating considerable distances away required large, slow-moving convoys, using inadequate or non-existent roads, frequently vulnerable to enemy attack. That they often failed to arrive in time, or even at all, is no surprise.

It was not until the closing months of the war, with the steady shrinkage of Royalist territory, the loss of Bristol, and the drying-up of supplies from the Continent, that the King again began to experience munitions shortages. But after the destruction of his major field armies at Naseby and Langport, this was no longer of any real significance.

SEVEN

LOGISTICS

'The Duke of Friedland's masterpiece is to be a good provisioner,
and he hath a singular good catering wit of his own.'

Swedish Intelligencer,
1635, pt iii, p. 11

FINANCE

Although ultimately King and Parliament would attempt to finance their war efforts by broadly similar means, the latter began the war with distinct advantages both in resources and because it possessed much of the machinery by which finance was raised. By contrast, Royalist money-raising methods had an air of improvisation that they never completely lost.

At the start of the war the King relied heavily upon contributions from his supporters. Some of his wealthier benefactors provided considerable sums. Although postwar claims of the Marquesses of Newcastle and Worcester to have each contributed in the region of £900,000 were inflated by the inclusion of their lost revenues and value of confiscated estates,[1] without such support it would have been impossible to field a significant Royalist army in 1642.[2]

Towns and institutions under Royalist control also provided financial support, usually in the form of 'gifts', voluntary or otherwise. Thus, in September 1642, a visit by Charles to Chester resulted in a contribution from the City Assembly of £300, less than the King had hoped for.[3] Although surviving financial records are scanty, it is known that between November 1642 and October

1643, the Treasurer of War, John Ashburnham,[4] received a total of £180,768. This included £12,000 from the cities of Oxford and Bristol, £17,000 from the Universities of Oxford and Cambridge, £13,000 from the King's Mint (mostly in the form of plate subsequently melted down to make coinage) and the rest from a variety of sources, including individual contributions, which do not incorporate the considerable amounts provided in the opening months of the war.[5] Of this sum, £117,000 was spent on the army, mostly paid to the Oxford Army Paymaster General, Matthew Bradman, and the Muster-Master-General. Of the remainder, £22,000 went on the upkeep of the royal household, and the rest on various expenditures ranging from gratuities to wounded soldiers to paying off the King's debts at cards.[6]

Also vital, particularly in buying munitions abroad, were the proceeds of selling and pawning the personal and royal jewels that Queen Henrietta Maria took with her to Holland in February 1642. This raised in the region of £180,000, increased by other means, including the loan of 300,000 guilders negotiated for the Queen by the Dutch Stadtholder, Prince William Henry.[7]

Although voluntary contributions remained a major, if inevitably diminishing, source of finance for the King throughout the war, prolonged conflict forced him to seek other ways of paying for it. Existing orthodox sources of revenue, such as the proceeds of customs, were mainly in the hands of Parliament, which controlled most of the major ports and whose naval supremacy severely hindered the trade of those harbours in Royalist hands. As a result, during the period 1642–6, Edward Hyde, Chancellor of the Exchequer, usually in direct competition with John Ashburnham, raised by pre-war methods, including customs dues, no more than about £97,000, compared with an average peacetime yearly income of £500,000.[8]

As well as confiscating the revenues of the estates of opponents, or 'delinquents', under their control[9] (by the process termed 'sequestration'), both King and Parliament introduced broadly similar systems of raising revenue. Early in 1643 Charles began appointing commissioners (often the original Commissioners of Array) for the counties under his control. Officially they were responsible for measures for 'the guarding of the county', but also for levying local taxes by means of the 'assessment'. A meeting between the commissioners and the local gentry would agree on the amount to be raised by a county, and the high constable, and through him the local constables, would be informed of the sums required from each local community. Prominent members of these, known as 'assessors', decided how the required sum was to be raised according to the means of each individual, and delivered it by a stipulated date to the constable, for forwarding to the commissioners. There was, in theory, an appeals procedure for those who felt that they had been unfairly assessed.

The effectiveness of the assessment system is open to debate. In its early stages, fifteen largely or partially Royalist-controlled counties were said to be producing £6,700 a week, of which £6,000 was going to the army. In 1643 the weekly levy demanded from Oxfordshire was £1,176, seventeen times greater than that required under the pre-war Ship Money tax.[10] In 1644 the amount had risen to £1,200, while Worcestershire was asked for a monthly levy of £3,000 for the maintenance of troops in the county, costs swollen by the need to supply escorts for convoys to Oxford. In general, despite the burdens imposed, the assessment system seems to have been fairly stoically accepted, provided it was administered with reasonable fairness and without undue force. Problems would arise in the latter stages of the war, with the breakdown in civilian administration in contested areas leading to direct – and often heavy-handed – military involvement in tax collection. These grievances, rather than active anti-Royalism *per se*, played a major role in the 'Clubmen' risings of 1645.[11]

A major failing of assessment from the viewpoint of the Royalist command in Oxford was that a large part of the proceeds were syphoned off for the needs of various local forces, and never reached the main field army. Though the whole system of Royalist finance was supposedly administered from Oxford, initially by the Privy Council and later by the Council of War, in this, as in other matters, their writ did not effectively run in outlying areas. Regional commanders were in practice largely responsible for their own financial provision, often employing a brutality that was devastating for the Royalist cause. 'Know you', the Governor of Worcester informed one local community, 'that unless you bring to me the monthly contributions for six months, you are to expect an unsanctified troop of horse among you, from whom if you hide yourselves, they shall fire your houses, without mercy, hang up your bodies wherever they find them, and scare your ghosts.'[12]

In March 1644, following the example of Parliament, the King introduced an excise duty on a range of commodities, including, unlike his opponents, basic necessities of living such as meat, bread, butter and cheese. As with the Parliamentarian tax, the new duty met with widespread opposition, and frequently could only be enforced by use of troops. Although statistics are scarce, it seems unlikely that the proceeds of the excise outweighed the hostility that it aroused. In Bristol, for example, instead of the £10,000 which various levies imposed on the surrounding area should have produced over a 29-week period, only £2,490 actually materialised.[13]

The effectiveness of the Royalist financial machinery in comparison with that of Parliament is still the subject of debate. Although there were examples, notably under Rupert and Maurice on the Welsh Border, of an administration that functioned reasonably smoothly even in adversity,[14] the overall impression is one of increasing shortages as the war went on. The problems of administering the system in disputed areas could never be overcome, and by the spring of 1645 the growing chaos and civil discontent resulting from the increasing exactions of the now dominant military were as great a threat to the King as that presented by the New Model Army, and one which was equally impossible to overcome.

SUPPLY

Though given little attention in contemporary military manuals, supplying the countless needs of a seventeenth-century army was a gigantic task. Indeed, the reputations of such eminent Continental practitioners of the art of war as Wallenstein were built as much upon their administrative skills as their prowess on the battlefield.[15] The business of feeding, clothing, housing, and caring for the men of an army that might number 20,000 men would test a commander with much greater resources than those of the King.

On campaign, a field army lived off the country in a system of more or less legalised looting, and, although most of its men frequently went hungry, they usually avoided starvation. When in garrison or billets, particularly if, as was usually the case, pay was in arrears or non-existent, the system known as 'free quartering' was adopted. A householder had a number of soldiers, based on available accommodation, lodged with him and was obliged to provide them with food at a specified rate, normally calculated on army ration levels. In return, he was given a ticket or receipt by the regimental commissary or other officer specifying what was owed to him, which theoretically could be redeemed at a later date. This, if it actually occurred, would normally be from money deducted from what was eventually paid to the troops, usually about half a private's pay and one-third that of an officer. Unfortunately for their hosts, soldiers frequently forcibly demanded much better provisions than they were theoretically entitled to, and for which their hosts would never be compensated.

Existing alongside 'free quarter', and still more unpopular with the civilian population, was a system of directly requisitioning supplies from an area, sometimes with a promise of future repayment, although this became increasingly rare as the war went on. This practice was widely abused by individual commanders. Clarendon wrote of Sir Henry Bard, in early 1645 Governor of Camden House, that the garrison brought 'no benefit to the public than the enriching of the licentious governor thereof, who exercised an illimited tyranny over the whole country'.[16] The arrival of a large field army could be a disaster for a local community. In September 1643, as well as unauthorised requisitioning and looting by his troops, the King demanded a loan of £7,000 from the city and county of Worcester. The royal presence during the Cropredy Bridge campaign of the following June cost them another £1,200, while in May 1645 they were forced to part with £100, as well as large quantities of supplies and wagons.[17]

In addition to these major demands, the civil authorities in towns such as Bristol, Worcester and Shrewsbury, in unenviable situations along lines of military communications, were forced to make frequent 'gifts' to passing commanders, in the form of money, overnight accommodation, food and drink. The corporation of Worcester found Prince Maurice and his officers particularly demanding. The Prince's success at Ripple Field in April 1643 cost them £16 17s. 10d. for claret, sack, white wine and other delicacies for the victors' celebrations, and during Maurice's time in 1645 as Lieutenant General of Worcester, Herefordshire, Salop and Staffordshire, the city of Worcester had to meet his daily living expenses of £3 15s. 6d. Even as late as 29 June 1646, when the New Model Army was closing in on the town, in an attempt to ensure his good will, the by now thoroughly war-weary corporation presented the ruthless, feared and hard-drinking Governor, Henry Washington, with £100 'whereof £50 ready, for his especiall care and love towards the City, towards the maintenance of his Table etc.' The foredoomed hope was that this bribe 'being done freely, it engageth him the more to preserve them'.[18]

If they were paid, troops might be left to buy their own provisions, but more often they would be supplied by the Commissary of the Army, usually with bread and cheese. In Oxford the accommodation afforded by the buildings of the University once again proved invaluable. Grain was stored in the Law and Logic Schools and general supplies in the Guildhall. Although some regiments had their own wagon, in general the task of moving these rations, and most other transport needs, fell to the Wagon-Master-General.

The first Wagon-Master-General of the Oxford Army was Winter Graunt, a son of the Gunpowder Plotter Robert Winter. He and his successor, Henry Stevens, paid 10s. a day, were responsible for the maintenance of the army wagon park in Oxford, and obtaining the horses or oxen (less popular because of their poorer stamina) required to move them. Vehicles and livestock, as well as carters, were also hired from civilian sources, with a carter being paid a hiring fee of about 2s. 6d. a day, and the owner of a packhorse proportionately less. Once again, payment was often in vouchers, uncertain of redemption. In times of crisis, such as the threat from the armies of Essex and Waller in June 1644, horses, wagons and carters were forcibly requisitioned from the parishes surrounding Oxford (those used to bring food supplies into the town were exempted), with the civilian drivers theoretically facing the death penalty if they deserted, though in practice most would have stayed with the army in the hope of preserving their wagon and horses, often their only means of livelihood.[19]

The main uses of wagons were in moving arms and munitions (in which role the Wagon-Master liaised closely with the Ordnance Office and individual regimental commanders), general supplies and the sick and wounded. The Wagon-Master was also responsible for transporting requisitioned food stuff to where it was required.

The other main supply need of the army was clothing. It is unclear how often the soldiers were issued with items of uniform, though it certainly happened on a number of occasions, notably the summer of 1643. Contracts were given to major suppliers such as Thomas Bushell, who in turn subcontracted to woollen merchants. The supplied cloth would then be made up into uniforms, usually of poor quality, by a network of tailors in Oxford and the surrounding villages, and stored in the Music and Astronomy Schools of the University until issued. In the army of the Protectorate a soldier was issued one suit a year, normally in October, and it seems likely that the Oxford Army attempted to follow a similar pattern, though in the autumn of 1644 at least, recourse was had to collecting garments from among the civilian population of the West Country.[20] The 'suits' issued to troops intended for Ireland in 1642 actually consisted of cap, doublet, cassock (a sleeveless variety of coat, fastened with tapes), breeches, two pairs of stockings, two pairs of shoes and two shirts per soldier,[21] and this was probably the ideal aimed at, if rarely achieved. Cavalry had their own requirements. Saddles (at about 16s.), harness and pistol holsters (2s. 6d.) had to be manufactured or purchased.[22]

Headgear and shoes were manufactured both at Oxford and further afield. Bewdley in Worcestershire was famous for its woollen 'Monmouth' caps, and these, along with many other supplies of all kinds, were carried down the River Severn by barge to the great Royalist clearing house of Worcester.

MEDICAL CARE

When considering the health of the King's soldiers, and the medical provision available, it should be remembered that they lived in a society in which the average life expectancy was no more than thirty-two years, with 40 per cent of the population aged under twenty and about a third dying before the age of fifteen. Tuberculosis, dysentery and cholera were among a host of diseases that – to modern eyes – took a horrendous toll but led to early death being a more readily accepted fact than is sometimes appreciated.

Even so, there is no doubt that the Civil War hit hard. There are no accurate statistics for casualties in the war as a whole, still less for those in the Royalist armies, but it has been reasonably suggested that between 10 and 25 per cent of total deaths were a direct result of combat. The horrific nature of the wounds that were suffered are illustrated in the description by the Parliamentarian chronicler John Vicars of the injuries inflicted by Parliamentarian cavalry swords on some unfortunate Royalist infantry: 'most woefully cut and mangled, some having their ears cut off, some the flesh of their heads sheared off, some with their very skull hanging down and ready to fall'.[23]

Surgeons generally knew how to treat wounds, with instruments remarkably similar to those in use today, and the main cause of death was from infection leading to gangrene. Cuts, if not infected, usually healed fairly satisfactorily. Gunshot wounds were more problematic. Even with the prompt and generally better treatment afforded to officers, the results were frequently fatal as gangrene set in, as in the case of Colonel Sir Nicholas Slanning, shot in the thigh at the storm of Bristol; the wound 'swelled, grew black, stank, whereof he died about midnight'.[24] Even so, some remarkable recoveries did occur, although more from luck and a strong natural constitution than medical skill. Colonel John Owen was one example; also wounded at Bristol, he informed his wife: 'I was unfortunately shot through the right side of my nose under the left ear, through all the jugular veins and mouth, and did bleed extremely, but God be praised I am in a pretty good state, if it doth not turn to fever.'[25] It did not, and Owen made a full recovery.

Doctors and surgeons were generally well aware of their limitations; Richard Wiseman, one of the most able of the Royalist physicians, wrote of a Cornish soldier 'without Eye, Face, Nose or Mouth', and admitted 'I did not know where to begin'.[26] But it was recognised that medical provision, however basic, was good for morale, and most regiments endeavoured to have a surgeon, usually with two mates, on their establishment. The surgeon would be paid 4 or 5s. a day, and was given £25 to provide a medical chest and equipment. Surgeons were difficult to obtain, most preferring the relative safety and comfort of civilian practice, and could be conscripted. They were treated with some respect, assisting the wounded of both sides without distinction. Henry Johnson, surgeon to the King's Lifeguard of Horse, wrote to Sir Samuel Luke, Parliamentarian Governor of Newport Pagnell, asking for the release of his captured apprentice:

It is very well known how careful I have ever been in dressing your wounded men, whensoever they have fallen into our hands. Therefore if you will give him a speedy release, and a safe pass to Oxford, I am very confident the favour shall not pass without an earnest endeavour of recompense, for if at any time any chirgeon or wounded man of yours should fall into our hands, my care of getting releasement, or dressing those that have need thereof, shall manifest how great a favour you have done to your obliged servant.[27]

The number of casualties suffered in a major action generally overwhelmed the medical resources available. Many of those wounded at Edgehill lay out in the open without treatment throughout a bitterly cold night, but a still greater problem arose from the outbreak of sickness, most probably typhus (called at the time 'camp fever', or the 'new disease'), that swept through the Oxford Army and the forces of the Earl of Essex in the Thames Valley in the spring of 1643. It would be a recurring feature of the war, exacerbated by the crowded conditions in Oxford, packed with soldiers and refugees. As a Royalist doctor, Thomas Willis, explained: 'It being seldom or never known that an Army, where there was so much filth and nastiness of diet, worse lodgings, unshifted apparell etc should continue so long without contagious disease.'[28] In May the 'Humble Desires of the Collonells' at Culham Camp included the request that 'a Phistian and Apothecary may Continually attend the Leaguer, and that some Village neere the Leaguer may be appointed, in Regard that the Souldiers that are sent to Oxford are neglected, and seldome or never return to their Colours'.[29] The officers also asked that each regiment should have a wagon to carry its sick and injured.

The outcome was that the Wagon-Master-General was instructed by the Council of War to provide such transport, and a military hospital was set up in a manor-house belonging to Sir William Spencer in the village of Yarnton, 4 miles north-west of Oxford. Though details of its administration are scanty, it was probably partly staffed by wives or widows of soldiers, and the parish records of the village not only include the burials, between May 1643 and January 1645, of about forty soldiers from four regiments, but also the marriage of two of the staff.[30] On at least one occasion, wounded from Maurice's Western forces were brought to the hospital by wagon, though the care of the wounded in the regional forces as a whole remains obscure. Most commonly, they would be placed in the care of local civilians, the costs of their treatment being deducted from their pay, and supposedly paid to the carers.

King Charles had a genuine concern for the welfare of his sick and wounded troops (and those of the enemy who fell into his hands), but as usual, the good intentions of that unfortunate monarch fell foul of reality. He appointed John Bissell as King's Commissary for the sick and wounded, though it is unclear what regular financial provision was made to him. On at least one occasion, Charles granted him £100; on 20 June 1644 Wagon-Master Henry Stevens was ordered to deliver to Bissell out of the magazine wheat and malt 'for the sick souldiers their provision and support',[31] and at one point Bissell was granted increased powers to press boats and carts 'in order to hasten the arrival of provisions' for the sick.[32]

On 2 May 1643 the King issued a proclamation 'For the Reliefe of all such Souldiers as are or shall be maimed in His Majestie's Service'. It ordered that 'every Officer and common Souldier . . . maimed and wounded should either be rewarded with some liberall pension, whereby the remainder of his life might be thought less grevious, or be received into such Hospitals and alms houses, as are within His Majestie's Disposing'. Regimental colonels were to submit the names of deserving cases, and local authorities and JPs were to give them priority, making sure that no such benefits were bestowed upon any wounded in the service of Parliament.[33] Unsurprisingly, the scheme met with limited success. Many of the charitable institutions tasked with the care of the wounded were under enemy control, and there were evidently continuing abuses in Oxford. Information on patients was not being recorded properly, so that the correct amounts were not deducted from their pay, or they deserted once their treatment was completed. On 8 June 1644 a further proclamation was issued, specifically relating to the Oxford area, ordering that a 'Governor or Over-seer' be appointed over the sick and wounded:

> who should have power both to receive such monies as were or should be raised for the reliefe of those Souldiers, and to dispose thereof accordinge to their necessities, in paying of Chirgeons, Nurses, and other attendants; that as oft as any of the Souldiers were cured of their wounds, and were fit for service, he should returne their names unto the Governour of the City of Oxford, by whom they were to be sent to their severall Colours; but if unfit for service then to returne their names to the chief Justice of the King's bench, who is thereby appointed to commend them to the Treasurers for the Counties in which they were borne, by them to be relieved with annuall Pensions, according to their severall merits and necessities: and finally that the Vicechancellor should take order to appoint some Minister to visit the sicke and wounded Prisoners, and read prayers unto them.[34]

It was, said the author of *Mercurius Aulicus*, 'a very seasonable, just and religious care'. Some of those unfortunates being prayed over, or crippled in the King's service, far from home and facing an uncertain future, might have thought differently.

EIGHT

THE HIGH COMMAND: ROYALIST LEADERSHIP AND STRATEGY

'War is not capable of a second Error; one fault being enough to ruine an Army; And therefore a General ought to be careful even of possibilities, accounting always that which may happen, to be as certain as anything which he doth most expect.'

George Monck, *Observations upon Military and Political Affairs*, 1671, p. 81

THE ROYALIST COMMAND STRUCTURE

On the outbreak of war in 1642, Parliament had all the material advantages. Only in his command structure did the King appear to have the edge.

While Parliament's Commander-in-Chief, the Earl of Essex, was frequently hamstrung by instructions from Westminster, not to mention by his own deficences, the main Royalist field army set out from Shrewsbury, with King Charles, its undisputed head, and all his principal military commanders and civilian ministers marching with it. This might have been expected to result in speedy and effective decision-making. But such would not be the case.

King Charles was 'Captain General', or supreme commander, of the Royalist forces for the duration of the war. Aged forty-two, Charles had gained some knowledge of the administrative and logistical aspects of war during the ill-fated Scots campaigns of 1639 and 1640, but otherwise he was inexperienced. He did understand that if the war was prolonged it would be impracticable to run a nationwide conflict from one headquarters. The result was that until the middle of 1644 there were effectively two independent Royalist commands, with the Earl of Newcastle, with the rank of Lord General, having largely independent authority north of the Trent.[1] The powers of this title varied. In Newcastle's case (and on the opposing side, Essex's), 'Lord General' meant 'Commander-in-Chief'. But it could also approximate to the modern role of 'Chief of Staff', in which an experienced soldier was appointed to act as mentor to a militarily untried superior.

The first holder of this post to King Charles was sixty-year-old Robert Bertie, Earl of Lyndsey. Socially impeccable, Lyndsey's military credentials, dating back to 1597, were not particularly current or impressive.[2] His speedy resignation, on the morning of Edgehill, after a quarrel with Prince Rupert over deployment, had the immediate advantage of the appointment of a more suitable replacement.

Patrick Ruthven, later successively Lord Brentford and Earl of Forth, was an excellent example of the Scottish professional soldier. Aged about seventy, Ruthven was 'a hard man, made for the hardship of Souldiers'.[3] Vastly experienced, he had served extensively on the Continent with the Swedish forces, and was promoted to major general by Gustavus Adolphus. In Ruthven's case, the frequently mercenary outlook of the professional soldier was overridden by genuine devotion to the Royalist cause, and he had joined the King in 1642 as a volunteer.

Ruthven is one of the most underrated military figures of the Civil Wars. Frequently dismissed as a uncultivated drunkard – he had been known in the Swedish service as 'Pater Rotwein' and as a man who 'could drink immeasurably and preserve his understanding to the last',[4] – there is no evidence that this hindered his military performance. During the two years in which he acted as Charles' Lord General, Ruthven usually succeeded in controlling an extremely difficult team of subordinates. To his credit must stand the remarkable series of manoeuvres in the spring and summer of

1644, which, aided by enemy blunders, resulted in the victories at Cropredy Bridge and Lostwithiel, as well as the escape from disaster at Second Newbury. Though increasing age, deafness and the effects of wounds and indulgence brought about Ruthven's retirement that November, it is a tribute to this unsung old Scotsman's ability that before his departure the Oxford Army never suffered a major defeat, but afterwards never enjoyed more than transitory success.

General of Horse of the Oxford Army in 1642 was the King's 23-year-old nephew, Prince Rupert. At first glance his might appear the honorific appointment of a royal relative. This assumption was quickly overturned by Rupert himself. But the Prince's tactlessness and intolerance of views contrary to his own quickly made him enemies, and the situation was worsened by the King's decision to allow Rupert to by-pass the Lord General and answer directly to him.

Assessing the impact of Rupert on the Royalist high command, and what if any harm he did to his uncle's prospects of winning the war, is made difficult by the fact that the 'romantic' image of the Prince tends to colour treatment of the subject. Despite the Prince's undoubted abilities as a cavalry leader, the Oxford Army generally performed more effectively in Rupert's absence. There is little direct evidence of disagreement between Rupert and Ruthven, or between the Prince and his old tutor, Sir Jacob Astley, Major General of Foot. But the tensions and conflicts that arose between Rupert and many of the King's military and civilian advisers frequently came close to paralysing decision-making, and in the Naseby campaign of 1645 would prove fatal.

THE COUNCIL OF WAR

The general of an army usually took advice from a council of war.[5] Initially at least, King Charles was no exception. The incomplete nature of surviving records make a full assessment of the role of his Council of War impossible, but the broad outline is clear.[6] Like those of lesser commanders, it had no executive powers but was intended to act as an advisory body to the King, who was invariably present at its meetings. In Oxford it customarily met in the King's quarters at Christ Church College, and on campaign wherever appropriate. Membership varied, but normally the Council consisted of high-ranking military officers, the Lord General, General and Lieutenant General of Horse and Major General of Foot, and those civilian officials, such as the Secretary of State, Lord Treasurer and Chancellor of the Exchequer, who were available, together with currently favoured courtiers, such the King's cousin, the Duke of Richmond, who held no formal position in army or government. Also called in as required were various 'experts', normally lower ranking military officers.

Usually numbering between ten and seventeen, the role of the Council varied according to circumstances. On campaign, where its numbers were generally smaller, it might meet daily to discuss strategic and logistical matters. In Oxford, when immediate military matters were less pressing, meetings took place once or twice a week and were mainly administrative in nature. Increasingly, aspects of this work were hived off to other committees, whose actual standing was sometimes unclear.[7]

The effectiveness of the Council of War was increasingly limited by two major factors. Its authority never really extended beyond Oxford and the West Midlands, and did not run at all in Newcastle's northern command, while, depending upon their distance, attitude of mind or circumstances, regional commanders were little influenced by the Council's wishes. This lack of authority resulted partly from difficulties of communication, but the overriding factor was the attitude of the King himself. All major decision-making revolved around Charles. Without his approval no important order could take effect, and decisions were increasingly made by the King without reference to most, or even any, of his councillors. In the intrigue-ridden Royalist Court the opportunities for 'special interest' groups to put their case directly to the royal ear were endless. Charles' well-known tendency to be unduly influenced by his current favourite, and his preference for subterfuge and behind-the-scenes dealing, led to a dangerous lack of continuity and clear decision-making. Open discussion was increasingly replaced by intrigue.

From quite early in the war, differences of opinion developed between the military and civilian leadership.[8] Rupert, perhaps because his views often met reasoned and cogent opposition from experienced senior commanders such as Wilmot and later George

Goring, tended to surround himself with younger *beau sabreur* types such as Charles Gerrard and Henry Bard, the unquestioning, unimaginative 'Honest' Will Legge, and his own ever-faithful younger brother, Prince Maurice. This group, aptly termed the 'swordsmen' by a modern writer, provided a largely uncritical 'Court' for the Prince, but served to distance him still further from the majority of the King's advisers.[9] Among the civilians, tensions grew between 'established' officials like Secretary Nicholas and Edward Hyde, and the younger 'courtier'-based grouping of Lord Digby and Treasurer John Ashburnham. From the summer of 1643, the ultra-Royalist faction of Digby and his associates, allied with the Queen, grew in influence, especially after Digby became Secretary of State following Lord Falkland's death at Newbury.

THE DELEGATION OF COMMAND

The lessening of the Council of War's influence was hastened by the devolution of military command that took place from the spring of 1643 onwards. In April a Lieutenant General was appointed in North Wales and its Border (Lord Capel), in South Wales and the Marches (Lord Herbert), and in the South-west (revived command of the Marquess of Hertford). To these were added Newcastle in the North, the Earl of Derby in Lancashire, who, though nominally under Newcastle's control, in practice operated independently, and the increasingly autonomous Colonel General Henry Hastings in the Midlands.[10] The essentially conservative nature of the Royalist administration is clearly demonstrated by these appointments. Newcastle, Derby and Herbert were the leading Royalist magnates in the regions where they commanded, and were expected to harness the existing power structure to the King's cause without altering the social fabric too drastically. While from a similar background, Capel, an Essex man, was appointed because of the lack of a suitable local candidate, and encountered considerable difficulties as a result.[11] With the exception of Newcastle and Derby, the new regional commanders were subject to direction from Oxford, but communication difficulties and, in the case of Hastings, independence bordering on insubordination greatly diluted its effects. In practice, only a direct order from the King held much sway.

By early 1644, relations between Rupert and the majority of the King's advisers in Oxford, especially Wilmot in the inquest over the failure at Newbury, had considerably worsened. This, and the deteriorating military situation in Wales and the North led to Prince Rupert's appointment as Captain General and President of Wales. His arrival at Shrewsbury also signalled the failure of what has been termed the 'grandee' phase of Royalist command.[12] Henceforward, although Newcastle would retain his Northern empire until Marston Moor, the 'professional' soldier came increasingly to the fore. Hertford had been honourably removed in the summer of 1643 after a dispute with Rupert and Maurice over the governorship of newly captured Bristol, and was replaced in the West by Maurice and other commanders, with unclear and overlapping authority pregnant with dispute. In South Wales, Herbert, discredited by the reverse at Highnam, had been given Sir William Vavasour as a mentor, soon to be followed by the 'swordsman' Charles Gerrard, with Nicholas Mynne, a soldier from Ireland, commanding in the south-west Marches, while Capel was summarily replaced by John, Lord Byron, then a supporter of Rupert.

Thus, by the spring of 1644, a series of more or less autonomous military commands – Rupert in Wales and the Borders, Maurice in the West, and Hopton and Brentford (Ruthven) in the South – had appeared. Each commander competed for the limited resources available, maintaining agents in Oxford and vying for the ear of the current 'favourite', whether it was the Queen or Lord Digby, and through them the support of the King. Rupert, hitherto largely dominant, found that absence strengthened the hand of his opponents. In the spring, Lord Hopton, operating in Hampshire, obtained the lion's share of available resources, so that Rupert's agent, the cynical Welshman Arthur Trevor, wrote to his master on 24 March: 'I find they that act for my Lord Hopton's interest are almost ashamed to see all things pass for him, and nothing for your Highness.'[13] He added that he hoped for news of a victory by the Prince 'for I find no court physic so present for the opening of obstructions as good news'.[14] Rupert, meanwhile, had duly obliged with his relief of Newark on 21 March, and his standing at Court improved considerably.

ROYALIST STRATEGY 1642–4

The constantly shifting centres of influence in the Royalist high command hindered the development of a coherent long-term strategy. The failure of the march on London of November 1642 spelt the end for any slim hope of taking the capital by direct assault, and the impracticality of such an operation was underlined by heavy casualties suffered in the storm of Bristol (26 July 1643). In the early part of that year, Royalist efforts were mainly directed towards clearing communications between Oxford and outlying areas. Oxford served both as a central collection point for men and supplies and as a forward base from which to maintain the threat to London. At this stage, lack of ammunition ruled out any major offensive by the Oxford Army.

After the fall of Bristol the time might have seemed propitious for a renewed attempt on London. It is to this period that historians, headed by the great S.R. Gardiner, have assigned the famous three-pronged advance on the capital, with Newcastle pressing down through the Eastern Association, Hopton advancing through Hampshire and Sussex, while the Oxford Army attacked along the Thames Valley and engaged Essex in a great battle at the gates of London. Though a superficially attractive scenario, it presents difficulties. Apart from being militarily unsound faced by an enemy with the advantage of interior lines, and still leaving the Royalists with the difficult task of forcing London's strong defences, supporting contemporary evidence is both scanty and unconvincing.[15]

A more gradual strategy is better documented. In this the Royalist regional forces would first consolidate their position, and then Newcastle and Hopton would move to close off the mouth of the Thames while the Oxford Army blocked the western approaches to London. A winter without the comforting warmth of imported coal, and facing growing starvation, might trigger off rebellion among the citizens or force Parliament to a negotiated settlement.[16] But Newcastle was stalemated in his attempt to capture Hull, and the Oxford Army was left marking time until the Northern forces could join them.

To occupy this waiting period it was decided in August 1643 to lay siege to Gloucester. When its defenders proved unexpectedly stubborn, the Royalist commanders hoped to use the besieged town as a lure to draw Essex's army out of the defences of London and into a decisive battle. However, the encounter at Newbury on 20 September revealed that the Royalist army was too weak to defeat Essex, still less take London, and the campaigning season closed with the Cavaliers reverting to the strategy of consolidating existing territory, while Prince Maurice reduced remaining isolated Parliamentarian strongholds in the West such as Lyme and Plymouth.

Imminent Scottish intervention on the side of Parliament also had far-reaching effects on Royalist plans. Newcastle would have difficulty in holding his own in the North, and English troops from Ireland, whom it had been hoped would provide valuable infantry 'muscle' for the King's main field army, would largely be absorbed in defensive operations. The only major offensives planned during the winter were for what was effectively a new army under Hopton to clear Dorset, Wiltshire and Hampshire, and 'point forward as far as he could go towards London',[17] in the hope of triggering off an uprising among Royalist supporters in Sussex and Kent. In the North-west, Byron and the 'Anglo-Irish' forces were to attempt to regain some of the ground lost to the enemy since the start of the war.

The outcome was disappointing. Although Rupert succeeded in relieving Newark in March, the defeat suffered by Byron at Nantwich in January weakened the Prince's forces and put back his support for Newcastle by perhaps two months. Hopton made little progress against Sir William Waller, and managed to lose some 2,000 of his foot. As a result, he had to be reinforced, and effectively superseded, by Lord Forth (Ruthven), with reinforcements from the Oxford Army.

The Royalist defeat at Cheriton on 29 March was claimed by Clarendon and Sir Edward Walker to have forced the King to adopt a defensive strategy in the South during the first part of 1644. But the Royalists got off quite lightly at Cheriton in terms of casualties, and Waller proved unable to follow up his success.[18] The King was actually obliged to go on the defensive because he was heavily outnumbered by the combined armies of Essex and Waller, and because of events in the North.

The Royalist strategy for the first part of 1644 seemed to have been agreed at a conference held at Abingdon in April. The Oxford Army, in a plan proposed by Prince Rupert, would remain on the defensive, putting its infantry into Oxford and the surrounding garrisons, while the horse harried enemy communications. In the meantime, Rupert would join Newcastle, deal with the Scots and Northern Parliamentarians, and Maurice would take Lyme, prior to both brothers reinforcing the King.[19]

Despite the approval which Rupert's scheme has received from most of his biographers, its viability is questionable. The Oxford Army had insufficient foot to garrison adequately all of the ring of fortresses around Oxford, and the horse no longer had clear superiority over their opponents. Royalist resources were becoming increasingly stretched. A quick decision by Rupert in the North, preferably by inflicting a crushing defeat on the allied forces there, seemed the only realistic hope of staving off defeat, short of taking the militarily advantageous but politically unacceptable decision to abandon Oxford except as a garrison, and transfer the Royalist headquarters to Bristol. The only other possibility was that 'miraculous conquest' in the South which the King talked of in his well-known letter of about 14 June to Rupert.

The full Council of War was increasingly involved in logistical matters, and strategic considerations were becoming the province of the King and a small group of advisers. However, close examination contradicts Clarendon's portrait of an indecisive monarch, and a deaf drunken old Lord General in his dotage, dominated by the scheming and unscrupulous Wilmot, while Secretary of State George Digby suffered from 'an excess of fancy' which caused him to alter orders before they were issued.[20]

In fact, the conduct of operations by the Royalist forces in the South during the summer of 1644 displays remarkable boldness and imagination. The oft-criticised decision to abandon Reading, taken after Rupert's departure, was a realistic assessment of Royalist capabilities. The evacuation of Abingdon close upon its heels, though bitterly condemned by King Charles, who blamed Lord Wilmot for a decision taken without his knowledge,[21] was a similar recognition of the inevitable. By slipping out of Oxford in the face of the advancing enemy, King Charles maintained his liberty, an army 'in being', and the hope of spinning out time until Rupert settled matters in the North. As Digby informed the Prince, the decisions reached had been taken after 'mature deliberation to await your success in the North or Prince Maurice's before Lyme',[22] after King Charles' own fears were eased by the victory over Waller at Cropredy Bridge (28 June) and after Essex's decision to plunge ever deeper into the West Country. The King's situation had so much improved, that, although the Council of War was left 'as in a wood'[23] by news of Rupert's defeat at Marston Moor, its decision to go in pursuit of Essex was by no means an act of desperation. It led, at Lostwithiel, to the greatest Royalist victory of the war.

Credit is sometimes ascribed to King Charles himself.[24] But, although the King's confidence in his military abilities had grown, there is little to suggest that Charles possessed the skills to handle such a large-scale operation. It is more likely that victory at Lostwithiel was owed to those underrated soldiers, Lord Forth, Jacob Astley and Prince Maurice. An increasingly discontented Wilmot had little share in the success. Since at least the evacuation of Abingdon, Charles had been seeking an excuse to be rid of him, writing to Rupert as early as 22 June asking for Goring to be sent as a replacement.[25] Wilmot's dismissal[26] was only the first stage in a radical overhaul of the Royalist high command. It had probably already been decided that Forth's age and growing infirmities required his replacement at the end of the 1644 campaigning season, and his post was earmarked for Rupert.

The Prince's defeat at Marston Moor, whatever its effect on Rupert himself, did nothing to shake his uncle's confidence in him. Rupert's hold over his critics in the Oxford Army was strengthened by the near-disaster at the Second Battle of Newbury on 26 October, when Charles succumbed to the over-confident urgings of Goring and Digby, and broke a promise to Rupert to avoid battle until the latter arrived. The penitent monarch was for the moment ready to grant the Prince most of his demands, especially after Rupert reached a superficial reconciliation with Digby.

THE FAILURE OF REFORM:
RUPERT IN COMMAND 1644–5

On 6 November the Prince of Wales was appointed 'first Captain-General of all our Forces'. This was a purely honorific title made on Rupert's recommendation. Real control lay with Rupert himself, as Lieutenant General. He appeared to have gained complete authority, yet almost unrelieved disaster followed, finally dooming the Royalist cause. How much of this was Rupert's fault was vigorously debated by his contemporaries, with the verdict tending to go against the Prince. Modern writers largely exonerate Rupert, and indict Digby, Goring, the 'courtier' faction, and indeed the King himself. Yet even a superficial examination of the evidence raises serious questions not only about Rupert's conduct of the war, but of his suitability for the command.

Rupert was a controversial and abrasive figure, capable of inspiring loyalty and dislike in equal measure. By the end of 1644, someone of remarkable experience, tact and authority was needed to pull things together, and Rupert had so far shown little evidence of possessing all of the qualities required. His intolerance of the opinions of others was notorious; even before Marston Moor, his officers had complained of his reluctance to consult them, while Sir Phillip Warwick condemned his tendency 'with a pish to neglect all another said'.

Even if tales of Rupert sinking into debauchery and despair after Marston Moor are exaggerated or fabricated,[27] there is no doubt that his first major reverse had a profound effect on the young man, still only twenty-five years of age. The Prince's suspicion and dislike of the King's other councillors now at times approached paranoia. As early as 16 October, Rupert was writing to his confidante, Will Legge : 'Digby and Rupert [are] friends, but I doubt they trust one another alike. . . . Great factions are breeding against Rupert under a pretence of peace: He being, as they report, the only cause of war in this kingdom.'[28] Prospects for 1645 were bleak, with Parliament largely free to concentrate against the Royalist heartland of Wales and the South-west. Rupert seems to have hoped at best to achieve a compromise peace, and pinned his hopes on reversing the verdict of Marston Moor and restoring a Royalist presence in the North.

Yet even such a limited objective required the same kind of root-and-branch 'remodelling' of the Royalist forces as the Parliamentarians were currently carrying out. It is clear that Rupert was aware of the need. But it never progressed far, and even basic problems were not addressed. Command of the Royalist horse, for example, was left unclear. Unsurprisingly, this quickly became a bitter dispute between Rupert and Goring,[29] which the King allowed to fester before indulging Goring by accepting his appeals directly over Rupert's head.

Nor was there any fundamental shake-up of the senior command. Rupert's supporters – Bernard De Gomme as Quartermaster General, and Will Legge as Governor of Oxford – took over some posts, but other changes were few. There was none of the relative social flexibility that, on Parliament's side, allowed comparatively low-born commanders such as Fairfax and Cromwell to rise on grounds of merit. Rupert may be accused of failing to make full use of the talent that was available. That excellent cavalry commander, Sir Charles Lucas, was made Governor of relatively unimportant Berkeley Castle, when his true role should have been to replace the unsatisfactory Goring. Rupert spent the critical spring of 1645, when the New Model Army was taking shape at Windsor, attempting to salvage his brother's faltering campaign on the Welsh Border, and complaining bitterly to Legge of the machinations of his opponents in Oxford: 'if the King will follow the "wise" Counsel, and not hear the soldier and Rupert (according to his promise to me at Bristol, which he may remember) Rupert must leave off all.'[30] As Arthur Trevor ruefully informed Ormonde: 'In Oxen we are at great faction.'[31]

Not all the blame was Rupert's. The King's decision to attempt to restore order in the West by establishing a separate council at Bristol under the Prince of Wales, while not entirely unsuccessful, did draw off a number of the King's best advisers, and removed a significant part of Royalist military strength from Rupert's control. During the critical days leading up to the Battle of Naseby, it also allowed Goring to use the Council of the West to help him avoid Rupert's orders.

Matters came to a fatal head in the Naseby campaign. The decision at Stow-on-the-Wold on 10 May to detach Goring and his horse back to the West, often held to have cost the King the Battle of Naseby, was not in fact unreasonable. In April it had been agreed that Goring should keep the New Model in check while the main field army attempted the relief of Chester and the recovery of the North. While Clarendon may well be partially correct in his claim that Rupert was motivated by a desire to remove the persuasive Goring, whom he regarded as a dangerous rival, from the side of the King, the main error lay with Charles granting Goring a more extensive commission in the West, causing considerable upset among the commanders there, and giving him further excuse to ignore Rupert's instructions.

Rupert, with the wavering support of the King, got his way over the Digby faction, who, arguably correctly, wanted to concentrate on defeating the New Model, and made the recovery of the North the main object of the campaign. But his was a hollow and transient victory. First forced to turn back by Fairfax's threat to Oxford, the Royalist army, perhaps awaiting ammunition supplies from Oxford, then delayed at Daventry long enough for the New Model to come up.[32] Though Rupert opposed battle, he was overruled by Digby and his supporters – though it was too late to avoid action. On 14 June at Naseby, in what may have been as much a gesture of disgust as a rational military decision, Rupert abandoned his role of commanding general, and put himself at the head of his cavalry to lead it into action for the last time. The lack of any other suitable available cavalry commander was an indictment of both Rupert and King Charles.[33]

Naseby was effectively the death-blow of the Royalist cause. Once the remaining slim hope of prolonging the war by linking up with Goring in the West was passed up, coherent Royalist strategy broke down. Rupert accurately surmised of Naseby, 'doubtless the fault of it will be put upon Rupert'.[34] His decision to concentrate personally upon the defence of Bristol, while in part based upon sound military considerations, was equally a desire to remove himself from criticism and the intrigues of the Court. Having advised the King to seek terms, Rupert chose to surround himself for the last time with many of his remaining 'swordsmen' in a role which more properly belonged to a subordinate. In so doing, he met with inevitable defeat and disgrace, and gave Digby the hollow triumph he desired. But by then it no longer mattered.

CONCLUSION

Why did the Royalist high command, which had begun the war with such an apparent advantage, in the end fail so completely? Part of the problem was undoubtedly the over-rigid and hierarchical command structure, which slowed or prevented the rise of able officers. The frequently expressed contempt of the courtier and civilian councillor for the professional soldier probably reflected the view of the fastidious monarch himself. As a result, men of real talent such as Sir Marmaduke Langdale, Sir Richard Grenville and Sir Charles Lucas were never fully utilised. All too often, they became embittered and operated as often insubordinate provincial 'warlords'.

The influence of Prince Rupert was on many occasions a malign one. From the beginning, the Prince, by his intellectual arrogance and intolerance, and the favour shown him by his uncle the King, alienated many of the soldiers and civilian officials whose support was essential. As a result his very real abilities were frustrated by intrigue and infighting, and the situation was worsened by promotion to a responsibility for which Rupert was insufficiently experienced and psychologically unsuitable.

Ultimately, however, responsibility must lie with the Captain General himself. The same defects of character, a mixture of stubbornness and irresolution, an over-dependence upon self-motivated councillors, and an inability to stick to an agreed strategy, which had done much to bring about the war, also helped the King to lose it.

NINE

DAILY LIFE

'I cannot but think that the life of the private or common soldier is the most miserable in the world, and that not so much because his life is in danger – that is little or nothing – but for the terrible miseries he endures in hunger and nakedness, in hard marches and bad quarters.'

Thomas Raymond, *Autobiography*,
1917, p. 46

THE NEW RECRUIT

According to George Monck, the perfect private soldier was one who would:

avoid all Quarrelling, Mutinies, Swearing, Cursing or Lying, and . . . content with his wayes, . . . a good husband in the well managing of his meanes, keeping himself neat and handsome in his apparell; avoiding Drunkenness, and all manner of Gaming; truely to serve and fear God, and be obedient to all the commands of his superiors, cheerfully going upon all duties and to be loving, kind and courteous unto all his fellow Soldiers.[1]

Such an unlikely paragon would surely have met with the derision of his comrades and the incredulity of his officers!

Evidence regarding the background of the rank and file of the Royalist armies is incomplete. Many of the men recruited during the summer of 1642 were from the trained bands, so might be expected to have been from such backgrounds as tenant farmers and reputable estate and household servants. While including many of the above, 'volunteers' came from a much wider spectrum, encompassing the unemployed and others down on their luck or seeking to better their existing condition. Many were very young; there must have been Royalist counterparts of the regiment of 'poor little boys' in the garrison of Plymouth in 1643.[2] When conscription was introduced, it was theoretically limited to those aged between eighteen and fifty and excluded both the gentry and more prosperous middle-class occupations, so that inevitably the first choice of the parish constables responsible for providing the demanded quotas fell on vagrants, criminals, the unemployed and the half-witted, and then on poorer labourers and servants.

Any illusions held by the new recruit about the realities of war did not survive long after his enlistment. He reached the army, assuming that he had not deserted en route, wearing either his own civilian clothing or some basics provided by the parish. Whether he now received a uniform depended on current circumstances. The newcomers would be drafted into a company of an existing regiment, whose original regional connections, if any, rapidly became diluted, though, for example, Welsh soldiers, whose knowledge of English might be limited or non-existent, would perhaps be kept together under an NCO who at least understood the basic commands in their language.

William Barriffe devised a six-day refresher course in weapon handling and drill for men with some previous military experience,[3] but adequate training for a raw recruit would have taken about two months, and was usually carried out after morning parade.

DISCIPLINE

As well as learning how to fight, the new soldier would be instructed in other aspects of military discipline. Both sides produced detailed *Articles of War*.[4] Those of the Royalists were slightly more lenient, with thirteen offences punishable by death as opposed to about twenty-eight for Essex's army. Headings covered such matters as 'duties martiall', 'duties in camp and garrison', and 'duties of commanding officers'. As well as obvious offences like murder, mutiny and desertion, the death penalty could be imposed for such crimes as throwing away one's weapon, sleeping on sentry duty, abandoning the colours, killing a prisoner, and (mainly applicable to officers) surrendering a garrison 'without the utmost necessity'. Blasphemy was punishable by boring a hole with a hot iron in the tongue of the offender, while other crimes were liable to various forms of corporal punishment, ranging from the lash, often performed by wagoners from the train, running the gauntlet, riding the wooden horse (in which a man was seated for a specified period of time on a wooden 'horse', made of two angled planks with its 'back' forming a sharp ridge, his legs weighted by a varying number of muskets according to the degree of his offence) or, burdened in similar fashion, suspended by the thumbs.

For common soldiers, execution was normally by hanging, though officers, like the unfortunate Frank Windebanke after his surrender of Bletchingdon House in 1645, might face the firing squad. The army Provost-Marshal, supported by regimental provosts, was responsible for enforcing discipline. A regimental court martial could impose non-capital punishments, though the death penalty could (in theory) only be passed by a full Army Court Martial of senior officers.

Strictness in enforcing the *Articles of War* varied considerably in the Royalist armies. Bowing to reality, desertion was often treated quite leniently, offenders merely being rounded up and returned to the army, though occasional examples might be made or at least threatened. On 30 March 1643 in Oxford, 'three souldiers were brought to the gibbet . . . to be hanged for runninge away from their collours; but then word came from the court that but one of them was to suffer for all the rest and that the dice should be cast to trie who that one should be: but when all came to all, other word was brought, that the Prince [of Wales] had begged all their lives and so they were pardoned all three.'[5] Possibly some of the leniency in the Oxford Army was the result of the King's own attitude; Lord Byron, for example, in his more remote command at Chester, hanged a number of his Irish soldiers after the fall of Liverpool, though more for their part in the surrender of the town than for their subsequent desertion,[6] and Hopton was noted for his willingness to 'hang well'. In the Oxford Army, where evidence, though still scanty, is slightly more plentiful than for the regional forces, the impression is of a somewhat erratic policy regarding the death penalty. Actively suspected of treason in his surrender of Reading in May 1643, Colonel Richard Fielding was reprieved on the pleas of Prince Rupert, while Frank Windebanke, lacking similar intervention by the Prince, suffered the supreme penalty.

Looting was also punishable by death, but recognising that such unpleasantness was in practice often essential for their men's survival, most Royalist commanders seem to have tacitly ignored it unless too blatant. There were exceptions, usually when protests came from a sufficiently influential quarter, such as those of the Chester Assembly to Lord Byron early in 1644 regarding the indiscipline of the troops from Ireland,[7] or from time to time in the Oxford Army, perhaps when particularly serious examples were brought to the notice of King Charles himself. On 13 July 1644, for example, during the Royalist pursuit of Essex in the West Country, Richard Symonds records the hanging at the army's morning rendezvous of two soldiers for 'pillaging of the country villages', with another for a similar offence a fortnight later.[8] On 20 August, when straggling in search of provisions was seriously weakening the infantry strength of the Royalist forces around Lostwithiel, a proclamation was issued 'that all straggling foot presently repair to their colonels, upon payne of death',[9] though there is no confirmation that the threat was actually carried out. Drunkenness, like looting, was so widespread as to be largely ignored unless resulting in grave dereliction of duty.

If murder was punishable by death, the tendency, particularly among officers, to settle their differences by duelling, also in theory a capital offence, was a more difficult problem to tackle. The practice seems to have been more common in the early stages of the war, though it was never eradicated. On 15 March 1643, 'at the further end of Christchurch Meadows' in Oxford, the King's cousin, Lord John Stuart, fought Treasurer John Ashburnham, without injury to either, and at around the same time Secretary of State Nicholas warned Prince Rupert that 'there is here no punishment and therefore nothing but disaster may be expected'.[10] In the summer of 1643 Colonel Sir Nicholas

Crispe killed in a duel friend and fellow officer, Sir James Enyon. Though as an act of contrition he is said to have worn mourning for the rest of his life, he escaped any formal penalty.[11] The following July Symonds reported: 'This morning was a duel inter the Earl of Peterborough and Captain Thomas Willoughby . . . Willoughby wounded in the shoulder and thigh, the Earle safe without hurt. Willoughby challenged.'[12] There could evidently sometimes be a fine distinction between a 'legitimate' killing in a duel and one regarded as murder. Symonds reported, again in July 1644, that: 'On Satturday night two of the King's captaynes of horse: viz Captain Plowman and Captain [blank] fell out, and P. basely ran him through on horseback, but fled immediately.'[13]

Seldom mentioned, and seemingly more rarely punished, were offences of a sexual nature. Symonds records only one such episode. On 24 May 1645 'a foot soldier was tyed (with his shoulders and breast naked) to a tire and every carter of the trayne and carriages was to have a lash; for ravishing two women'.[14]

PAY

One of the problems in imposing effective discipline resulted from difficulties in paying the troops. The Earl of Newcastle wrote that 'The common soldier is encouraged with nothing but money or hopes of it.'[15] There were never any standard rates of pay throughout the Royalist armies. In December 1642 the King was offering 6s. a week to a musketeer, 12s. 10d. to a dragoon and 17s. 10d. to a trooper of horse, the latter being expected to provide his own arms and equipment. At about the same time, the Earl of Derby was hoping to pay his Lancashire forces at the rate of 10s. a day for a captain of foot, 4s. for a lieutenant, 18d. for a sergeant, 15d. for a drummer and 9d. for a common soldier.[16] Such rates were too high to be sustainable in the parlous state of Royalist finances, and by 1644 a foot soldier's pay was fixed at 4s. a week, with a captain being paid £2 12s. 6d., a lieutenant £1 8s. 0d., and an ensign £1 1s. 0d. A gentleman at arms and a sergeant were to receive 10s. 6d.,while corporals and drummers were both paid 7s.[17] Even if payment had been made regularly, a soldier did not actually receive the stated amount, deductions being made for food and clothing.[18]

As we have seen,[19] pay was frequently replaced, entirely or in part, by 'free quarter'. This seems to have been generally popular with the men. They were being fed on the same diet as their hosts, and thus fared better than they would from army supplies; it also provided opportunity to indulge in some semi-legitimate plundering.[20]

Pay arrears were one reason for allowing troops to sack captured towns and loot enemy prisoners. In the Parliamentarian forces this was sometimes replaced by the payment of 'storming money' to those taking part in such an operation, though it is difficult to believe that this prevented victorious troops from helping themselves to any available spoils as well. The Royalists never seem to have been in a position to make such offers credible, and loot, or the hopes thereof, played an important part in motivating their troops, particularly, it seems, those from the less prosperous 'celtic fringes'.

The storm of a large town could bring a considerable windfall to the soldiers taking part. In 1643 regulations laid down for the government forces in Ireland decreed that booty should be shared out according to a carefully graduated system, with a cornet of horse receiving three troopers' shares, a captain of foot that of six privates, a drummer two, and a sergeant one and a half.[21] The reality seems to have been a policy of every man for himself, often with considerable success. It was said that after the sack of Leicester in May 1645, one of the most profitable operations of its kind, no Royalist taken later had less than 40s. about his person – almost three months' pay for a private. Such a bounty resulted in large-scale desertion among the recipients, as they made off to a place of safety with their booty.

The division of the spoils could itself cause problems, particularly among soldiers who felt that they had missed out on their share. On 27 July 1643, after the storm of Bristol, Sir John Byron wrote to Rupert saying that there were very few men left with his brigade of horse (which had not taken part in the actual storm), 'the reason whereof is their discontent, in that they think they are sent away at this time to lose their shares in the pillage of Bristol. I shall therefore humbly beseech your Highness that I may have authority from you to assure them that they . . . shall have their parts as well as others. . . .'[22]

DIET

In the mid-seventeenth century there were four staple items in the diet of the poorer classes – cheese, beef (and/or fish), bread and beer, sometimes supplemented by peas and beans. The daily rations laid down in the Oxford Army for the common soldier, comprising 2 lb of bread, 1 lb of cheese or meat, a bottle of wine or two bottles of beer, compared very well with their sustenance in civilian life, and have been estimated as the equivalent of 4,500 calories, sufficient for heavy manual labour.[23]

While there was a good chance of regular rations being maintained in garrison or long-term billets (one of the reasons that such postings were so popular), the situation on campaign was often very different. Though the troops of the King's army were supplied in their winter quarters with bread freshly baked in the Royalist ovens in Oxford, regular delivery was impossible in the field, and soldiers were frequently reduced to stale bread and water, and whatever they could steal, beg or more rarely buy from civilian sources or forage from the fields and orchards. Observers remarked upon the large herds of plundered cattle and sheep that accompanied Royalist troops on the march, but even this source was not to be relied upon. Before Edgehill, Clarendon admitted that there were 'many companies of the common soldier who had scarce eaten in eight and forty hours',[24] while during the Lostwithiel campaign of 1644 straggling by common soldiers in search of provisions threatened the Royalist ability to continue their operations. Even on campaign there was usually a variety of food and drink available for those able to buy it from the victuallers who accompanied the main field armies. Officers would have fared best, and some were accompanied by a servant in charge of a 'sumpter horse' bearing a wider range of provisions.

CAMP AND CAMPAIGN LIFE

In winter quarters or garrison a soldier might expect to have a roof of some kind over his head, but this was not always the case on campaign. The foot of the Oxford Army were fortunate in the spring of 1643, when most of them were billeted in the fortified Culham Camp. Here, they were provided with timber huts as barracks, as well as fairly regular supplies. But this was exceptional; more commonly they slept in the open, whatever the weather. The field armies were on the move for most of the time during the campaigning season, which in normal circumstances extended roughly from April to the end of October (though operations in the depth of winter, such as the Nantwich Campaign and the fighting in the North-east in early 1644, were not unusual). Between 9 April and 23 November 1644, King Charles covered some 949 miles. By the time they entered battle, troops were frequently not only thirsty and hungry, but also cold, wet and exhausted. Captain John Gwynne vividly remembered conditions on the eve of the First Battle of Newbury: 'When we drew off it proved to be the most miserable, tempestuous rainy weather, that few or none could take little or no rest, and the creasing winds the next morning soon dried up our thorough wet clothes we lay pickled in all night.'[25] Cavalry units, sending their mounted quartermasters ahead in search of billets, were sometimes better off than the foot, but most available space in civilian households was taken up by the officers, with the best accommodation reserved for the King and his most senior commanders, the rest taking shelter wherever was available. Even the supposedly pampered King's Lifeguard of Horse quartered where they could, Lord Capel relating how on the Edgehill Campaign he and 100 other gentlemen of the Lifeguard had slept 'tumbled in the straw' in a barn.[26]

During the Lostwithiel Campaign the Lifeguard once more camped in the open. In his diary entry for 28 August, Richard Symonds described how the King's Troop 'returned to our quarters in the field, as the two nights before, the mornings and evenings very misty: though the night starlight'.[27] On the night of 31 August, as the Royalists moved in for the kill against Essex's trapped infantry, the King shared the discomfort of his troops: 'This night the King lay under the hedge with his servants in one field. The troopes of lifeguards lay in the next, it being very wyndy . . . and rayned much and great stormes.'[28]

Particularly during active operations, soldiers must have been exhausted for much of the time. In the retreat of the Royalist horse from Devizes to Oxford in July 1643 Captain Richard Atkyns paused in Faringdon to have his horse re-shod, 'when leaning upon a post I was so sleepy that I fell down like a log of wood, and could not be awakened for half an hour'. When he eventually staggered into his lodgings, Atkyns slept for fourteen hours.[29]

Though battle was the terrifying climax of a soldier's life, it was probably its aftermath that most exercised his mind. We have already looked at the treatment afforded to the wounded; the dead tended to receive even shorter shrift. Senior officers and other notables whose friends took the trouble to identify them might be returned to their family or buried with some ceremony. In August 1643 the burial of a Royalist major at Over in Shropshire was a formal affair: 'They buried him in a warlike manner, with his sword upon his coffin, and a drum beating before him to the church, where he was buried . . . men giving two volleys of shot there for him and afterwards the same drum beat before them home again. . . .'[30] After Marston Moor, the victorious allies took the captured Sir Charles Lucas around the field to identify dead Royalists. When King Charles' cousin, Lord Bernard Stuart, was killed at Rowton Heath, a Parliamentarian officer, Colonel John Booth, reported finding his body to the Governor of Chester, Lord Byron, who arranged for its collection and kept it embalmed in the city until it could be taken to Oxford and interred alongside Lord Bernard's brother.[31]

Other ranks could expect no such niceties. Bodies would be stripped of valuables and clothing and, though occasionally buried in neighbouring churchyards, were most commonly disposed of unceremoniously in mass grave pits dug by conscripted local countrymen, sometimes paid a fee according to the number buried. Unless a comrade eventually returned home with the tale, in many cases families would never learn the details of their loved ones' fate.

RELIGION

Religion did not play quite as prominent a role in the Royalist forces as among their opponents. Many regiments had a chaplain on their establishment, and in 1643 the King ordained that prayers be said in front of his troops twice a day, with a sermon on Sunday and communion once a month. Sir Ralph

Hopton's Cornish held prayers before going into battle at Braddock Down. At Edgehill, Sir Jacob Astley apparently found time only for his own famous brief prayer: 'Oh Lord, thou knowest how busy I must be this Day. If I forget Thee, do not Thou forget me. March on, Boys!' The chaplain of Sir Ralph Dutton's Regiment of Foot, while realistically admitting that 'soldiers are not at leisure for long prayers', nevertheless produced a 'Manual of Prayer', including ones for the King, Peace, one's officers, against swearing and 'for a good end'. The reaction of the troops is unrecorded.[32] Parliamentarian accounts frequently portray Royalist chaplains in an unflattering light. At Bristol in July 1643 it was claimed of the victorious Cavaliers that: 'Wheras the chaplains that go with them should teach them better, some of them swear as bad as the soldiers. . . .'[33]

PRISONERS

A captured soldier faced an uncertain fate. The status of 'prisoner of war' did not exist. In the opening weeks of the war, the Royalists briefly considered executing Parliamentarian prisoners as 'rebels', and though this was for obvious reasons not proceeded with, the King's prisons such as Oxford Castle, and in the West Country the notorious Lydford Castle under the sway of the ruthless Sir Richard Grenville, had a fearsome reputation, with prisoners suffering from 'violence to person, extortion, denial of rations, beds, access to friends and surgeons to dress their wounds. Lodging in heaps not only on the ground, upon bare boards, and in loathsome and filthy dungeons.'[34] Sometimes deliberate, this could also result from lack of resources. The first Governor of Oxford Castle blamed this as the cause of any problems and, though the Royalists officially allowed each prisoner 6d. a day for subsistence, at Oxford they were only actually being given 1½d.

There was often little real animosity between the ordinary soldiers on opposing sides once the fighting was done, but prisoners could nonetheless expect initial rough handling. They would generally be stripped of their valuables and much of their clothing, and subjected at least to verbal abuse. On the fall of

Bristol in July 1643, an infuriated Rupert waded in with his sword among some of his soldiers who, in breach of the agreed surrender terms, were pillaging the men of the garrison as they marched out, and similar scenes, described with some complacency by Richard Symonds, occurred when Essex's foot surrendered at Lostwithiel on 3 September 1644:

They all, except here and there an officer (and seriously I saw not above three or four that looked like a gentleman) were stricken with such a dismal feare, that as soone as their colour of the regiment was passt, (for every ensign had a horse and rid on him and was so suffered) the rout of the soldiers of that regiment presst all of a heape like sheep, though not so innocent. So durty and dejected as was rare to see. None of them, except some few of their officers, that did looke any of us in the face. Our foot would shout at them, and bid them remember Reading: Greenland House[35] (where others that did not condition with them tooke away all prisoners) and many other places, and then would pull their swords etc away, for all our officers still slash't at them.[36]

The King, however, as usual too late to make any difference, was outraged. When his unpopular Secretary at War, Sir Edward Walker, jested that 'our Souldiers freed them of the Burthen of their Cloathes', the unamused monarch retorted, 'Fie, that is ill said and was worse done!'[37]

Royalist prisoners fared much the same. In March 1643 some of Lord Herbert's unfortunate raw Welsh levies captured at Highnam were penned into a Gloucester church for ten days and allowed only ¼d. a day, with the result that they were fed on cabbages, turnips and whatever scraps were available. By the summer of 1645, prisoners were officially being allowed 1¾d. a day by Parliament, compared with its own ration rate of 6d., clearly insufficient for more than bare survival.

There were several possible eventual fates for prisoners. Officers, and occasionally some particularly valued other ranks such as the troops from Ireland and, in 1645, some of the Lifeguard of Foot, would eventually be exchanged for Parliamentarian prisoners in Royalist hands, according to a carefully graded scale of values.

Officers might be paroled in order to arrange their exchange, and wounded were sometimes released. Faced with the alternative of prolonged captivity in jail or the dreaded prison hulks of the River Thames, most ordinary soldiers quickly took the path of least resistance and enlisted with their captors; some of the veteran troops from Ireland taken at Nantwich did so and were greatly valued by their new employers. In 1645 the large numbers of Royalist foot taken at Naseby and in the string of surrendered garrisons proved something of an embarrassment to their captors. Many were handed over to agents of the armies of France and Spain, and others either sent to fight in Ireland or drafted into the ranks of the New Model Army, making little objection to a change in loyalty, for as New Model chaplain Richard Baxter explained: 'For the greatest part of the common soldiers, especially of the Foot, were ignorant men, of little religion, the abundance of them such as had been Prisoners, turned out of Garrisons, under the King, and had been soldiers in his army. And these would do anything to please their Officers.'[38]

REWARDS

Though many officers, and perhaps more of the rank and file than sometimes suggested, served the King from religious or political conviction as well as reasons of self-interest, Charles was not a figure to inspire much personal loyalty among the men. There is no evidence of his having any direct contact with them, and he lacked the charisma of a Rupert or Grenville and the social ease of a Goring or Wilmot. Though the King did introduce, with the financial assistance of Thomas Bushell, a number of medals, such as the 'Forlorn Hope' award for gallantry, these were probably mainly awarded to officers. The most that an ordinary soldier could expect was a monetary award if his action drew the attention and approval of a senior officer. On the whole, some loot, and an eventual safe return home, was the best he could hope for.

PART TWO

TEN

'WESTERN WONDER': THE CORNISH ROYALIST ARMY, 1642–3

'These were the very best Foot that ever I saw, for Marching and Fighting . . .'

> Captain Richard Atkyns, 'The Vindication of Richard Atkyns', in Peter Young (ed.), *Military Memoirs: the Civil War*, 1967, p. 29

Of all those who fought for King Charles, the little army, largely raised in Cornwall, that played a leading role in conquering much of south-west England for the Royalist cause earned perhaps the greatest reputation.

Cornwall in 1642 was still deeply linked to its Celtic past, isolated geographically and psychologically from the mainstream of English affairs by the River Tamar and poor communications. The inhabitants of its rocky coasts and rugged interior were regarded with distrust and dislike by many elsewhere, and this feeling was fully reciprocated. Although the majority of the population understood English, Cornish was still spoken west of Truro, though it was largely a language of the poor, who were 'laughed at by the rich that understand it not'.[1] The Cornish were noted for their fierce local nationalism, matched by an adventurous spirit. In peacetime this characteristic was apparent in their tendency towards disorder and lawlessness, which in war made Cornish troops notoriously unwilling to obey any but their own officers, and not always even them. Richard Atkyns, whose tribute to the Cornish infantry heads this chapter, added that they were 'so mutinous withall, that nothing but an alarm could keep them from falling foul upon their officers'.[2]

On the whole the Cornish gentry were not as prosperous as their counterparts elsewhere in England. Much of their income came from tin mines and foreign trade, which entered a period of decline during the 1630s, though agriculture was increasing in importance. The relationship between the Cornish gentry and their tenants had feudal and patriarchal overtones that, at this time, were largely disappearing in other parts of England. Sir Edward Walker noted in 1644 that the Cornish people had 'that obedience to their superiors which the rest have cast off. For the Gentry of this Country retain their old possessions, their old tenants and expect from them their ancient reverence and obedience.'[3]

Cornwall was by no means a rural arcadia. Although, on the whole, the relationship between the Cornish gentry and their tenants was a reasonably amicable one, even such a reputedly benevolent landlord as Sir Bevil Grenville ruled with a firm hand. His tenants were expected, for instance, to grind their corn in his mill and were sued if they failed to do so. The life of the average Cornishman and his family was harsh. Tin miners, for example, earned no more than £3 to £4 a year, and rarely lived to old age.

This semi-feudal society, together with Cornwall's geographical isolation and separate racial identity, resulted in a close-knit and deeply conservative community. These factors in themselves tended to result in sympathy for the King's cause, added to which were the close links with the Crown as a result of Cornwall's status as a royal duchy, which owned some forty-five manors in the county and was a reasonably good landlord. During the period 1624 to 1640, for example, only 2 out of a sample of 145 tenements saw any increase in rents.[4] While not necessarily resulting in fervent support for the King, this certainly helped ensure that there was no major political discontent such as existed elsewhere. Ultimately, however, it would be the local landlord or employer who decided the allegiance of the ordinary Cornishman.

While the Cornish gentry, with their relatively greater cosmopolitanism, were influenced by national issues, the feelings of the mass of the population are not so clear-cut. It was less than a century since the last great Cornish rebellion against rule from London. A desire to preserve the remaining unique features of Cornish society, its privileges and traditions, against external threat was a factor that increased in significance during the course of the war.[5]

There was nothing in the years prior to the Civil War to indicate that the King could rely automatically upon the support of the majority of the Cornish gentry. In the 1620s Cornish MPs had been in the forefront of opposition to royal policies, heightened by the imposition of Ship Money and conscription during the Bishops' Wars. A notable exception was Sir Bevil Grenville, whom the crisis caused to support the King, explaining 'I cannot contain myself within my doors, when the King of England's standard waves in the field upon so just occasion: the cause being such as must make all those that dye in it little inferior to martyrs'.[6] At the time, this was a minority view, but the growing constitutional crisis of 1640–1 caused a shift of opinion, with the majority of the innately conservative Cornish gentry, apart from a relatively small Puritan element, becoming uneasy at developments.

The Act of Attainder against the Earl of Strafford in April 1641 was decisive. Eight Cornish MPs, including future leaders of the Royalist party Richard Arundell, Sidney Godolphin, Sir Nicholas Slanning and John Trevanion, voted against the Bill. Fears of the parliamentary opposition's religious policy were growing, not just among Catholic families such as the Arundells. Yet, although by the summer of 1642 Royalist sentiment was dominant within Cornwall, this did not result in a desire to become involved in the fighting. In June the King issued Commissions of Array to his leading supporters in the county – Grenville, John Arundell of Trerice, John Grys the High Sheriff and Lord Mohun – but there remained a significant pro-Parliamentarian faction, particularly in the eastern part of Cornwall, headed by the county's leading magnate, Lord Robartes, while the Cornish boroughs were neutral.

Although at the Cornish Assizes in August the Sheriff read out his Commission of Array, he met with a lukewarm response. According to a Parliamentarian version, Grenville only raised about 180 men in an initial levy on Bodmin Racecourse on 17 August, instead of the 500 expected, some of whom came from Devon while 80 others were retainers of Sir Bevil himself. This, reportedly, was even after he had summoned recalcitrants 'upon pain of death'.[7]

Some of the apathy resulted from the imminent harvest, and also reflected the reluctance, common in many parts of the country, to plunge into the abyss of total war. However, in Cornwall, as elsewhere, community interests were overwhelmed by national events.

RAISING AN ARMY

Ironically, Cornwall was brought fully into the Royalist camp by the failure of the King's supporters to secure Somerset. Himself retiring across the Bristol Channel into South Wales, the Marquess of Hertford, commanding Royalist forces in the West, sent Sir Ralph Hopton, accompanied by 160 horse and dragoons and a number of leading West Country Royalists, to raise support in Cornwall. Hopton was to be the dominant military figure in West Country Royalism for the next year. A veteran of the Continental Wars, he would prove, until injured in July 1643, to be one of the most successful of the King's generals. The arrival of his cavalry, in the view of one contemporary Cornish observer, proved decisive in tipping the scales in favour of the Royalists.[8] Hopton appeared before the Cornish Assizes, where, with the jurors possibly influenced as much by his troops as by his arguments, he successfully pleaded the legality of the Commission of Array and was given control of the Cornish Trained Bands.

Sir Ralph may have hoped to take the offensive with these men, 3,000 of whom were mustered on 4 October at Bodmin. But, though the bandsmen proved willing enough to help Hopton chase the Cornish Parliamentarian leadership across the Tamar into Devon, they stood firm on their legal right not to serve outside their home county. Hopton had to turn to the alternative of a volunteer force.

Initially, this included five regiments of foot, and the main role in recruiting them was taken by the Cornish Royalist gentry. Details of the process are sparse, but certain features are clear.

The close ties between landlords and tenants were critical. Four of the regiments were recruited mainly from on and around their commanders' estates. This bond of community encompassed both officers and men. In Sir Bevil Grenville's Regiment, for example, all but one of the officers came from its home area of north-east Cornwall, while eight of Colonel John Trevanion's originated from around his estates in the south and centre of the county. All of the colonels were men of considerable local influence. Grenville was the leading landowner in north-east Cornwall, and was noted as a mildly reforming landlord. Trevanion's father had been High Sheriff and was a Deputy Lieutenant of Cornwall. Lord Mohun, whose Royalism was initially a little ambivalent, was a major landowner, and for this reason rather than any evidence of ability he was given the largely honorific post of Lord General of the Cornish Army. Two other colonels, Sir Nicholas Slanning and William Godolphin, had extensive interests in tin mining, and most of their recruits seem to have been miners.

All five of the Cornish colonels were men of substance and some education, although only Slanning, who had served on the Continent in the First Bishops' War and was Constable of Pendennis Castle, could be described as an experienced soldier.[9] The same pattern recurs among their subordinates. Only one of Grenville's officers, his major, George Lower, is known to have had previous military experience, serving with Sir Bevil in 1640. Most officers of the five volunteer regiments seem to have been amateurs.[10] The same applied to the majority of the rank and file; apart from some trained band experience, and those of Grenville and Slanning's men who served with them in the Bishops' Wars, all were new to war.

The impression given by many writers, taking their lead from Clarendon, is of a 'band of brothers', with the entire Cornish Army united and inspired by bonds of loyalty. Although it is true that the colonels and many of the officers were linked by kinship and the interests of their class and background, it is misleading to suggest that all of the rank and file flocked eagerly to arms. Some volunteered for much the same reasons as recruits elsewhere, among them apparently a number of sailors and Frenchmen.[11] But there is also plenty of evidence of coercion. Whatever Grenville's peacetime attitude to his tenants and dependents, he had no compunction about compelling them to serve him in war. A Parliamentarian newsletter reported: 'Sir Bevill Grenvile hath been a tyrant, especially to his tenants, threatening to thrust them out of house and home if they will not assist him and his confederates.'[12] Grenville's own correspondence confirms this. He wrote angrily to his wife, Grace: 'My neighbours did ill that they came not out, and are punishable by the law in high degree; and though I will do the best I can to save some of the honester sort, yet others shall smart.'[13] And, he added: 'If we proceed I shall expect they should yet come forth, or they shall suffer.'[14]

Recruitment proved disappointingly slow. Although Hopton wrote optimistically that the new regiments were 'formed into some reasonable show of an Army',[15] by the end of October they totalled no more than 1,500 men with five guns, instead of their theoretical establishment of 1,200 each. But recruits continued to come in, and Grenville's and Slanning's Regiments eventually each mustered about 1,000 men.

If recruiting had been brisker, Hopton would have encountered difficulties in arming and paying them. Grenville, Trevanion and later Jonathan Trelawney all maintained their own regiments, and their efforts were supplemented by contributions from other Cornish gentry, sometimes in the form of plate, and Sir Francis Basset, who coordinated financial affairs, established a mint at Truro. The new regiments originally 'were armed, partly out of the Gentlemen's particular stores, and partly out of those that belonged to the Trained Bands of the county',[16] but the quantity that could be spared was insufficient for Hopton's needs. Basset and Slanning organised the import into Cornish ports of munitions from France, paid for by the sale of tin, and Slanning was also responsible for a growing flotilla of privateers, which preyed upon merchant shipping in the Channel.

The Parliamentarian navy sought, with some success, to stifle the arms trade. In November 1642, for example, a relative of Sir Bevil Grenville employed by him to purchase arms in France was captured with a cargo including 300 muskets, 500 cases of pistols and 3 guns.[17] By then, most of the volunteers were probably adequately armed, though none of them apparently received uniforms for a considerable time afterwards, relying upon ribbons, such as the Grenville family colours of blue and white, to distinguish the different regiments.[18]

INTO BATTLE

In December Hopton felt strong enough to move against Plymouth. But his 'volunteers' were almost as unwilling to leave their native county as the trained bands had been, until in effect they were bribed to do so.[19] The campaign proved a débâcle. The defences of Plymouth were too strong, and after a rendezvous of Devon Royalists was broken up at Modbury (7 December) Hopton had no option, 'in that bitter season of the year', but to fall back across the Tamar. Sir Ralph was later described as 'a man superior to any temptation . . .',[20] with a policy of 'pay well, command well, and hang well'[21] displayed as early as November 1642, when he hanged twenty looters at Launceston.[22] But he found imposing discipline on the Cornish Army a long and difficult task. During the December retreat, he complained, the Cornish foot were 'through the whole marche so disobedient and mutinous, as little service was expected from them if they should be attempted by the Enemy'.[23]

During January the Cornish Army endeavoured to build up its strength for the coming campaign. Grenville wrote to his wife on 6 January:

I am of a mind to billet some companies in the parishes about you as namely five companies five parishes, by one in a parish for defence against plunderers. Wherefore Mr Rous to prepare the inhabitants of Kilkhampton, Morewenstow, Stratton, Poughill and Lancells to diet a hundred men a parish in several houses. They should be allowed for each man two shillings by the week which is enough from a poor soldier, and to be brief if they will not do it willingly, they shall do it whether they will or no . . .[24]

In mid-January the Parliamentarian commander in Devon, General Ruthin, anxious to make a name for himself before he was superseded by the Earl of Stamford, invaded Cornwall. Hopton was critically short of arms, ammunition and money to pay his men, but on 17 January, in what must have seemed to the anxious Royalists like intervention by Providence, two Parliamentarian ships, laden with arms, ammunition and enough money to pay the Cornish troops for a fortnight, were driven by bad weather into Falmouth. The Royalist commanders, aware that Ruthin, at Liskeard, was about to be reinforced, decided to attack first. Early on 19 January the two armies confronted each other on Braddock Down. Knowing that the brittle morale of his men would not withstand a reverse, Hopton took the offensive. He decided, in his own words, 'to leave the decision to the mercy of God and the valour of his side',[25] and, after prayers at the head of each division, launched a charge. Grenville described the action:

> I led my part away, who followed me with so good courage, bothe downe the one hill and up the other, it strooke such a terror in them, while the second came up gallantly after me, and the winges of horse charged both sides, but their courage so failed them, as they stood not our first charge of the foote but fledd in great disorder and we chast them . . . many were not slaine because of their quick disordering . . .[26]

The Royalists killed about 200 of the enemy, and took 1,200 prisoners and 5 guns, in this quick and complete victory that revitalised the Cornish Royalist cause. Their own casualties were remarkably light. Among them perhaps was the soldier of whom Grenville instructed his wife, 'If my soldier Hugh Ching continues sick, pray let there be care had of him, and let him not want what you can help him.'[27] It was an example of the paternalistic care that helped form a strong bond between the Cornish commanders and their men.

Braddock Down had been predominantly a victory for the foot, who formed the most significant part of the Cornish Army. It was never particularly strong in cavalry. In the spring there were no more than about 300 of them, later reportedly expanded to about 1,400, of whom a Parliamentarian report reckoned only Hopton's original two troops of 150 men to be 'very serviceable'.

Hopton followed up his victory with a renewed thrust across

the Tamar, but encountered the same difficulties as before. Not for the last time, Plymouth proved too strong, while the Cornish Trained Bands still declined to serve beyond the county boundary. A reverse at Modbury was followed by a truce, with both sides anxious to play for time to prepare for the next round, and it was extended until 22 April, by which time the Parliamentarians were ready to resume the offensive.

The Royalists made use of the breathing space to expand and reorganise their forces. A weekly assessment of £750 was set in Cornwall to maintain the army, and, symptomatic of the continued difficulty in obtaining volunteers, a limited form of conscription was introduced in May, by means of which the third man in every 100 of military age was enlisted. Two new foot regiments, those of Charles Trevanyon and Francis Basset, were commissioned, though no regiment seems to have mustered more than 1,000 men, with detachments absent on garrison duty.[28] The overall strength of the Cornish foot fluctuated between approximately 3,000 and 4,000 men.

CORNWALL SECURED

On 23 April 1643, hard on the expiration of the truce, a Parliamentarian force under Major General James Chudlegh crossed the Tamar, heading for Launceston. After a hard fight they were repulsed, but the Cornish Army displayed its besetting vice when the foot 'according to their usual custom grew disorderlie and mutinous'.[29] When the success at Launceston was eventually followed up, the Cornish were routed in a somewhat farcical encounter on Sourton Down (25 April) when they were thrown into panic as much by the effects of a thunderstorm as by the efforts of the enemy, crying in terror as they fled that 'the militia fought not against them but the Devil'.[30]

Hopton remained at Launceston until early May, when the Earl of Stamford advanced with an army of 3,400 foot and 200 horse, set on the final destruction of the Cornish Army. The decisive action came on 16 May at Stratton. Hopton was outnumbered, mustering some 2,400 foot and 500 horse, and the Parliamentarians were strongly positioned on a hilltop. The encounter that followed was a demonstration of the dogged fighting qualities of the Cornish foot. Advancing up the hill in four columns, they were repeatedly thrown back until, with their ammunition almost exhausted, the Royalist commanders, concealing the full extent of their plight from their men, resolved on a final drastic effort. The foot were ordered forward again, reserving their fire until they reached the crest of the hill.

Stamford's men, many of them raw levies, were almost as exhausted as their opponents, and began to crumble as the Royalists approached. Major General Chudlegh led a desperate counter-attack:

> with a good stand of pikes upon that party which was led by Sir John Berkley and Sir Bevill Grenvile, and charged them so smartly that he put them into disorder; Sir Bevill Grenvile in the shock being borne to the ground but quickly relieved by his companion, they so reinforced the charge, that having killed most of the assailants and dispersed the rest, they took the Major General prisoner. . . . Then the enemy gave ground apace, insomuch as the four parties, growing nearer and nearer as they ascended the hill, between three and four of the clocke, they all met together upon one ground near the top of the hill, where they embraced with unspeakable joy . . .[31]

Stratton was a decisive victory for the Cornish Royalists, gained at very light cost. Perhaps 80 of their men were killed, of whom 46 were common soldiers, while the Parliamentarians lost 300 dead, 1,700 prisoners, 70 barrels of powder, 13 guns and £5,000. Sir Francis Basset wrote in tones of incoherent ecstacy to his wife: 'Dearest Soule, Oh Deare Soule, prayse God everlastingly. Reede ye inclosed, Ring out your Bells, Rayse Bonfyers, Publish these Joyfull Tydings. Beleeve these Truthes. Excuse me writing larger. I have not tyme. We march on to meete our Victoryus ffriends, and to sease all ye Rebells lefte if we can ffynde such Lyvinge.'[32]

APOTHEOSIS

With Cornwall secure, the Cornish Army was now free to march over the Tamar and link up with the main Royalist forces. It is a remarkable tribute to Hopton's leadership, and the bond that had developed among his soldiers and their officers, that troops who only a few months previously had mutinied at the prospect of leaving their home county were now prepared to march the length of south-west England.

On 4 June the Cornish Army, totalling 3,800 men plus officers, linked up with Prince Maurice and the Marquess of Hertford at Chard in Somerset. Hertford was Captain General of the Royalist forces in the West, but a formula was devised whereby Hopton continued to exercise effective command in the field. The looser discipline of the troops under Maurice and Hertford, and the effect it had on his own men, concerned Hopton. He explained: 'There began the disorder of the horse visibly to break in upon the prosperity of the publique proceedings . . . the Generals were never able to repress the extravagant disorder of the horse to the ruine and discomposure of all.'[33] An officer of these cavalry, Richard Atkyns, described the reaction of the Cornish soldiers, who 'could not well brook our Horse (especially, when we were drawn up upon Corn) but they would many times let fly at us . . .'.[34]

Several days skirmishing with the Parliamentarian forces, under Hopton's old friend and comrade in arms Sir William Waller, followed around Wells and Bath, and climaxed with the bloody Battle of Lansdown. So far, the Cornish troops had achieved their victories at a remarkably light cost. Though exact figures will never be known, total losses in action had probably not exceeded 500.[35] Lansdown changed all this.

On 4 July Waller had outmanoeuvred the Royalists, and taken up a defensive position outside Bath on Lansdown Hill. Its natural advantages were further improved by earthworks, and the approaches covered by cannon, with musketeers positioned in the woods on either flank. The only line of approach lay along the winding lane from Tog Hill, with an attacker exposed to the full weight of the defenders' fire. On 5 July the Royalists approached, eyed the magnitude of the task confronting them and, at about 3 p.m., began to withdraw. Waller reacted with a cavalry counter-attack, which was beaten off. The exultant Cornish foot, fired with memories of success at Stratton, were eager for action, for, as Lieutenant Colonel Arthur Slingsby explained, 'did our foote believe noe men their equal, and were soe apt to undertake anything that the hill upon which the Rebells stood well fortifyed, from whence they racked us with theire cannon could not deterre them, and they desired to fall on and cryed "let us fetch those cannon"'.[36]

It must have been a difficult decision for Hopton. But he had perhaps become convinced of his men's invincibility, or felt that a refusal would have serious effects on their always brittle morale. Perhaps the attack even began spontaneously. The Royalists, with the Cornish foot in the centre, supported by Hertford's infantry, and with the horse operating ineffectively on the flanks, began a long slow advance up the hill under heavy fire, making what use they could of the cover offered by hedges and banks. Grenville's massed pikes, possibly drawn from several regiments, and a particularly vulnerable target, were able to shelter for a time behind a low stone wall at right angles to the enemy fire, until the musketeers on their flanks slowly pushed back their opponents.

As Grenville's men approached the crest of the hill, with perfect timing Waller's horse – including Haselrigg's heavily armoured cuirassiers, the 'Lobsters' – counter-attacked. The outcome of the battle hung, literally, in the balance. Slingsby likened Grenville's pikes to 'a heavy stone on the very brow of the hill which with one hasty charge might well have been rolled to the bottom'.[37] Atkyns arrived in time to witness the climax:

When I came to the top of the hill, I saw Sir Bevill Grenvile's stand of pikes, which certainly preserved our Army from a fatal rout with the loss of his most precious life. They stood as upon the Eaves of a House for steepness, but as unmoveable as a Rock, on which side of the stand of Pikes our Horse were, I could not discover, for the air was so darkened by the smoke of the powder that for a quarter of an hour together there was no light seen, but what the fire of the volleys of shot gave, and 'twas the greatest storm I ever saw.[38]

Grenville fell, mortally wounded in the head by a blow from a pole-axe, as his pikemen repulsed the third successive attack by Waller's horse. His epic stand had been just enough. The Royalists carried the first Parliamentarian defensive position, although Waller hung on behind the cover of stone wall until darkness, when he quietly withdrew to Bath.

By virtue of their possession of the field, the Royalists could technically claim Lansdown as a victory. But it had been won at a terrible cost. The loss of Grenville was 'a universal grief to the army', and the overall casualties of the Cornish had been horrendous. With Grenville, from his own regiment had fallen Major Lower, Sir Bevil's Captain Lieutenant, and 200 foot, while another 300 were badly wounded. In all something like one in six of the Cornish Army were casualties at Lansdown. Morale slumped still further next day, when Hopton was badly injured in an accidental powder explosion. The army took refuge in Devizes, and played little part in the sweeping Royalist victory at Roundway Down on 13 July which led to their relief.

The survivors of the Cornish Army went on to take part in the storming of Bristol on 26 July. Stationed on the south and west sides of the town, the Cornish officers had opposed an assault because of the heavy casualties likely to be suffered, but were overruled. In the event, with a resurgence of the over-confidence of Lansdown, or perhaps succumbing to the strain of waiting, the Cornish troops began the assault prematurely at 3 a.m.

Casualties were heavy; according to Slingsby most were the result of the defending ditch being too wide for the Royalists' scaling ladders to bridge, and too deep to fill. But the Cornish 'fell on with that courage and resolution as nothing but death could control'.[39] All attempts to scale Bristol's defences failed and, after three hours of bitter fighting, the Cornish sullenly fell back, having lost a third of their numbers. It was left to the troops of the Oxford Army to complete the capture of Bristol, but the Cornish took little joy from the victory. They were stunned by the loss of perhaps another 200 dead, and especially by the appalling casualties among their officers. Slanning and Trevanion, who had the belief of young men in their own apparent immortality, were both mortally wounded, and Clarendon paid tribute to them in a moving elegy: 'They were both very young . . . of entire friendship to one another, and to Sir Bevill Grenvile . . . they were hurt in almost the same minute and the same place, both shot in the thigh with a musket ball, their bones broken, the one dying presently, the other some few days later. . . .'[40]

Trevanion, said Clarendon, was a quiet man 'of good understanding, great courage, but few words, but what he said has always been to the purpose'. Slanning, in contrast, was small and lively, 'of a very handsome and of a lovely countenance, of excellent parts and an invincible courage'.[41] He died, according to Clarendon, without regrets, not knowing that his only son had been born the same day, and commenting wryly 'that he had always despised bullets, having been so used to them, and almost thought they could not hit him'.[42]

THE WAR GOES ON

The original Cornish Army died with its leaders. Mary Coate, the historian of Cornwall in the Civil War, reached a verdict that the years have rendered no less valid:

> The army which Grenvile and Hopton had led so triumphantly across the Tamar after Stratton had perished as surely as if it had fallen with Grenvile on the heights of Lansdown, or with Slanning by the walls of Bristol. For the life of the Cornish army had been in its leaders; they had inspired it with enthusiasm, they had given it its unity, and when they died its history ended. Lansdown and Bristol might be numbered among the Royalist triumphs, but for the Cornish army they were its Ichabod.[43]

Bristol was not the end of Cornwall's part in the Civil War. But the survivors of the old Cornish Army had lost that essence of spirit that had hitherto carried them to victory. They relapsed into a mutinous sullen condition, and refused to serve with the main Royalist army, citing fears of incursions into Cornwall from unconquered Plymouth. A few remained with Hopton in Bristol garrison, while others marched back to the West with Prince Maurice. They fought, without particular distinction, at the capture of Exeter, the ill-fated siege of Lyme, and at the Second Battle of Newbury, where they were worsted by Skippon's foot. The King continued to place ever more unrealistic hopes on the war-weary Cornish population, dismayed and discouraged by the proportionately heavy casualties they had suffered.

For a brief interval, the invasion of Cornwall in the summer of 1644 by the Earl of Essex revitalised Cornish efforts, and Charles hoped to exploit this when he appointed Sir Richard Grenville, brother to Sir Bevil but with the family charisma cast in a coarser and more brutal mould, to raise new forces in the county. Unfortunately, though having remarkable success in recruiting men, notably the four foot regiments known as the 'New' Cornish Tertia,[44] Grenville proved to be working partially towards his own agenda. Few of the new recruits were prepared to march eastwards with the main field army, and Grenville may have been bowing to the inevitable when he chose instead to concentrate on Plymouth.

Though he proved an excellent disciplinarian, and one of the few Royalist commanders by this stage of the war able to maintain the strength of his forces, Sir Richard failed to take Plymouth. His cruelty towards prisoners and personal enemies, and ruthlessness towards those who failed to cooperate, alienated many influential Royalists, though not the ordinary Cornish people, with whom Grenville's popularity apparently increased.

By the time he had grudgingly obeyed the Council of the West's orders, and had taken his New Tertia into Somerset to join the operations against Taunton in the early summer of 1645, Grenville knew the reluctance of many Cornish to make further sacrifices for the Royalist cause. Desertion was rife among both 'old' and 'new' Cornish forces, and after Grenville was temporarily put out of action by wounds, there were armed clashes between his troops and Goring's horse.

Consequently, Cornish troops played little part in the Langport campaign of July 1645. Grenville eventually rallied many of the deserters, and there was a brief resurgence of loyalty to Prince Charles, as Duke of Cornwall, when he took refuge across the Tamar. Increasingly, Grenville was the only man able to rely upon the obedience of the Cornish, and it has been suggested that by the end of 1645 he was assuming the mantle of Cornish 'nationalist' leader aiming at a separate settlement between the Duchy of Cornwall, under his effective control, and Parliament.[45]

In February 1646 Grenville's insubordinate stance led to his arrest and final collapse seemed imminent, despite the New Cornish Tertia fighting manfully at Torrington, the last major engagement of the war in the West. Lingering support for the Royalist cause received its death blow after the influx into Cornwall of disorderly Royalist troops from elsewhere and this, coupled with reaction to Grenville's arrest, resulted in large-scale Cornish desertions. Though a handful of Cornish activists, under John 'Jack for the King' Arundell, held out at Pendennis Castle long into the summer, on the whole an exhausted, war weary and devastated community would fight no longer for a doomed cause. Yet the Cornish troops had played a major role in the tide of Royalist success that had crested at Bristol in July 1643, and their contribution was recognised in September 1643 in the rare honour of a Proclamation from the King, still to be seen in some Cornish churches:

That so long as the History of these Times and this Nation shall continue, the Memory of how much that County hath merited from Us and our Crown may be derived with it to posterity.[46]

ELEVEN

'NURSERY OF THE KING'S INFANTRY': WALES AND THE ROYALIST ARMY

'That land of promises, but never of fulfillment.'
John, Lord Byron, 'Account of the Siege of Chester',
in *Cheshire Sheaf*, 1971, p. 3

Wales and its inhabitants followed close upon the heels of the Irish as a propaganda topic for the London-based pamphleteers of the 1640s. But whereas the Irish – particularly after the Rebellion of 1641 – were the subject of lurid accusations of massacre and atrocity, the Welsh were treated more as objects of contempt. Given 'humorous' names – 'Thomas ap Shinkin' and 'Shon ap Shones' – they were credited with outlandish customs and language, an obsession with leeks and toasted cheese, and a tendency to run away in battle.[1] Dislike of the Welsh was a common English prejudice, shared by many Royalist officers who served with them.

But Parliament had well-founded fears of the amount of support that the King was likely to receive from his Welsh subjects. In September 1642 a London newsletter opined that the men of North Wales 'would flock to the Standard like Wild Geese'.[2] Despite publically expressed derision, there was an underlying respect for Welsh military prowess. Soldiers from Wales had been heavily involved in England's wars since early medieval times, and the Tudor dynasty, playing up its Welsh connections to the full, had employed troops from the Principality at home and abroad. This reached a peak during the Irish Wars of Queen Elizabeth, with nearly 3 per cent of the population estimated to have served – over twice the figure for England.[3] The military tradition had been continued by impoverished Welsh gentry seeking their fortunes in the Continental Wars, and most recently by troops raised in Wales for the Scots Wars, and to suppress the 1641 Rebellion.

Contemporaries assumed that Welsh troops were vital for the Royalist war effort, and this has also been a virtually unquestioned article of faith among modern historians.[4] While generally correct, it is a belief deserving closer examination.

THE EVE OF WAR

Wales in 1642 was regarded by most English people as poverty-stricken and backward. Its mountainous interior would mostly be untouched by the war, fought for possession of the coastal plains and towns, where most of Wales' estimated population of 400,000 lived. Although there was some small-scale mining and iron-working, the Welsh economy was predominantly agricultural. Trade with England was vital, especially the export of cloth and the great herds of cattle driven as far as London to be sold, likened by that influential Welshman, John Williams, Archbishop of York, to 'the Spanish fleet of North Wales, which brings hither that little silver and gold we have'.[5]

Welsh society was dominated by the native gentry, undisputed masters of their estates and tenantry, who might total a handful or hundreds. Despite their fierce pride, claiming ancestral links with the ancient princes, most Welsh gentry, with the exception of the great Herbert family of Monmouthshire, were poor by English terms. It was perhaps inevitable that this strongly conservative and traditionalist society, many of whom spoke only Welsh, should react with alarm to the political, religious and social convulsions in London. One writer went so far as to warn: 'These things are signs . . . that the end of the world is not far off; God prepare us for it.'[6]

Though there was a small pro-Parliament element in Wales, notably in the far south-west and among the tiny Puritan community, the vast majority of the Welsh gentry, and by association the bulk of the population, reacted to war with varying degrees of commitment to the King, sometimes more out of fear of the social consequences of a Parliamentarian victory than from enthusiasm for Charles. Exceptional were activists such as Sir Thomas Salusbury in Denbighshire, who, as well as fearing a repetition on Welsh soil of the horrors of the contemporary conflict in Europe, was motivated by belief in the divine right of the monarch against the machinations of the 'filthy dreamers' of Parliament.[7] But there was a potentially significant neutralist sentiment in Wales, which the impact of events would gradually activate.

WALES FOR THE KING

The arrival of King Charles I at Shrewsbury in September 1642, and his appeal for support, met with a ready response in Wales. It is impossible to say how many individual Welshmen enlisted with the 'English' regiments mustering at Shrewsbury, for the surviving evidence relates mainly to units that the Royalist Commissioners of Array, firmly in place throughout Wales by the summer of 1642, were instructed to raise. In all, it seems, ten colonels were commissioned to recruit in Wales before the end of 1642, with varying degrees of success.[8]

The main problem was finance. Few Welsh gentry, with the exception of the Herberts of Raglan, could meet the costs of arming, equipping and paying a full-sized regiment. In Denbigh and Flintshire the pro-Royalist gentry formed an association that 'persuaded' the inhabitants to contribute £1,500 to raise a regiment of foot. This was placed under the command of Sir Thomas Salusbury of Llewenni. Enough evidence survives to provide a fairly detailed picture of the origins of this unit, the only complete regiment from North Wales at Edgehill. With nine companies, Salusbury was fortunate in obtaining the services as officers of a number of professional soldiers, as well as Denbighshire gentry, including his lieutenant colonel, John Royden, who had been a lieutenant in 1640, and his major, George Boncle, who combined the skills of professional musician and soldier.[9] Despite it being harvest time, recruiting for the regiment went well, Salusbury telling Anglesey squire Thomas Bulkley on 6 August:

> our companyes of men are near full . . . I gave all my Captains leave to be forward before I began presuming upon ye beating of my drummes. I should soone rayse my company, but I have stayed soe long that besides myne owne servants and tennants very few that will goe but have already taken entertainment with one or other of my captains, soe that I am like to be ye last provided unless I may be well helped by my friends from other parts. I have sent to Montgomeryshire, but there I hear they are raysing a Regiment themselves,[10] yet I doubt not but Sir Edward Lloyd [his brother-in-law] will help me to some; if you can spare half a score or more lusty fellows out of your Country, that are reasonably well cloathed to be of myne owne company, you shall therein lay great obligation upon me, It falls to my share to rayse 350 for my self and Sergeant Major who is a stranger, my own company consisting of 200 and his 150, and this being harvest time will put me to it shrewdly . . .[11]

Bulkley sent ten men and, although probably not so well equipped as desired, Salusbury mustered some 1,200 troops, the largest regiment in the Royalist army mustered at Shrewsbury. Despite a contemporary description of Salusbury's men as 'poor Welsh vermin, the off-scourings of the nation',[12] they performed reasonably well at Edgehill.[13]

Less fortunate was the only other complete Welsh regiment to serve with the King's forces there. Sir Edward Stradling's men, raised mainly in Glamorgan, were routed, possibly because most of their officers were country gentlemen without previous experience.[14] Stradling's misfortune cast a slur on the fighting reputation of the Welsh troops that Salusbury felt keenly. In a speech before the attack on Brentford, he told his men: 'Gentlemen you lost your honour at Edgehill. I hope you will regain it here.' In the action that followed, Royalist foot, spearheaded by the Welsh, broke three Parliamentarian regiments and drove the remnants into the Thames.[15]

The prospect of a long war led King Charles to turn

increasingly to Wales for support. He had hoped at the start of the war for more assistance from his Welsh subjects than he actually received, and Ronald Hutton has commented that 'the King does not seem to have realised the potential of Wales'.[16] Certainly, the response to royal demands was by no means uniform throughout the country. The four counties of north-west Wales provided 60.5 per cent of Welsh colonels, and about half of the Welsh 'Indigent Officer' claimants came from there. Even here, difficulties were encountered in raising the 'second wave' of regiments for the Royalist army. At the end of October the King wrote to the Commissioners of Array in Caernarvonshire urging them to make greater efforts to provide funds for the foot regiment that John Owen of Clennau was raising there and in Merioneth.[17] Even then, it did not reach full strength, Owen having only eight companies with him when he set out in November to join the King.[18]

More successful, apparently, was Roger Mostyn in Flintshire, although claims that he was able to muster 1,500 men in twelve hours are probably an exaggeration. Using as a basis the Flintshire Trained Band Regiment, manned partly by his own lead miners, Mostyn was able to reinforce the garrison of Chester early in 1643. The influx of Welsh troops was not popular among the citizens, whose alarm was heightened when Mostyn's men got out of hand, and sacked the town house of the Cheshire Parliamentarian leader Sir William Brereton. Fears of the vengeance that Brereton might wreak would haunt Chester for the rest of the war.[19]

Two other North Wales regiments were raised at this time. William Wynne's Denbighshire Trained Band unit was used initially to garrison Shrewsbury, but during the winter was converted into a 'volunteer' regiment to serve with Lord Capel's army in Cheshire and Shropshire.[20] Colonel Robert Ellice of Gwasnewydd, one of Denbighshire's Commissioners of Array and a veteran of the Swedish service, was commissioned to recruit a regiment of foot. Though Ellice was highly thought of, his performance was a disappointment; after designing an over-ambitious system of defences for Chester, he and most of his regiment were captured in March 1643 at Middlewich.[21]

None of these troops were of direct assistance to the main

field army, but during the spring there were high hopes of reinforcement from South Wales, where the Herbert family were raising a new army, partly based on Welsh units that had joined the Oxford Army during the winter, and which were recalled in the spring.[22] Once again, Royalist expectations were dashed. Herbert's 500 horse and 1,500 foot – the 'mushroom army' – were trapped at Highnam by the combined Parliamentarian troops of Edward Massey and Sir William Waller, and were forced to surrender.[23]

Undaunted, Lord Herbert again began recruiting and, arming it rather inadequately from the ironworks of Glamorgan and the Forest of Dean, was able to despatch a similar sized force (largely based on Glamorgan Trained Band units), under Colonel General Sir William Vavasour, to take part in the siege of Gloucester during the summer. In the event, the Welsh troops proved ineffective.[24] After fighting, without distinction, at First Newbury, Vavasour's men returned to the Welsh Border.

For all his high hopes, the King's main field army received little direct reinforcement from Wales during 1643. The only Welsh regiments permanently serving with it were the foot of Sir Thomas Salusbury, John Owen and John Stradling,[25] none of them at full strength. Several companies of Salusbury's had been sent back home in the winter of 1642 to help bolster the ramshackle Lancashire forces of the Earl of Derby, and there were further losses through attrition. Salusbury went back to Denbighshire, purportedly to hasten financial contributions, and his men, now stationed in Reading and reduced to 800 in number, were, as Salusbury's regimental chaplain warned him, becoming increasingly disenchanted by their colonel's absence.[26] Sir Thomas had perhaps found the brutal realities of war a rude awakening, but he made his escape in an unexpectedly final way, dying in May 1643, possibly from the typhus currently raging in the Royalist forces.[27] His successor, Charles Lloyd, a Montgomeryshire professional soldier, quickly restored the regiment's confidence, and led it for the remainder of the war. Meanwhile, Owen's Regiment, about 600 strong, was with Rupert at Birmingham and Lichfield in April 1643, and in May, perhaps totalling five companies, was in Culham Camp, where it was issued with 112 pikes.[28]

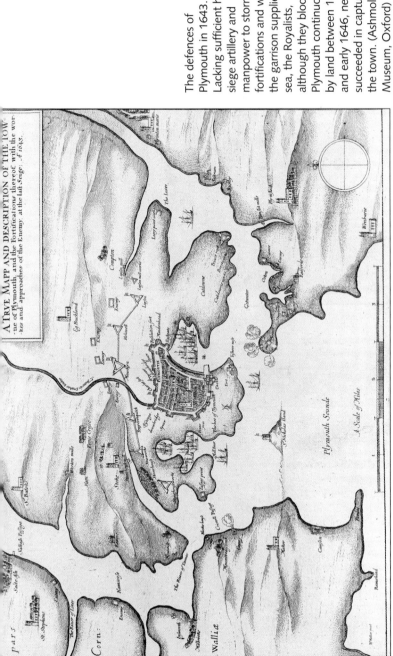

A TRVE MAPP AND DESCRIPTION OF THE TOWNE of Plymouth, and the Fortificatiõns thereof: with the workes and approaches of the Enemy, at the laſt Seige, ɅF 1643.

The defences of Plymouth in 1643. Lacking sufficient heavy siege artillery and manpower to storm the fortifications and with the garrison supplied by sea, the Royalists, although they blockaded Plymouth continuously by land between 1643 and early 1646, never succeeded in capturing the town. (Ashmolean Museum, Oxford)

Sir Richard Grenville (1600–52). Brother to Sir Bevil Grenville, a career soldier, originally returned from Ireland in the service of Parliament, but quickly changed sides, according to his own account from conviction, but also possibly through financial disillusionment with his current employers. A brutal but capable officer, Grenville arguably could have better served the King in a more senior command than he actually received.

Arthur, Lord Capel (1610–49). Lieutenant General in North Wales and its borders, 1643, Capel, as an outsider, proved both unpopular and unsuccessful. Though possessing no great military ability, his operations were frustrated as much by lack of cooperation from the local leadership as his own incompetence.

The VVelsh-Mans Postures,

OR,

The true manner how her doe exercise her
company of Souldiers in her own Countrey in a
warlike manners with some other new-found
experiments, and pretty extravagants fitting
for all Christian podies to caknow.

Vp Morgan.   up Shinkin.   Maurice
Taffie

fig: 10

'rinted in the yeare. When her did her enemy jeere, 1642.

'The Welsh-mans Postures'. This semi-pornographic Parliamentarian
propaganda sheet of 1642 lampooned the Welsh troops in the King's service,
and typified the attitude towards the Welsh of many of the English population.
(British Library)

William Cavendish, First Marquess of Newcastle (1592–1676). The leading Royalist magnate in the North of England, Newcastle was best known before the war for his wealthy lifestyle and his unsuccessful attempts to gain a prominent place at Court. Lacking military experience, he proved an acceptable Lord General in the North, and was a tougher and more capable commander than the dilettante courtier of legend. His suspicions of enemies at Court, though at times overstated, were not without foundation. (Courtesy of the Countess Spencer)

Sir Henry Slingsby (1602–58). A Colonel of Foot under Newcastle, Slingsby later served with the Northern Horse and was executed in 1658 for attempting to suborn the garrison of Hull. His *Diary* is a useful source for the war in the North.

Beeston Castle. This thirteenth-century fortress occupied a key position on the Cheshire Plain. Its capture by Sandford's firelocks in December 1643 was an important coup for the Royalists, who held the castle for the next two years.

James Graham, 1st Marquess of Montrose (1612–50). Montrose's undoubted military ability, which made him perhaps the greatest Royalist commander of the Civil Wars, was unfortunately not matched by the political skills that would have enabled him to exploit and consolidate his victories on the battlefield. (Scottish National Portrait Gallery)

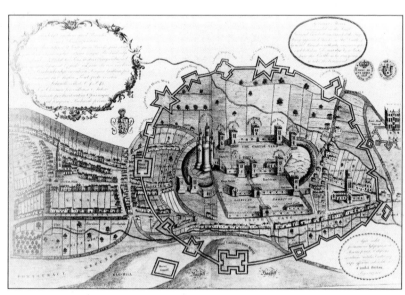

Pontefract. The siege works may relate to the second siege of 1648. The main action between Langdale and Lambert took place in the town fields just off the left of the picture.

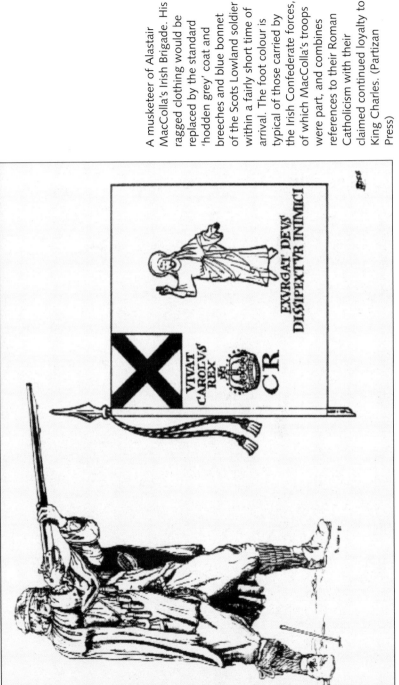

VIVAT CAROLVS REX

CR

EXVRGAT DEVS DISSIPEXTVR INIMICI

A musketeer of Alastair MaccColla's Irish Brigade. His ragged clothing would be replaced by the standard 'hodden grey' coat and breeches and blue bonnet of the Scots Lowland soldier within a fairly short time of arrival. The foot colour is typical of those carried by the Irish Confederate forces, of which MaccColla's troops were part, and combines references to their Roman Catholicism with their claimed continued loyalty to King Charles. (Partizan Press)

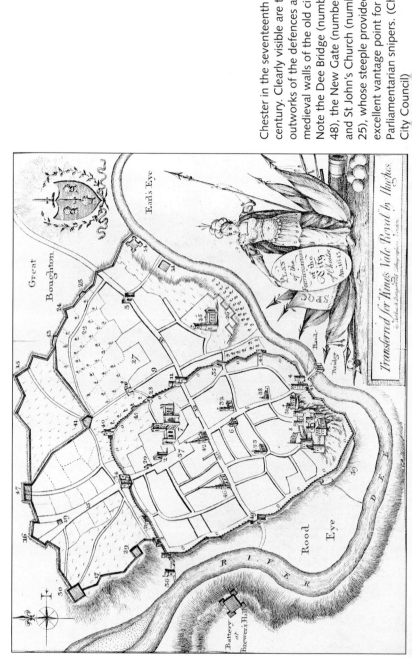

Chester in the seventeenth century. Clearly visible are the outworks of the defences and the medieval walls of the old city. Note the Dee Bridge (number 48), the New Gate (number 35) and St John's Church (number 25), whose steeple provided an excellent vantage point for Parliamentarian snipers. (Chester City Council)

Marmaduke Langdale (1598–1661). A former political opponent of royal policies, Langdale became a distinguished cavalry commander under Newcastle. Possibly the only man who could have held the Northern Horse together, Langdale's strong personality failed to endear him to many of his colleagues in the Oxford Army.

Sir William Brereton (1604–61). Leader of Parliament's Cheshire forces for most of the war, Brereton made the capture of Chester his primary task. An administrator rather than a battlefield commander, Brereton possessed qualities of determination and organisational skills which made him a formidable opponent. (Chester City Council)

John, Lord Byron (d. 1652). Proud, prickly and quarrelsome, Byron saw himself as primarily a soldier and, though unlucky in higher command, proved a resolute and inspirational leader for the Royalists in the prolonged 'leaguer' of Chester. (Ashmolean Museum, Oxford)

The site of the breach made by the Parliamentarian artillery in the bombardment of 22 September is still clearly visible in the present-day 'Roman Garden'.

The moſt Illuſtrious and High borne PRINCE RUPERT, PRINCE ELECTOR, Second Son to FREDERICK KING of BOHEMIA, GENERALL of the HORSE of H:s MAJESTIES ARMY, KNIGHT of the Noble Order of the GARTER.

'Prince Rupert's Burning Love for England. . . .' The sack of Birmingham provided ready propaganda material for Parliamentarian newsletters. (British Library)

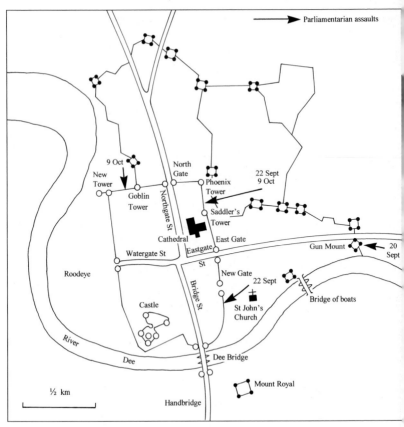

The siege of Chester, 1645–6.

Queen Henrietta Maria (1609–69). (Courtesy of the National Portrait Gallery, London)

As this contemporary cartoon of an English soldier in Ireland demonstrates, it was accepted that troops would steal anything if they had the opportunity.

Jacob, Lord Astley (1579–1652).
A tough practical soldier, not at ease in the intrigues of the Court, Astley was a fine infantry commander who, in the final campaign of the First Civil War, proved himself a capable general as well. (Courtesy of the National Portrait Gallery, London)

Sir Charles Lucas (d. 1648). One of the best of the Royalist cavalry commanders, though his rough manner alienated Clarendon, Lucas fought well at Newbury and Marston Moor before for some reason losing favour with Rupert.

Charles II (1630–85) during his exile in Flanders.

Richard Grace (c. 1620–91). An Irishman who, after serving with the Royalist forces during the First Civil War, led Irish troops in Spanish service and fought in Charles II's army in Flanders. Dying in the defence of Athlone against the Williamite forces in 1691, Grace was perhaps the last Royalist field officer to see active service.

George Monck (1608–71). A professional soldier who defected to Parliament after his capture at Nantwich (1644), and served them in Ireland, in 1659 Monck was Commander-in-Chief of the Parliamentarian forces in Scotland. His intervention played an important role in events leading to the Restoration, after which, as Captain General and Duke of Albermarle, he continued to play a leading part in military and naval affairs.

William Walker (1613?–1736). A Lancashireman, Walker supposedly fought for the King at Edgehill and died aged 123! While this seems highly unlikely, it is possible that Walker may have been involved as a youth in a later Royalist rebellion such as Booth's Rising of 1659. (Ashmolean Museum, Oxford)

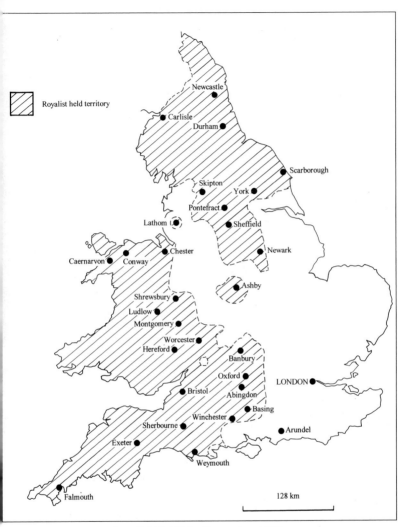

Royalist high tide, December 1643.

THE DESCRIPTION OF THE ARMIES OF
S.ᵉ Tomas Fairefax his Excellency, as they were dr
the Fower

NASBYE

Printed for John Patridge

Battle formation of the Civil War period. The foot are deployed in 'divisions', usually roughly 1,000 strong, with pikes flanked by bodies of musketeers. Note the light artillery pieces deployed in the intervals between divisions. The horse are in bodies of about 500 men. (Northamptonshire Record Office)

FOOT OF HIS MAJESTIES, AND [...]odyes, at the Battayle at NASBYE: June 1645.

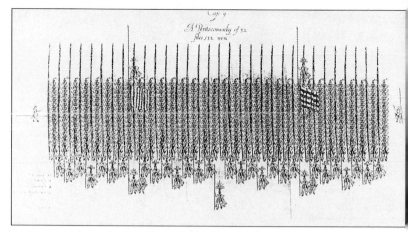

A massed formation of pikes, which might be formed from men of several regiments brigaded together. Note the officers and NCOs stationed on flanks and rear to help maintain formation and deter desertion.

James Stanley, 7th Earl of Derby (1607–51). The leading magnate in Lancashire, Derby's support enabled the King to raise large numbers of recruits there. Derby's own military abilities were limited, leading to the almost total defeat of the Royalist forces in Lancashire by the summer of 1643.

'Harquebusiers' as depicted by Cruso (1632). These figures are fully equipped with back and breast plates, 'pot' helmet, sword, pair of pistols and carbine. Carbines were probably rarely actually fired from horseback.

Prince Rupert (1619–82). (Portrait by Honthurst, *c.* 1642; courtesy of the National Portrait Gallery, London)

Cavalry in action (Cruso). The first ranks of both sides are discharging their pistols, and the body on the right, threatened in front and flank in a recommended cavalry tactic, is breaking even before contact is made.

Buff-coats. Normally made from ox-hide, these varied enormously in quality and price. An officer's version might cost £10, and that of a common trooper, generally made from thin leather, 30s. They were probably not as widely worn as sometimes assumed, as a set of back and breast plates was often less expensive. (Partizan Press)

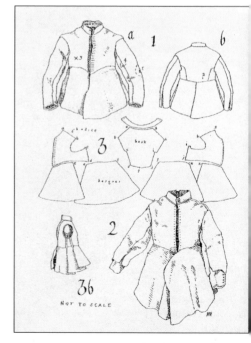

Lord George Goring (1608–57). One of the more enigmatic figures of the Civil Wars, Goring was potentially among the most able of the Royalist generals, but his talents were undermined by ill health, dissipation and self-seeking intrigue. (Bristol City Library)

Sir George Lisle (d. 1648). One of the outstanding infantry commanders of the war, Lisle was executed by Fairfax in controversial circumstances for his part in the Second Civil War. He was, wrote Clarendon, 'kind to all, beloved by all'.

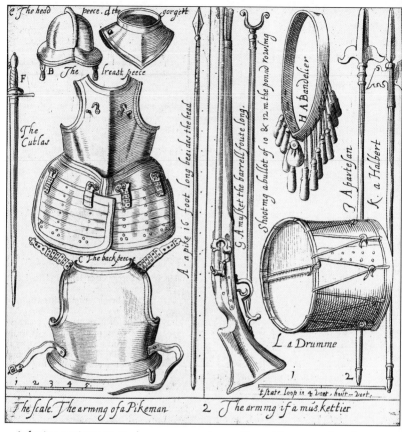

Within the illustration:
e The head peece. d the gorgett
B The breast peece
F
The Cutlas
C The back peece
A a pike 16 foot long besides the head
G A musket the barrell foute long.
Shooting a bullot of 10 & 12 in the pound rowing
H A Bandelier
I A partesan
K a Halbert
L a Drumme
1   2
The scale. The arming of a Pikeman   2 The arming if a muskettier
t state loop is 4 voet, hout voet.
1 2 3 4 5

Infantry equipment. Body armour was in practice seldom worn by pikemen during the Civil War. Halberds, and other pole-type weapons such as the 'brownbill', were useful in close-quarter fighting, and were commonly employed by garrison troops. They were also a badge of rank for NCOs and perhaps some officers.

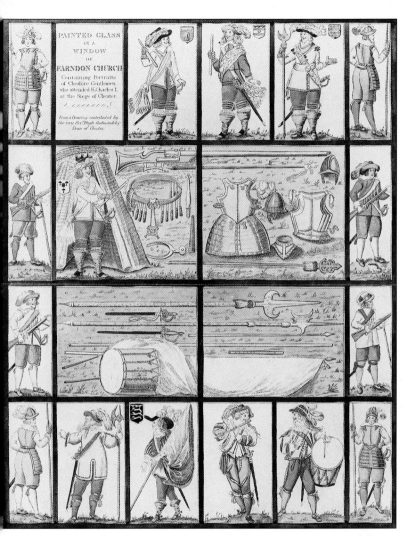

A memorial window in Farndon Church, Cheshire, to Sir Francis Gamull's Regiment of Foot, which played a leading role in the defence of Chester. Erected *c*. 1660, by William Barnston, a captain in the regiment, the window depicts some of the individual officers, with representations of pikemen and musketeers, heavily influenced by near-contemporary Continental illustrations. (Chester City Council)

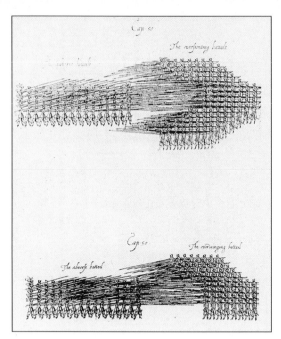

'Push of Pike'. Combat between opposing bodies of pikemen tended to resemble a giant 'scrum', in which injuries were more the result of falling and being trampled than from being caught by the pikes, of which only those carried by the leading ranks could actually reach the enemy. Only if one side lost its formation were serious casualties likely to result.

This contemporary illustration is probably intended to depict dragoons firing from horseback, a rarely adopted tactic.

Siege artillery. The gun at the top is probably a culverin, and the lower piece a demi-culverin, the lightest weapon likely to be effective in siege operations. Note the platforms of planks and wickerwork on which the guns are placed, to minimise the effects of recoil in embedding them in the ground.

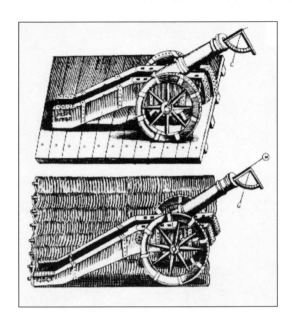

Edward Hyde, 1st Earl of Clarendon (1609–74) was Chancellor of the Exchequer from 1643, and one of the King's closest advisers, though an opponent of the influence of the Queen and Lord Digby. Later, he became one of the Council of the West under the Prince of Wales, and author of the major Royalist account of the war. (Bristol City Libraries)

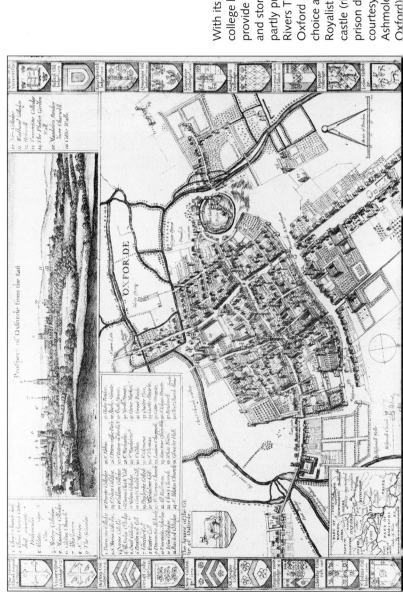

With its large number of college buildings to provide accommodation and storage facilities, and partly protected by the Rivers Thames and Isis, Oxford made an excellent choice as the 'temporary' Royalist capital. Note the castle (right), a notorious prison during the war. (By courtesy of the Ashmolean Museum, Oxford)

Medical instruments in use during the Civil War were in many cases very similar to those employed today. Those illustrated here include equipment used for 'trepanning' the skull in head injuries.

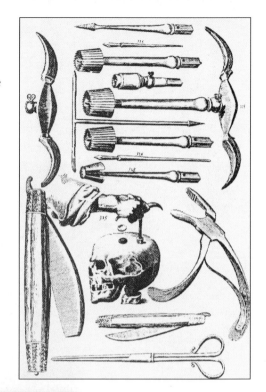

Patrick Ruthven, Earl of Forth and Brentford (1573?–1651). A Scottish professional soldier of great experience, Ruthven proved an extremely able Lord General of the Oxford Army from 1642 to November 1644. Although famous for his capacity for alcohol, it was probably a combination of the effects of wounds, deafness and old age, rather than his fondness for the bottle, which led to Ruthven's eventual retirement. (Bodleian Library, Oxford)

King Charles I and Sir Edward Walker. In this portrait (c. 1644–5), the King is wearing what may have been his usual campaign dress, including an ornamented buff-coat, with the 'close' helmet of a cuirassier close by. Walker, a generally unpopular figure because of his conceit and quarrelsome nature, was Secretary at War from 1642 and of the Privy Council from 1644, and wrote what was in effect the 'official' Royalist history of the 1644–5 campaigns. The drum depicted here may belong to the King's Lifeguard of Foot. (Courtesy of the National Portrait Gallery, London)

Ralph, Lord Hopton (1598–1652). Often held to be the most capable Royalist general after Prince Rupert, this assessment perhaps owes more to Hopton's own portrayal of his actions than to his actual performance, which at times displayed hesitancy and met with mixed fortunes. After his defeat at Cheriton in 1644, Hopton was appointed General of Ordnance in succession to Lord Percy, and only returned to active field command in the closing stages of the war. (The National Trust; print Courtauld Institute of Art)

Sir Bevil Grenville (1596–1643). Though not entirely the benevolent figure of legend, Grenville proved an inspiring leader of the Cornish forces in 1642–3 and, with Sir Nicholas Slanning, played a major part in their success.

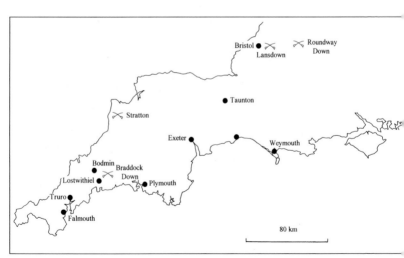

The campaign in the west, 1643.

The Welsh regiments took part in the storm of Bristol on 26 July. John Owen was seriously wounded in the face, and rendered unfit for service for most of the remainder of the year, but his regiment, along with Lloyd's and Stradling's, was in the thick of the action at the First Battle of Newbury in September. Here, Owen lost Captain William Byrnkir, killed, and fourteen men, 'hurt, unable to march'.[29] Captain John Gwynne, that colourful memorialist of the wars, had a narrow escape while acting as an ensign in Lloyd's Regiment. His men were thrown back into a neighbouring field by a counter-attack of Parliamentarian horse: 'There were several gaps to get to it, but not direct in my way; yet, with the colours in my hand, I jumped over hedge and ditch, or I had died by a multitude of hands.'[30]

GROWING DEMANDS

By the end of 1643 most Royalist foot were raised by impressment, and the usual assumption is that a large proportion of conscripts reaching the Oxford Army were Welsh. Peter Newman has suggested that although no complete new Welsh regiments joined the Oxford Army, a significant number of Welsh companies, under Welsh officers, were added. But analysis of the 'Indigent Officers' listings provides no clear support for this.[31]

This can partly be explained by reverses suffered by the Royalists in Wales itself. In the south, the militia-based forces of the King's Lieutenant General, the Earl of Carbery, rapidly lost ground to Parliamentarian troops based in Pembrokeshire. Further north, William Wynne was killed and his regiment destroyed in Capel's unsuccessful assault on Wem in October 1643, and this was followed by a full-scale invasion of north-east Wales by Brereton and Parliament's nominated commander for North Wales, Sir Thomas Myddleton. The raw and unenthusiastic local defence forces collapsed, including trained band units and Robert Ellice's recently re-formed regiment, and only the intervention of the first contingent of troops from Ireland stabilised the situation.[32]

The appointment, in January, of Prince Rupert as Captain General of Wales and the Border and later as President of Wales led to a full-scale reorganisation of the Royalist administration of the area. In particular, a number of (mainly) English professional soldiers were placed in key positions. Although the Prince attempted to ensure that increased demands for finance and manpower that he made on North Wales in particular were administered fairly,[33] friction increased between his men and the Commissioners of Array. Rupert's officers were exasperated by what they saw as the endless feuding of the Welsh and by their apparent unwillingness to cooperate. Lord Byron, based at Chester, seems to have been on poor terms with most of the Welsh, apart from John Owen, whom he respected as a fellow soldier, while Sir John Mennes, appointed to command in north-west Wales, was a hard-drinking former sailor, who upset the local gentry, ever-vigilant for a grievance, by his demands and his lifestyle.[34]

In South Wales, Charles Gerrard, a capable but ruthless soldier, and protégé of Rupert, was tasked with regaining the ground lost by Carbery. Arriving in March 1644, he brought with him his own regiments plus Stradling's to act as the core of a new army of over 2,000 men that was raised in South Wales by conscription. His demands for men and his scorched earth policy, while militarily effective in the short term, cost Gerrard dearly in popularity and eventually support.[35]

As early as the spring of 1644 there were ominous portents in Wales for the King. Much rested upon the outcome of the coming season's campaigning. Large numbers of men were conscripted in Wales, but few reached the Oxford Army, used instead either to form Gerrard's new army or to fill out the ranks of Rupert's own depleted units in preparation for his operations in Lancashire and the relief of York.[36] Ellice's re-recruited regiment took part in the Lancashire campaign, and there must have been a high proportion of Welshmen among the rank and file of the Royalist foot at Marston Moor.

Rupert's crushing defeat cost the Royalists the war in the North. It also struck a savage blow at Welsh morale. The Prince soon discovered just how badly support had eroded when, back at Chester, he launched a new impressment drive to rebuild his shattered army. Levies were slow in appearing but much more rapid in deserting, and after a few weeks Rupert apparently despaired of the situation and headed south to Bristol.[37]

MONTGOMERY: THE 'MARSTON MOOR' OF WALES

In Mid- and North Wales, the Royalist position had already been weakened on 23 June when Parliamentarian troops captured Oswestry, aptly likened by Myddleton to 'the key which opens the door to Wales'.[38] Its loss threatened communications between the key garrisons of Chester and Shrewsbury, and cleared the way for a Parliamentarian thrust into Central Wales, aimed at severing communications between North Wales and Royalist England, and perhaps cutting the Principality itself in two. Setting out to seize 'some place of advantage', on 4 September Sir Thomas Myddleton and his small army appeared before Montgomery Castle, strategically situated in the valley of the Severn. Lord Herbert, its eccentric and scholarly owner, promptly surrendered, either because he recognised his situation as untenable or on the promise that his library would be left undisturbed. The Royalists reacted swiftly. On 7 September a hastily mustered force under Sir Michael Earnley laid siege to Montgomery. They were reinforced by Lord Byron, with a contingent from Chester including Robert Ellice's Welsh regiment, raising total Royalist strength to about 2,500 foot and 1,500 horse.

In the meantime, Myddleton, who had remained outside Montgomery with most of his cavalry, had been reinforced by Brereton's experienced Cheshire foot and a contingent of horse from Lancashire and Yorkshire under the highly competent Scottish professional Sir John Meldrum, who assumed overall command of the combined army of perhaps 3,000 men. He came within sight of the castle late on 17 September, and deployed in open fields some 2 miles north-east of Montgomery, with the little River Camladd and its bridge to his rear. The Parliamentarians decided to collect supplies for the Montgomery garrison before attempting to relieve them, and early on 18 September Meldrum despatched about a third of his horse on a foraging expedition. For Byron, who had taken up a strong defensive position just west of Montgomery, the opportunity seemed too good to miss, and he ordered a general attack, with the object of seizing the Salt Bridge over the Camladd, so cutting off Meldrum's escape.

At first the tide of battle flowed Byron's way; the Parliamentarians admitted, 'It came to push of pike, wherein they [the Royalists] were much too hard for us, having many more pikes.'[39] The Parliamentarians were pushed back for several hundred yards, but then the Cheshire foot rallied under Major General Lothian. The Royalists were probably short of both muskets and ammunition, and the Parliamentarian foot, predominantly musketeers, checked them with concentrated 'salvee' fire. The Royalist cavalry apparently recoiled without putting up much of a fight, and the rot quickly spread to the infantry. Possibly discouraged by the unexpected enemy rally, and unable to reply to their heavy fire, Byron's men broke. The pursuit continued for several miles, the Royalist infantry suffering heavy casualties. Perhaps 500 were killed, and another 1,500 taken prisoner. Robert Ellice's Regiment was once more destroyed, this time finally.

Archbishop Williams assessed the defeat as, in Welsh terms, worse than Marston Moor,[40] while Meldrum hoped that 'North Wales (which formerly hath been the nursery for the King's armies) in all likelihood will shake off that yoke of servitude which formerly did lie upon their necks and will be reduced to the obedience of the King and Parliament. . . .'[41]

'WARPING TO THE ENEMY': THE FALL OF ROYALIST WALES

Though Meldrum's hopes were not initially realised, Montgomery represented a turning point. During the winter and spring of 1644/5 war-weariness and disaffection in Wales increased steadily. The dwindling strength of the Oxford Army foot in particular made it essential both to strip garrisons of every man who could (or even could not) be spared, and also to squeeze every available conscript out of Wales.

In the spring of 1645 Princes Rupert and Maurice managed temporarily to relieve pressure on Chester, though at the cost of losing Shrewsbury, but they also drew off most of the remaining veteran soldiers in Chester garrison, leaving Byron to complain bitterly that he had been left with Roger Mostyn's inexperienced Welsh regiment, who he had had to send out of town, 'finding them by reason of their officers, who were ignorant Welsh gentlemen, and unwillinge to undergoe any strict dutie, far more predjudiciall to us than usefull'.[42] This was partly an attempt to have the seasoned troops he had lost restored, but it also reflected the growing tensions between the King's mainly English military commanders and the Welsh community. By the spring of 1645, there was a stream of petitions and complaints from the Welsh Commissioners of Array concerning the demands placed upon them. Their resources in manpower, money and supplies were exhausted, and war-weariness was turning rapidly into outright hostility. The appointment of the now knighted John Owen of Clennau as Major General in North Wales quickly led to confrontation between him and Archbishop Williams, whose concern for the well-being of the Welsh and the wrecking of their economy met with little sympathy from Sir John.

Nevertheless, Wales provided one last major trawl of conscripts for the Oxford Army. At least 1,000 levies were raised in North Wales in the spring of 1645 and despatched to Rupert in Herefordshire, where they were incorporated into existing regiments.[43] At Naseby perhaps as much as one-third of the Oxford Army foot were Welsh.[44] Virtually all of them were captured and marched off to London, where the bewildered prisoners, many of whom had never left Wales before, were preached to in Welsh.[45]

Even now, the King had not finished with Wales. Taking up quarters, first at Hereford then in the Herbert stronghold of Raglan, the King and his Council issued a stream of orders for new Welsh levies to replace those lost at Naseby. At least 6,000 men were hoped for,[46] and Secretary of State Digby assured a correspondent on 10 July that 'we shall have an army fit to fight for a kingdom'.[47]

But it was not to be. Even before Naseby, Rupert had warned, 'I fear all Wales will be in rebellion', while one of his officers wrote despairingly of his difficulties in Monmouthshire: 'If your Highness shall be pleased to command me to the Turk, or Jew, or Gentile, I will go on my bare feet to serve you; but from the Welsh, good Lord deliver me.'[48] Two understrength regiments from South Wales, led by English professional soldiers, were despatched to join Goring in the West, while a few Welsh soldiers joined the defenders of Bristol.[49] But Goring's defeat at Langport on 10 July and the surrender of Bristol by Rupert doomed the

King's hopes of assistance from Wales. His Glamorganshire levies, under the leadership of the local gentry, formed themselves into the 'Peaceable Army', whose initial demands for the dismissal of the unpopular Charles Gerrard rapidly turned into active anti-Royalism.[50] The King's hold on Wales disintegrated almost without a fight. By early 1646, only the great Edwardian fortresses of North Wales, under diehard Royalists such as Byron at Caernarvon, the eccentric William Salusbury – 'Old Bluestockings' – at Denbigh, Sir John Owen at Conway, and a dwindling band of garrisons elsewhere, such as Raglan, would continue to bid defiance to Parliament.

One by one, with no hope of relief and assistance from Ireland proving a mirage, these last captains of King Charles yielded to the inevitable and accepted the usually generous terms that were offered. Last of all was Harlech, on the western coast of Merionethshire, where Colonel William Owen and the twenty-eight men of his garrison still fit to fight, the only Cavaliers remaining in arms in England and Wales, surrendered on 16 March 1647. The First Civil War in Wales was over.

CONCLUSION

Welsh support was of vital assistance to the Royalist war effort. As well as supplies and money, Welsh manpower had been an important part of the Oxford Army in 1642, and still more so three years later. Without recruits from North Wales, it is unlikely that Prince Rupert could have made his 'Yorke March' of 1644. Yet Hutton's verdict that the King did not fully realise the potential of Wales still stands. Division, internal threats, poverty, lack of sensitive handling and an underlying view by a significant minority that, as one Welsh writer put it, 'Heigh god, heigh devil, I will be for the strongest side',[51] meant that Byron's words quoted at the head of this chapter, though exaggerated, contain a grain of truth.

TWELVE

'THE POPISH ARMY': THE ROYALISTS IN THE NORTH, 1642–4

'as good men as were in the world.'
Sir Hugh Cholmley, 'Memorials Touching the Battle of York',
in *English Historical Review*, V, 1890, p. 352

ORIGINS

Though it was the largest and most important after the Oxford Army, the Northern Army is the least known of the King's major forces in the First Civil War. Despite the lack of surviving administrative records, this 'forgotten army' deserves closer study.[1]

In 1642 the North of England seemed remote from the scene of action. Nevertheless, it was of considerable importance. The city of York was regarded as England's second capital, and Yorkshire was one of its most populous counties. The port of Hull, with its arsenal, was a key strategic location. In Northumberland, Newcastle upon Tyne was important for overseas trade and for shipments of coal to London and the South. The West Riding of Yorkshire, with its textile towns, had growing economic value. On the outbreak of war, the North, with the exception of Hull, the West Riding, eastern Lancashire and Scarborough, was predominantly under the control of the King's supporters.

In February 1642 Queen Henrietta Maria had been sent to Holland to purchase munitions and recruit professional soldiers. After Charles' failure in July to secure Hull, the ports of the North-east were their only practicable landing point. The task of securing them was given to the leading Royalist magnate of the region, William Cavendish, First Earl of Newcastle. Aged fifty on the outbreak of war, Newcastle was later among the most vilified of Royalist commanders. The verdict of Sir Phillip Warwick, who served for a time on Newcastle's staff, is typical: 'His edge had too much of the razor in it, for he had the tincture of a romantic spirit, and had the misfortune to have something of the poet in him.'[2] Modern research, however, has modified this view.

Newcastle's considerable wealth and influence in the North had been placed at the King's disposal during the Scots Wars, and on 29 June 1642 he was appointed Governor of the town of Newcastle upon Tyne and General of Northumberland, Durham, Cumberland and Westmorland. His task was to consolidate control and establish a secure landing place for the Queen and her supplies. There seems to have been no plan for him to intervene further south. Newcastle carried out his initial assignment with considerable success. He found recruitment slow but was able to raise a troop of horse, and a regiment of foot drawn from his own tenants. Most importantly, the town of Newcastle was secured. The trained bands of Durham, who displayed reluctance to serve further afield, were brought into line by Newcastle's personal intervention with troops from Northumberland.

Although some arms arrived from Denmark, Newcastle had difficulty in equipping all of his recruits. In her laudatory life of her husband, the Duchess of Newcastle claimed that he raised in the four northern counties a total of 8,000 men, but the true figure was probably about 3,000 foot and 2,000 horse and dragoons, some of whom were absorbed by garrison duties.[3] Newcastle took the politically sensitive step of recruiting Roman Catholics, numerically strong in the region. The King was quick to make virtue of necessity, but the issue provided ready propaganda for the Parliamentarians, who emphasised the threat posed by Newcastle's 'Popish Army', despite the Earl publishing a *Declaration* justifying his actions on the dubious grounds that Parliament had recruited foreign Catholic mercenaries first![4]

Late in July 1642 the King greatly extended Newcastle's powers. In what was effectively a viceroyship, the Earl was commissioned General of all Royalist forces raised now or in the future in England north of the Trent, together with the counties of Lincolnshire, Nottinghamshire, Derbyshire, Lancashire, Cheshire, Leicestershire and Rutland. Eventually, Parliament's Eastern Association would be added. He was given far more independence than any other Royalist commander, with powers to grant commissions and confer knighthoods. Though this delegation was sound in principle, it soon became clear that the extent of Newcastle's command was too great, given his remoteness from Oxford. Newcastle seems tacitly to have accepted this; the Earl of Derby in Lancashire and Lord Loughborough in the Midlands were left largely to their own devices.

The first crisis to confront Newcastle came in Yorkshire, where the local Royalists were losing ground to the Parliamentarians. Their request for assistance was greeted unenthusiastically by the Earl, who laid down certain conditions. His troops were to be regularly paid and quartered, and Newcastle made clear that his overriding objectives remained unchanged: 'That since this army was levied a purpose to guard her Majesty's person, it shall not be held a breach of any engagement betwixt us if I retire with such numbers as I shall think for that service.'[5] Reluctance by the Yorkshire Royalists to pay Newcastle's officers brought an angry retort from the Earl that 'rather than come cheerfully to serve you, I will not come at all, for I see beforehand I shall either disband in a mutiny, or fall of plundering without distinction, either of which would be destructive to me'.[6] In fact, Newcastle had little option. The loss of Yorkshire would sever links with the Royalist South, and put all his operations in jeopardy. Nevertheless, his failure to obtain undisputed control of the Yorkshire forces had serious repercussions.

THE FIRST CAMPAIGN

Newcastle's intervention quickly stabilised the situation in Yorkshire. In mid-December 1642 the King informed him, 'The business of Yorkshire I account almost done', while the

Parliamentarian commander Lord Fairfax admitted that Newcastle was 'absolute master of the field'.[7] But Newcastle failed to capitalise on this apparent opportunity. He was still short of munitions, though he attempted to collect what remained in the magazines of the trained bands, and required time to organise his expanded forces.

Newcastle also remodelled his command structure, appointing as his Lieutenant General (or Chief of Staff) the most controversial figure of the war in the North. A Scottish professional, James King had served with the Swedes, though views on his abilities differed. Clarendon wrote of his 'extraordinary success' there, but Sir James Turner, a fellow Scots professional, commented that King was 'a person of great honour, but what he had saved of it in Germanie, where he made a great ship wrack of much of it, he lost in England'.[8] King's greatest claim to fame was his undistinguished role at Lemgo in 1638, when Prince Rupert had been captured by the Imperialists. As Newcastle's principal military adviser he seems to have been generally competent, if cautious.

Also despatched by the Queen were a number of other officers, including as General of Horse the erratically brilliant George Goring. The senior commanders of the Northern Army have been the subject of some critical comment, not least by one French historian, who wrote that: 'we find the army of the North therefore under a commander-in-chief who was utterly inexperienced, a drunkard for General of cavalry, a poet for General of artillery, and a very able divine for Scoutmaster-General'. This is an exaggeration. Newcastle's eighteen-year-old son was nominally General of Artillery, but the department was run by his Lieutenant General, Sir William Davenant, the dramatist and poet. There is nothing to suggest that Davenant, who had been Paymaster of the Ordnance in 1639, was unsuitable for the post. The Scoutmaster General, the Reverend Michael Hudson, certainly appears to have been competent.

While some criticisms of Newcastle's senior commanders may be overstated, his strategy during the winter of 1642/3 is more questionable. Even allowing for his various difficulties, Newcastle's passivity allowed the Fairfaxes to regain the initiative in the West Riding. Newcastle's main preoccupation remained the Queen and her foreign supplies, and the first stage of this mission was achieved on 4 March, when Newcastle and the bulk of his army escorted Henrietta Maria and her convoy into York. Though Newcastle obtained from this vast shipment munitions including the two Dutch-made demi-cannon 'Gog' and 'Magog' – otherwise known as the 'Queen's Pocket-Pistols' – the bulk of the convoy of 10,000 small arms, 32 guns and 78 barrels of black powder[9] was intended for the Oxford Army, and Newcastle had to supply an escort for them. Later complaints by the Duchess that this seriously weakened Newcastle's army are an exaggeration. The first detachment of 1,500 troops sent south with Lord Percy's convoy in April consisted of 'commanded men' from a number of units, so that Newcastle's regimental structure remained intact.[10] In June the Queen took another 3,000 to 4,000 men south with her, but many of these were either from Lord Derby's defeated forces in Lancashire or newly raised units, so that once again Newcastle's own field army was little weakened.

More inhibiting to Newcastle's operations had been the need to protect the Queen and her supplies for as long as they remained in York, although he was also preoccupied with covert, and ultimately fruitless, negotiations for the surrender of Hull. However, this did not prevent a number of Royalist successes, notably Goring's defeat of Fairfax at Seacroft Moor on 30 March, and incursions into Lincolnshire by Lieutenant General Charles Cavendish, which caused sufficient alarm in the Eastern Association to divert half of the 12,000 men who had been intended to reinforce the Earl of Essex's army in the South.[11] Newcastle himself secured Rotherham and Sheffield in South Yorkshire, the latter's ironworks providing the Northern Royalists with the basis of a small munitions industry.

These successes were counterbalanced by Sir Thomas Fairfax's surprise of Wakefield on 21 May, which temporarily cost Newcastle the services of the captured George Goring and nearly 3,000 men. But this reverse, while undoubtedly the 'very great loss and hindrance' claimed by the Duchess, was less serious than sometimes suggested. Freed for more active operations by the Queen's departure on 4 June, Newcastle was able to take the field with an army of about 3,000 foot and 4,000 horse, ready to strike a decisive blow in the struggle for the West Riding.

ADWALTON MOOR

The next few weeks witnessed the high tide of Northern Royalist success. On 22 June Newcastle moved in strength into the West Riding. A week later (30 June) Newcastle encountered the army of Lord Fairfax at Adwalton Moor, just outside Bradford. The action which followed, between armies numerically roughly equal, was not notable for tactical finesse. The enclosed nature of the terrain made it difficult for the Royalists to utilise their superior horse, while the Parliamentarians had considerably more musketeers. Successive Royalist cavalry attacks were beaten back, and for a time it seemed that a general Parliamentarian advance might carry the day. But a determined counter-attack by Newcastle's pikes, headed by Colonel Postumous Kirton, 'a wild and desperate man', swung the battle back in Newcastle's favour, and Fairfax's army, which included many untrained 'clubmen', collapsed in rout.[12] Bradford and Leeds both fell, and by the end of June Fairfax had been driven back into Hull.

Newcastle had fulfilled all of the objectives set him in the previous summer. The North-east was secure, the Queen and her vital convoys despatched safely to Oxford, and the local Parliamentarian forces for the moment crushed. Only on the periphery of Newcastle's 'empire', in Lancashire, had Derby's ramshackle forces been defeated, and this seemed a minor blemish on the fair face of Royalist success. Yet Newcastle's victory at Adwalton Moor carried within it the seeds of defeat. The prospect of the dreaded 'Popish Army' plunging deep into Parliament's heartlands hastened Westminster's alliance with the Scots. Unless he acted quickly, Newcastle would face the prospect of war on two fronts.

THE NORTHERN ARMY REVIEWED

Although Newcastle was accused of preferring the appearance and pomp of generalship to its unpleasant realities, on the whole he used his powers with moderation and discretion.[13] He usually had the sense to defer to his professional advisers. He conferred only twelve knighthoods, mainly for bravery in the field.

Complaints made by Sir Phillip Warwick[14] that he followed the common Royalist weakness of granting too many commissions have more substance. Lacking muster rolls, regimental estimates tend to be based on strength at Marston Moor, when the average foot regiment may have been only 200 or 300 strong, and the horse units even weaker.[15] But this was after a harsh and gruelling campaign, and is not an accurate guide to the situation earlier in the war. Like the King, Newcastle was handicapped by political considerations when granting commissions, though the Duchess's claims that he tried only to grant them to those with sufficient resources to maintain their units are dubious.[16] Yorkshire provided about half of the total strength of the Northern Army.[17] This reliance on forces that Newcastle only commanded on a conditional basis was a severe limitation upon his operations.

Newcastle understood the value of adequately paid and fed soldiers, and the Duchess, with less than total accuracy, maintained that as a result looting and disorder were rare. It should have been easier for Newcastle than other commanders to achieve this, for, as Dr Newman points out,[18] for at least the first year of its existence the Northern Army had a fairly easy war. It possessed a secure base area, and even in Yorkshire the Parliamentarians were operating on the strategic defensive.

It is unclear how well armed Newcastle's men eventually were. In the winter of 1642/3 and early 1644, when they were being rapidly expanded, the Northern Royalists claimed difficulties in arming all their foot, though Newcastle's complaints were generally discounted. By the middle of 1643 the situation had eased considerably. Newcastle had three main sources of arms: existing stores in trained band and private hands (plus captured weapons), imports from abroad, and locally manufactured materials. A considerable quantity of arms came from existing stores, but not as much as some felt was potentially available. The bulk of foreign imports was destined for the Oxford Army, but a significant proportion was utilised by Newcastle. For example, in December 1642 the Dutch merchant Johann Van Haesdonck, later to be a major Royalist arms supplier, contracted to land at Tynemouth 3,000 muskets, 2,000 pairs of pistols, 3,000 sword blades, 1,000 firelocks, 20 tons of match and 1,000 grenades.[19] Much was retained for the Northern Army.

Nor did arms imports cease after the Queen's departure. No complete records survive of the size of the imports, which mainly came via Newcastle, Tynemouth and Scarborough, but some shipments were quite large. In November 1643 a consignment landed at Scarborough included 1,390 matchlocks and bandoliers, 884 pairs of pistols, 100 carbines, 100 pair of holsters, 100 barrels of powder and 50 bundles of match.[20] However, this was probably one of the last to arrive because of the tightening Parliamentarian naval blockade of the east coast ports. There is similarly no detailed tally of locally manufactured material. But munitions were produced in the Sheffield area, and powder mills were probably established in other locations. Newcastle, despite some shortages, was usually able to arm and equip his forces adequately until July 1644.

Newcastle also managed to clothe most of his men. There was plenty of undyed woollen cloth available for coats (hence the famous 'Whitecoats' – a description that seems to have included several regiments, probably differentiated by ribbons or embroidered badges). Other coat colours, such as the red of Sir William Saville's Yorkshire Regiment, are also evidenced. Many of the Northern foot, and quite possibly the horse, were supplied with Scots blue bonnets.[21]

The Northern troops had a justifiably high reputation. Newcastle's foot proved themselves comparable to any opponent, and the Northern Horse, though perhaps not as well turned out as some of their opponents, were formidable adversaries.

THE HULL PHASE

After Adwalton Moor no effective opposition remained in Yorkshire outside Hull, and most historians have asserted that the Eastern Association lay open for the 'Popish Army'. But Newcastle displayed no apparent haste, and his eventual move into Lincolnshire, taking Gainsborough and Lincoln, came as a reaction to Cavendish's defeat. A continued advance seemed feasible, but Newcastle cited as a reason for delay opposition from the Yorkshire Royalists who were unprepared to march further south so long as Hull remained in enemy hands.[22] So at the end of August the Northern Army, reportedly 15,000 to 16,000 strong, turned back and laid siege to the town.

Newcastle has been generally condemned for this decision, often cited as one of the turning points of the Civil War, but it is unclear what pressure the Earl came under from the Royalist high command to continue his advance. Sir Phillip Warwick suggests that this was the King's wish, but no formal order survives. The nearest is in a letter from Henrietta Maria to the Earl in which she says: 'He [the King] had written me to send you word to go into Suffolk, Norfolk or Huntingdonshire. I answered him that you were a better judge than he of that, and that I should not do it. The truth is that they envy your army.'[23] This is significant because it not only shows the King's convoluted approach, but it also highlights an increasingly important influence on Newcastle's thinking.

The Earl resented what he felt to be lack of appreciation at Court of his problems. An example was the jibe that he lay in bed until 11, combed his hair until 12 and so the work was done[24] – significant less for its content than because the alleged source was the wife of Colonel John Russell, a leading supporter of Prince Rupert. Though he never appears to have said so openly, Newcastle probably believed the Rupert faction to be his main enemies at Court.

Criticism of Newcastle's generalship was widespread; Clarendon once described him as 'a lamentable man, and as fit to be a general as a bishop'.[25] Sir Phillip Warwick gives his own explanation for Newcastle's apparent procrastination during the summer of 1643: 'There was nothing he apprehended more than to be joined to the King's army, and to serve under Prince Rupert; for he designed himself to be the man who should turn the scale, and to be a distinct and self-subsisting army, wherever he was.'[26] Though Newcastle was greatly concerned with his own prestige and position, there is nothing in his record to suggest that he would have disobeyed a direct order from the King, had one been given, and the fact that in October he was created a Marquess does not suggest any shadow of royal displeasure at this time.

The reality was that Hull in enemy hands represented a threat to his rear and lines of communication in the event of a march south, which Newcastle could not ignore. The concerns of his Yorkshire supporters were well founded, and without them Newcastle was not strong enough to invade the Eastern Association. His problem, as he had probably known all along, was that the capture of Hull was almost certainly beyond his powers. On 3 September 1643 the Northern Army dutifully sat down before Hull, which was never seriously threatened by an enemy who lacked sufficient artillery to breach its defences, men to storm them, or ships to cut off its supplies by sea. Royalist efforts were further frustrated by heavy rain flooding their siegeworks, leading to one of Newcastle's few recorded jokes: 'You hear us called the Popish Army, but you see we trust not in our good works.'[27] It may have been an attempt to put a brave face on failure, for a major Parliamentarian sortie and the defeat on 11 October at Winceby of the Royalist forces in Lincolnshire spelt the final end of any hope of taking Hull.

THE COMING OF THE SCOTS

The failure not only cost Newcastle a considerable amount of equipment and an unknown number of men, it also rendered impossible direct assistance to the King. Even if Hull had fallen in October, the looming threat of Scottish invasion would probably have prevented Newcastle from launching a major attack on the Eastern Association. Newcastle had not dismissed the threat presented by the Scots. His problem was that he lacked the resources to fight a war on several fronts. Meeting the Scots in the far north would leave the remainder of his vast command frighteningly vulnerable.

The Scots crossed the Border on 19 January 1644, and the Marquess beat them to Newcastle with a few hours to spare. He had left a dangerously small army of 5,000 foot and 1,000 horse under Lord Bellasyse to defend Yorkshire, but still lacked the strength to defeat the Scots. On 28 January Newcastle warned Prince Rupert: 'I know they tell you sir, that I have great force, truely I cannot march five thousand foot, and the horse not well armed. . . . Since I must have no help, I shall do the best I can with this.'[28]

Newcastle's plan was to hold the line of the Tyne while relying on abysmal winter weather and raids by his qualitatively superior cavalry to wear the Scots down to the point at which he could bring them to battle with reasonable prospects of success. Newcastle was aware that he was engaged in a race against time to defeat the Scottish invasion before the vulnerable Royalist hold on Yorkshire collapsed. On 16 February he told the King, 'If your Majesty beat the Scots, your game is absolutely won . . .' but warned of 'a great army at Newark behind us, and a great Scotch army before us, and Sir Thomas Fairfax very strong for the West Riding of Yorkshire . . . , and his father master of the East Riding, so we are beset, not able to encounter the Scots, and shall not be able to make our retreat for the army behind us . . .'.[29]

Though Newcastle received a few reinforcements, his first attempt to bring the Scots to battle, at Bolden Hill on 7–8 March, ended in frustration when their canny commander, the Earl of Leven, declined to be tempted out of his carefully chosen defensive positions. Stalemated, Newcastle fell back on Durham, doubtless infuriated by the King's bland assurance, 'I profess the Scots rebelles to be in much worse case than your armie.'[30] A week later Newcastle was warning Rupert that: 'the Scots are as big again in foot as I am, and their horse, I doubt not, much better than ours are, so that if your Highness do not please to come hither, and that very soon too, the great game of your uncle's will be endangered if not lost'.[31]

Time was running out, but on 23 March a second encounter, at Hilton near Sunderland, failed to bring on the hoped-for decisive action with the Scots. Newcastle was plainly beginning to despair, and both he and General King, now ennobled as Lord Eythin, apparently offered their resignations. Charles implored them to reconsider, pleading, 'The truth is, if either you or my Lord Eythin leave my service, I am sure all the North is lost.' He went on, in apparent confirmation of Newcastle's fears, 'The Scots are not the only, or (it may be said) the least enemies you contend with at this tyme', and then urged him to remember that 'All courage is not in fighting; constancy to a good cause beeinge the chiefe, and the dispysing of slandrous tongues and pennes being not the least ingredient.'[32]

On 12 April came shattering, if not unexpected, news from

Yorkshire. Belasyse's small army had been smashed at Selby and, with York in peril, Newcastle had no option but to abandon the struggle in Durham and make another forced march to protect the northern capital. Once again he arrived in the nick of time, but had lost heavily en route and was soon besieged by the combined armies of Fairfax, the Eastern Association and the Scots.

THE ROAD TO MARSTON MOOR

Rupert relieved York on the evening of 1 July, and the events of the next few hours have excited more controversy than almost any other episode of the war. It is clear that Rupert allowed his impatience with the touchy and courtly Marquess to show by sending him peremptory orders to bring up the Northern Army as soon as possible, in order to give battle to the allies. Newcastle was deeply affronted by this slight, which seemed to confirm his worst suspicions, and the flames were fanned by Eythin, who had long-standing cause to dislike Rupert. Newcastle had other reasons to question the wisdom of Rupert's plans. He urged that battle be postponed. The allies, he said, were riven by dispute, and might separate of their own accord. He expected at least 2,000 reinforcements from the North. He also knew, though probably did not voice the thought, that his troops were effectively the last of the Northern Army, and his own command would die with them.

There was considerable delay before the Northern foot appeared on Marston Moor late in the afternoon of 2 July – a loss of time that disrupted Rupert's plans to attack an unprepared enemy. How far this late appearance was the result of confusion, a mutiny over pay, and whether the discontent was fomented by Eythin, with or without Newcastle's knowledge (perhaps in a last attempt to avoid the battle to which they were opposed), is now impossible to know. But it earned for the Marquess and his Lieutenant General the unenviable reputation of being the men who lost the North (and perhaps the war) for King Charles in the course of an afternoon. The final and oft-discussed acrimonious exchange on the field between Rupert and Eythin over the army's dispositions was, in fact, irrelevant; as

Eythin said, it was now too late to alter the Royalist deployment
– a situation that was largely his doing.

The story of the battle is well known but, in the gathering
darkness of that July evening, as the King's armies in the
North went down to defeat, Newcastle's whitecoated infantry
staged a grim fight that ranks among the classic last stands of
military history.

A body of up to 3,000 of the Whitecoats, the bulk of
Newcastle's foot, possibly commanded by Colonel Sir William
Lambton, were attempting to make an ordered withdrawal on
York, and cover the retreat of fugitives, when they were trapped
by Cromwell's advancing horse with their backs to a thick
hedgerow near the present-day Whitesyke Close. Reportedly
scorning an offer of quarter, the Whitecoats opened fire on the
enemy cavalry, 'peppering them soundly with their shot'. The
first charge of enemy horse was stoutly met, the musketeers
sheltering with clubbed weapons under the protection of their
pikes, and the Royalists 'stoutly bore up with their pikes, that
they could not enter to break them. Here the parliament horse
received their greatest loss, and a stop for some time to their
hoped-for victory, and that only by the stout resistance of this
gallant battalion.'[33]

Though the Royalists held out for up to an hour, there could
be only one end to their fight. As the musketeers ran short of
ammunition, Cromwell pushed forward some Scottish dragoons
to open gaps in the enemy ranks with their fire. These were
exploited by the horse, who broke up the Whitecoats into
isolated knots of struggling men. Yet 'they would have no
quarter, but fought it out until there was not thirty of them
living; those whose hap it was to be beaten to the ground as the
troopers came near them, though they could not rise for their
wounds, yet were so desperate as to get either a pike or a sword,
or piece of them, and to gore the troopers' horses as they came
over them. . . .'[34]

The Whitecoats, apart from a few who were 'saved against
their wills', seem to have refused quarter and gone down
fighting. They were, wrote the Royalist Sir Hugh Cholmley, in an
epitaph that might stand for Newcastle's Northern Army as a
whole, 'as good men as were in the world'.[35]

Newcastle declined Rupert's urgings to continue the fight and, with Eythin, opted for exile on the Continent – 'I will not endure the laughter of the Court' was his bitter and characteristic comment. This was perhaps not the impulsive decision sometimes suggested. We have seen that Newcastle and Eythin had both been threatening resignation since at least the spring, and Marston Moor, a defeat that they felt could have been avoided if their advice had been heeded, merely confirmed their intention.

Newcastle's abrupt departure probably made little difference to the outcome of the war in the North. Although Langdale's Northern Horse were to fight on in 'exile', it is hard to see how Newcastle's shattered forces as a whole could have been reconstructed. Significantly, no one, including the King, seems to have greatly blamed Newcastle for his decision. Clarendon sums up their view: 'All that can be said for the Marquis is, that he was so utterly tired with a Condition and Employment so contrary to his Humour, Nature and Education, that he did not consider the meanes or the way, that would let him out of it, and free him for ever from having more to do with it.'[36]

Despite his failings, William Cavendish, Marquess of Newcastle, had in many ways served his royal master well. By the early summer of 1643, he had achieved all of the initial tasks set for him. His ensuing setbacks and eventual defeat were as much the result of the weaknesses of Civil War armies in general, and overwhelming enemy superiority in men and resources, than any failure of Newcastle and his 'Popish Army'.

THIRTEEN

AN ARMY FROM IRELAND

'Bold Hardie men and excellently well officer'd'
Ralph Hopton, *Bellum Civile*, in *Transactions of the Somerset
Record Society*, Vol. 18, 1902, p. 62

ORIGINS

On 5 May 1640 the King's chief minister, Thomas
Wentworth, Earl of Strafford, until recently Lord Deputy in
Ireland, told Charles, 'You have an army in Ireland you may
employ here to reduce this kingdom.' His words (referring to
Scotland) were claimed by his political opponents to reveal an
intention to use Irish troops in England, and were a key
accusation in Strafford's later impeachment and execution.[1]
Three years later, Strafford's words would return to haunt the
Parliamentarians.

Many historians have regarded Charles I's use of troops from
Ireland as a fatal blunder.[2] Though this conclusion is debatable,
English distrust and fear of Ireland was deep-rooted and
centuries old. It was exacerbated in October 1641 by the
outbreak of rebellion there. England was swept by wild and
greatly distorted reports of massacres perpetrated against the
Protestant settlers.[3] To suppress the rebellion, Parliament
reluctantly authorised the King to raise in England 6,000 foot
and 2,000 horse[4] under the overall command of James Butler,
Earl of Ormonde (created Lieutenant General in November
1641). Response varied, with districts more affected by tales of

atrocities, such as Cheshire and North Wales and the area around Bristol, providing most men. The units raised contained a high proportion of experienced soldiers; in the nine foot regiments eventually sent to Ireland some 55 per cent of the captains and field officers had served in the Scots campaigns, and many in Europe.[5] Some of the rank and file also had previous military experience, although many were drawn from unemployed or semi-criminal elements. Complaints of 'divers insolencies and robberies' by the troops en route to Ireland abounded.

Estimates of total numbers raised for the war in Ireland vary, partly because of difficulty in calculating figures for the 'loyalists' recruited there, mainly, though by no means entirely, Protestant. A considerable Scots force serving in Ulster also needs to be included. By 1642 between 40,000 and 45,000 men may have been serving in Ireland, of whom perhaps 8,000 to 10,000 were raised in England.[6] Despite shortages of virtually all necessities, the army in Ireland enjoyed considerable success, and by the outbreak of the Civil War represented the largest source of trained military manpower, and the only standing army within the British Isles.[7] Its intervention might radically alter the course of the war.

THE COMING OF THE 'IRISH'

In early 1643 both King and Parliament began to seek further afield for military assistance to break the threatened stalemate. While Parliament turned towards Charles' opponents in Scotland, the King pinned his hopes on assistance from Ireland, initially by making use of English troops but with the longer term aim of obtaining military aid from the Irish Confederates as well. From the early spring of 1643, Charles was pressing the Earl of Ormonde, now Lord Deputy in Ireland, to reach a truce, or 'cessation', with the Confederates which would free government troops for service in England.[8]

The Irish Confederacy claimed loyalty to the King, and its leadership hoped to use Charles' current necessities in order to squeeze maximum concessions from him, knowing that a Parliamentarian triumph in England was likely to face them with a much more implacable foe than would a Royalist victory. For his part, the King felt that the military advantages of using troops from Ireland would outweigh any resultant loss of support in England. On 7 September he instructed the Royalist-controlled Council in Dublin: 'That you doe consider and advise of the best means of transporting the rest of our army in that our province of Leinster [the area around Dublin] (excepting such as are to be kept in our garrisons) into our kingdom of England.'[9] A week later, on 15 September, Charles' first objective was realised when the 'Cessation' between Ormonde and the Confederates was signed.

TRANSPORTING THE ARMY

Making effective use of the troops was another matter, and Ormonde was faced by several problems. First was the attitude of the men themselves. Since arriving in Ireland, the English forces had suffered from woeful neglect, blame for which was placed on the Parliament that had authorised their enlistment. Accounts of their miserable condition are numerous. The ordinary soldier rarely received his promised pay of 8d. a day, while in 1642 the Lord Justices in Dublin had complained that 'many of them, especially the English, fall sick daily through cold for want of clothes and shoes'. It was hoped that guarantees that they would receive clothing, free quarter, and regular pay of 12d. a week[10] once they reached England would ensure the soldiers' loyalty to the King. The allegiance of the officers, it was anticipated, might be secured by the oath they were required to take. A number of dissidents were weeded out as a result, while other individuals who sympathised with Parliament had already found means to return to England.

The Royalists acknowledged that they were taking a considerable risk. The King's Secretary of State, Lord George Digby, admitted to Ormonde that 'the army that is transporting hither, [is] considered as fatal to the rebels here, in case it come over and continue with hearty and entire affections, but fully as fatal to his Majesty's affairs in case it should revolt'.[11] Ormonde, with better knowledge of the attitude of his men, warned that any desertions on arrival would not be from sympathy with Parliament, but because the soldiers will be apt to fall into disorders, and will think themselves delivered from prison, when they come on English ground, and that they may make use of their liberty to go whither they will. . . . And if the case be such, that plentiful provision cannot be instantly ready, it is absolutely needful that a competent strength of horse and foot, of whose affections you are confident, should be in readiness by force to keep the common soldier in awe; and whatever provision is made for them, this will not be amiss.[12]

The other point at issue, with implications for their destinations, was how the Irish forces were to be employed, particularly the main contingent from Leinster. The intention seems to have been to retain the separate identity of this latter force. Its obvious use was to counter the imminent Scottish invasion, and this was uppermost in the mind of Arthur Trevor in Oxford, who told Ormonde on 21 November that: 'The expectation of English–Irish aydes is the dayly prayers, and allmost the dayly bread of them that love the Kinge and his business; and putt into the dispentory and medicine booke of state as a cure for the Scotts.'[13] The Irish troops might (as Newcastle himself seems to have expected) be used to reinforce the Northern Royalists in countering the Scottish invasion of north-east England. Alternatively, they could spend the winter consolidating Royalist control of the North-west by clearing Cheshire and re-establishing a Royalist presence in Lancashire. A further option was to retain them as a strategic reserve pending the opening of the spring campaign. However, Ormonde was insistent on the need to keep the troops fully occupied from the moment they landed, and in reality their use was governed by events and decisions taken by commanders on the spot.[14]

The Leinster forces needed to arrive where they could be most effective, and also be supplied and reinforced. For these reasons, as well as the rapidly deteriorating Royalist position resulting from a Parliamentarian offensive into north-east Wales, it was decided to land them in the Chester area. Transporting the troops across the Irish Sea proved less problematic than feared. Parliamentarian naval strength in the area, consisting mainly of half a dozen armed merchant ships operating out of Liverpool, proved insufficient to oppose Royalist vessels reinforced by a flotilla from Bristol. Even so, shortage of shipping forced Ormonde to despatch his troops in several contingents.[15] The first arrivals consisted of 1,500 foot and a few horse, under Major General Sir Michael Earnley, who landed on 20 November at Mostyn in Flintshire. The mere arrival of these first troops from Ireland caused the collapse of the Parliamentarian invasion of north-east Wales, and the Royalists quickly reoccupied the area.

Meanwhile, strenuous efforts were made in North Wales and Chester to provide sufficient food and money to maintain 4,000 troops for a fortnight, together with shoes and clothing for 1,300 men. When the main body of the Irish troops entered Chester on 29 November, it was noted that they were 'in very evill equipage . . . and looked as if they had been used hardship, not having either money, hose or shoes . . . faint, weary and out of clothing . . .'.[16] Collections of clothing from citizens relieved for the moment by their rescue from the imminent threat of enemy attack eased the worst of these shortages, and when a second wave of troops, 1,300 foot of the regiments of Henry Warren and Robert Byron, with a few dragoons, arrived at Neston early in December, they too were provided for.[17]

But problems remained. It had been intended that Ormonde should command the Leinster forces in person, but the need of his presence in Ireland and dissension among the leadership at Oxford prevented this. In the event, command went to John, Lord Byron, nominally as Field Marshal General or deputy to Ormonde, leading a contingent of 1,000 horse and 300 foot from the Oxford Army, which had been sent north to support the troops from Ireland.

Byron was a soldier of considerable experience with a fine record as a cavalry commander, but his somewhat abrupt assumption of command ruffled Royalist feathers in Chester and North Wales, where the welcome for the troops from Ireland was already wearing thin. They had a fearsome reputation, magnified by Parliamentarian propagandists and apparently confirmed by the bloodthirsty threats of officers such as Captain Thomas Sandford,[18] and though no worse than expected from professional soldiers fresh from a harsh theatre of war, their behaviour even in Royalist-held territory soon rendered them unwelcome guests. There were widespread complaints of theft, cattle-stealing, drunkenness, and that some of the troops promptly sold the clothes they had been given in order to obtain beer money. On 1 December 1643 the Chester City Assembly offered £100 of the city's plate if the 'soldiers bee removed forth of this Cittie to quarters elsewhere by Monday next'.[19]

Byron was equally anxious to leave. He had over 1,000 horse and some 4,000 foot, the great majority of the latter from Ireland, a force too large to be maintained in Chester, even if it had been wise to leave the men, among whom desertions had so far been encouragingly light, unemployed for long. On 12 December Byron and his army headed out of Chester, their objective the Cheshire Parliamentarian headquarters of Nantwich, before moving north into Lancashire.[20]

THE NANTWICH CAMPAIGN

Byron's operations were initially successful. Beeston Castle was surprised on 13 December in a classic 'special forces'-type operation by Thomas Sandford's firelocks, and on 26 December 1643, in a hard-fought action at Middlewich, Sir William Brereton's Cheshire forces suffered a damaging reverse. Lord Byron was now free to commence operations against Nantwich itself, and his troops spread out across the neighbouring countryside, earning a reputation for looting and brutality that is impossible to put down entirely to enemy propaganda. Most notorious was the 'Bartholmley Massacre' of 25 December.[21]

Byron wrongly believed Nantwich to be poorly provisioned and likely to fall quickly. But the siege dragged on, and a major assault was repulsed on 17 January 1644, with heavy loss to the troops from Ireland.[22] By this time, Parliamentarian Sir Thomas Fairfax had collected an improvised relief force at Manchester and had set off through bitter winter weather to the rescue of Nantwich. Fairfax had no illusions regarding the opposition that he faced. They were 'Men of great experience who had run through all sorts of services, and were not new to the Policies of Warre . . . acquainted with the greatest hardship, habituated to cold and want, and whatever suffereing a winter siege could require. . . . They were put in heart by their former successes, and that would make them the more desperate, and they were valiant before, being used to nothing but conquests. . . .'[23]

Byron's plan seems to have been to maintain the siege until the last possible moment, and then to engage the relief force at a safe distance from Nantwich, but his strategy was wrecked by a sudden thaw that left his army divided by the River Weaver. By about noon on 25 January, when Byron had managed to bring his isolated units over to the western bank of the Weaver, Fairfax's army was closing in on Nantwich. The Royalists had no option but to launch a piecemeal general attack.

The battle, between two armies closely matched in numbers, was hard fought, and hung in the balance for over an hour. Two incidents decided the outcome. Some of Byron's 'Irish' foot, apparently from Henry Warren's Regiment, 'upon an instance unexpected' gave ground. Byron alleged treachery, claiming that at least sixty men suddenly switched sides and opened fire on their former comrades, but this is not borne out by other sources and it is equally possible that ammunition shortage was a key factor. As the Royalists faltered, the garrison of Nantwich made a well-timed sortie and struck them in the rear. Byron's forces were broken, with the loss of about 200 dead and 1,500 prisoners, mostly from the Leinster troops. The Irish-Royalist Army, as an independent force, had suffered a fatal blow.[24]

An inquest on the defeat followed. Lord Byron and his brother Robert, anxious to portray their own actions in the best light, accused their troops of lack of enthusiasm and outright treachery. Lord Digby seemed to confirm this, telling Ormonde that the men recruited in Cheshire and North Wales had been 'very subject to bee corrupted in theire owne countryes',[25] while Lord Byron was more outspoken, requesting Ormonde that if reinforcements were sent, 'I wish they were rather Irish than English, for the English we have already are very mutinous, and being for the most part these countrymen are so poisoned by the ill-affected people here, that they grow very cold in the service.'[26] Other evidence suggests that these accusations were exaggerated. Sir John Mennes, Lieutenant General in North Wales, told Prince Rupert that only about 200 of the troops from Ireland had deserted prior to the Battle of Nantwich, and about 500 of the prisoners taken there enlisted with the Parliamentarians.[27] This total of about a third of those captured was not unduly high, particularly as the troops were professional soldiers, who might have been expected to place their own welfare above the cause. Many of the remaining prisoners seem to have remained obdurate. Fairfax offered them to the Scots for service in Ulster, but most of them were probably 'ransomed' for a month's pay in the spring of 1644, and joined Prince Rupert's forces along the Welsh Border together with some of their comrades who had changed sides and been placed in minor garrisons in North Shropshire, but had returned to Royalist allegiance when these were taken by Prince Rupert.[28] The same trend may be discerned among captured officers. Though some of the most prominent, such as George Monck and Colonel Richard Gibson, remained as prisoners, a number of more junior officers were captured, and exchanged, on more than one occasion, having resisted any persuasions to change sides.[29]

AFTER NANTWICH

The defeat at Nantwich, though a grievous blow, was not the end of the troops from Ireland. Until about April 1644, when Parliamentarian naval control of the Irish Sea, together with lack of available English troops, effectively halted convoys from Ireland, a trickle of reinforcements continued to arrive. Most significant were two regiments of foot, totalling 1,700 men, under Colonels Robert Broughton and Henry Tillier, the latter a military tactician of note who became Major General of Foot in the army Prince Rupert was raising on the Welsh Border. Operating mainly from Shrewsbury, these troops became the core of Rupert's forces, once some initial 'growling' over pay and conditions had been settled.[30] Their musketeers were mounted for the relief of Newark on 21 March, and helped strengthen the Royalist position along the Welsh Border prior to the Prince's advance north. In the meantime, the regiments that had been defeated at Nantwich were refitted and recruited, in part with new levies and also with exchanged prisoners. The Irish units made up about four-fifths of the 5,000 foot in the army that

Rupert led northwards in May for his offensive into Lancashire and march to relieve York.[31] Without the troops from Ireland, it is difficult to see how the operation would have been possible.

The foot from Ireland suffered heavily at Marston Moor; Tillier's 'Greencoat' Regiment, for example, apparently lost most of its men there.[32] A further blow came in September at the Battle of Montgomery,[33] when some 1,500 'Irish' foot were lost almost 'unto a man'.[34] Yet remnants of the Leinster regiments lingered on; possibly again recruited and reinforced by exchanged personnel, they formed a division, perhaps 500 strong, known as the 'Shrewsbury Foot', at the Battle of Naseby in June 1645.[35] Few of the 'Irish' foot present at Naseby escaped death or capture; only a small number of detachments, such as the company of Earnley's men in Bridgenorth garrison, remained, and for most the end came with the surrender, at Stow-on-the-Wold on 21 March 1646, of the last Royalist field army.[36]

In other parts of the country the impact of troops from Ireland was less apparent. From the autumn of 1643 English troops serving in the province of Munster were despatched to the West Country. Among them were two weak regiments of foot under Charles Vavasour and Sir John Paulet, perhaps 1,000 men in all, who were sent to reinforce Lord Hopton in his operations in Hampshire and Sussex. Hopton described the newcomers as 'bold hardy men and excellently well officer'd, but the common men were mutinous and shrewdly infected with the rebellious humour of England, being brought over meerly by the vertue, and loyalty of theire officers, and large promises, which there was then but small meanes to performe . . .'.[37]

A mutiny by Vavasour's men was swiftly crushed by Hopton, who executed two or three of the ringleaders. Though the troops from Ireland fought at Cheriton and elsewhere, and served with the Oxford Army until Naseby, they were too few in number, and perhaps too poorly motivated, ever to have the impact of the army from Leinster.[38] More valuable were two regiments, under Sir William St Leger and Colonel Nicholas Mynne, that also landed at Bristol and were sent to bolster operations against Parliamentarian-held Gloucester. St Leger's strong unit, renamed the Duke of York's Regiment, later served effectively with the Oxford Army, while Mynne was appointed Colonel General of the

Royalist forces in the south-west Midlands, where he and his regiment were destroyed by Edward Massey on 2 August 1644 at Red Marley in Worcestershire.[39]

In all about 8,000 'English' foot from Ireland, with a few hundred horse, arrived in England between October 1643 and February 1644, and virtually none after that date.[40] But while their numbers and impact are relatively easy to determine, there is much less certainty regarding the use of 'native' Irish soldiers by the Royalist forces in England.

'ENGLISHMEN-BORN OR NATIVE IRISH'

After his defeat at Nantwich, Lord Byron urged Ormonde to send over Irish-born troops, and on 6 February reiterated: 'I must renew my suit concerning the sending over of a considerable number of Irish natives with as much speed as may be; the English excepting such as are gentlemen not being to be trusted in this war.'[41] It was felt that military expediency overrode any loss of English support that their use might incur; as Lord Digby told Ormonde on 8 February: 'We are past scruples long since.'[42] The Lord Deputy himself responded encouragingly that if provided with sufficient arms and ships he was confident that he could send over 'considerable numbers of Irish with little noise'.[43]

These and similar statements have encouraged some historians to conclude that large numbers of Irish troops served with the Royalist forces,[44] but this was not so. The problems faced from the spring of 1644 onwards were two-fold: steadily increasing Parliamentarian naval supremacy in the Irish Sea, which Prince Rupert's capture of Liverpool in June 1644 did little to alter,[45] coupled with the reluctance of the Irish Confederates actually to provide troops to support the King, despite tortuous negotiations.

Some soldiers certainly arrived, recruited by agents such as Colonel Thomas Napier from among men who had served with Strafford's 'Irish Army' prior to the war. Among them, appropriately enough, were perhaps 500 men who reached Chester in April 1644 to form part of Lord Byron's Regiment of Foot, under English and Welsh officers, and two more small detachments of reinforcements landed later in the war.[46] The foot regiments of Lords Inchiquin and Broghill (possibly raised from 'loyalists') served in the South-west of England in late 1643 and early 1644, but on their colonels' defection to Parliament made terms and were shipped home.

There is evidence that a few more 'native' Irish landed. A number of officers serving with Prince Rupert's Regiment of Firelocks, for example, have Irish names, and as late as February 1646 attempts were still being made to raise Irish forces for the relief of Chester.[47] But even though the King's envoy, the Earl of Glamorgan, eventually reached agreement with the Confederates, and wrote optimistically of the despatch of 10,000 men, both Parliamentarian seapower and Irish reluctance made them no more than another Stuart pipedream. Probably no more than a couple of thousand 'native' Irish soldiers ever set foot on English soil.[48]

However, there is no doubt that Westminster was seriously alarmed by the prospect of the King receiving significant Irish assistance, and responded sharply to the threat. In April 1644 a consignment of soldiers from Lord Willoughby's Regiment, raised at the start of the 1641 rebellion from among loyalists in the Cork area, was intercepted by the Parliamentarian navy and about seventy men and two women were thrown overboard to drown.[49]

This atrocity had a profound effect in Ireland, especially among the Confederates, and their reluctance to risk their men deepened. In October 1644 Parliament passed an Ordinance instructing its commanders to give no quarter to 'any Irishman, or to any Papist born in Ireland which shall be taken in arms against Parliament in England'.[50] This ignored the practical difficulties in determining the exact status of prisoners, such as the complicated definition of 'an Englishman by descent but an Irishman born', as well as probable reprisals (speedily enacted by Prince Rupert), and was opposed, or quietly ignored, by many commanders. Sir William Brereton, for example, yielded to the persuasions of his officers, and executed relatively few prisoners. When Chester fell in 1646, despite Byron's Irish foot being excluded from the surrender terms, they were actually allowed to leave the city 'as free as any other soldiers'.[51] At Liverpool in November 1644, where the 'native' Irish foot of Byron's Regiment and the 'English-Irish' regiment of his brother Robert were both in the garrison, Robert's men, fearful of falling victim to the Parliamentarian ordinance, arranged to mutiny and turn over the town to one of their former officers now serving with the besiegers.[52] In the event, even the 'native' Irish were spared and shipped back to Dublin.[53]

Other commanders were less forbearing. At Conway in August 1646 Colonel Thomas Mytton caught up with the survivors of Byron's foot and had a number of them 'sent home by water' – taken out to sea and drowned. By this stage in the war, Mytton regarded further enemy resistance as stubborn and unjustified, or it may have been a result of the prisoners being captured in action rather than surrendering on terms.[54]

When considering the significance of Ireland to the Royalist war effort, we must also take into account the large numbers of individual officers of Irish origins or experience who took service with the King. Among them were notable commanders such as Sir Richard Grenville (who defected from the Parliamentarians) and capable men who occupied a lesser role, such as the cavalry commander Colonel John Marrow and Lieutenant Colonel Dan O'Neill of Rupert's Regiment of Horse. They provided a leavening of experience – and sometimes ruthlessness – that spread widely through the Royalist forces.

It is sometimes claimed that the King's use of troops from Ireland cost him far more than he gained.[55] But, in fact, relatively few supporters were permanently alienated by the landing of Ormonde's men, who, at least in the areas where they mainly operated, were well known to be English or Welsh. Not enough native Irish landed to have any great impact. Despite the disaster at Nantwich, the troops from Leinster not only prevented a Royalist collapse in north-east Wales that would have led to the loss of Chester, but also made possible Prince Rupert's offensive of 1644.

Nonetheless, it is clear that King Charles' 'Irish' troops did not have the impact he had hoped. Seasoned veterans as they were, their arrival in the autumn of 1642 or the following spring, when the bulk of their opponents was still relatively inexperienced, might have been decisive. But by late 1643, their margin of superiority had considerably diminished and they proved too few, and too dispersed, to turn the tide of the war.

FOURTEEN

A METEOR IN THE NORTH: MONTROSE'S ARMY, 1644-6

'He either fears his fate too much, or his deserts are small,
who dares not put it to the touch, to win or lose it all.'
Verse by James Graham, Marquess of Montrose

GENESIS OF A LEGEND

James Graham, Marquess of Montrose, is the greatest romantic figure of the Civil Wars. Subject of more biographies than any other participant save Oliver Cromwell, his chroniclers, from his contemporary, George Wishart, an unashamed Royalist propagandist, to the twentieth-century giants John Buchan and C.V. Wedgwood, have all succumbed, at least in part, to the lure of the Graham legend.[1]

Montrose's earlier career, his political and religious ambivalence in the years of gathering conflict, and a hedging of bets that at times seems more calculating than principled, may sit uneasily alongside the chivalric paragon of later years. But these flaws are forgotten in the epic of the *Annus Mirabilis* – the sensational year of victories of 1644–5 that saw Montrose smashing army after army sent against him by the Scottish government and which was crowned by the years of exile and Montrose's return, capture and execution, events turned by propagandists and the Marquess's own theatrical courage into a Royalist martyrdom. As a result, the nature of Montrose's victories, and the men who won them, have themselves become clouded in legend. This is unfortunate, for the truth is remarkable enough.

A REBELLION BEGINS

Born in 1612, James Graham received the customary education of a young man of his class, though there is, in his case, no evidence of any military experience on the Continent. His somewhat indifferent educational record suggests a rather slapdash approach that would cost him dear in his later military career. In 1638, as political and religious tensions grew between King Charles and his Scottish subjects, Montrose was one of the first to come out in favour of the party opposing royal plans. The First Bishops' War gave Montrose an early taste of warfare, and the first sign of his ability, at the Covenanting victory at Bridge of Dee.

But by the outbreak of the Second Bishops' War of 1640, Montrose's enthusiasm for the Covenanting cause was already waning, though whether from growing sympathy with the King or as a result of rivalry with the other leading Covenanting magnate, Archibald Campbell, Earl of Argyll, remains debatable. By 1643, despite being offered a senior command in the army being raised to fight on the Parliamentarian side in the Civil War in England, Montrose's alienation from the Covenanting regime was complete. He made his way to Oxford and offered his services to King Charles.

But in Court circles Montrose was regarded as one more importunate Scottish exile, and it was not until after the Scottish invasion in January 1644 that the King began to treat him more seriously. On 1 February he was given the title of Lieutenant General in Scotland, and became involved with the cloudy schemings of the Earl of Antrim to create a pan-Celtic Catholic alliance in support of the King.[2] In the short term, this did nothing to forward Montrose's plans, and his first incursion into Scotland, in the spring of 1644, with a handful of cavalry drawn mainly from Scotsmen serving with the Royalist forces in England, quickly ended in inglorious retreat, while the pro-

Royalist rebellion of the Gordons under the Marquess of Huntley in north-east Scotland petered out.

The Royalist defeat at Marston Moor seemed to signal the end of Montrose's hopes. Prince Rupert has been blamed by historians for declining to provide Montrose with the cavalry support he requested, but there was nothing at the time to suggest that someone with James Graham's equivocal political track record could be expected to carry out his extravagant promises, and Rupert required every man to salvage what he could in England.

Montrose's schemes were rescued by the only practical result of Antrim's scheming. Moving on to Carlisle, the Marquess heard of the landing in the Western Highlands of 1,600 troops from Ireland under Alastair MacColla, and linked up with them on 29 August at Blair Atholl. The apparently spontaneous support received from a number of Highlanders was, in fact, probably the result of prior planning, but the outcome gave Montrose the basis of a field army. On 1 September, at Tippermuir, he won his first great victory, and the Royalist rebellion in Scotland achieved credibility.

MONTROSE'S ARMY

The backbone of Montrose's army throughout most of its existence was the Irish Brigade of Alastair MacColla. These troops are frequently confused with Highland clansmen and are portrayed as being equipped and fighting in Highland fashion. In reality, however, they were mostly professionals, 'brockt up in West Flanderis, expert souldiouris'.[3] As well as these veterans of the Spanish Army of Flanders, others were recruited in Ulster, and there was at least one company of 'Old English' from the Dublin area. Only about four of the total of twenty-nine companies seem actually to have been Highlanders, serving mainly in MacColla's Lifeguard. The suggestion that the Irish wore Highland dress is also misplaced. Though some initially had trews, and the blue bonnet was universal among Scottish soldiers on both sides, MacColla's men seem quickly to have adopted the 'hodden grey' coats and breeches, together with items of looted civilian dress. The largest of the three Irish regiments, commanded by Thomas Laghtman, was probably equipped on the usual 2:1 musket/pike ratio, but the two smaller units may have been all-musketeer.[4]

The 'Irish' quickly gained an unenviable reputation for cruelty and brutality, heightened by the notorious sack of Aberdeen after Montrose's victory outside the town on 13 September. Though the extent of the atrocities carried out, apparently by one of the Irish regiments while Montrose, MacColla and the remainder of the army stayed outside the town, remain unclear,[5] there is no doubt that Montrose made little effort to prevent them, and as a result his cause suffered a serious, perhaps ultimately decisive, loss of support from the Lowland Royalists and many members of the Scottish aristocracy whose adherence would have transformed his prospects. Instead, his opponents found it easier to portray Montrose as the leader of a band of Irish and Highland cut-throats, and thus marginalised him from the mainstream of Scottish politics.

Yet Montrose had no option but to rely upon the support of the Irish Brigade. It was certainly to them that he owed his earliest victories. The idea of the Irish engaging in a wild and impetuous charge after the popular image of the Highland clansman is far removed from reality. At both Tippermuir and Aberdeen they adopted the standard tactics of the regular troops they were. In the first of these actions, the government forces, mostly raw levies and considerably fewer in numbers than Royalist propaganda suggests, broke under the concentrated and accurate fire of the Irish, who then completed their victory with musket butt and pike.[6]

The Royalist army at Tippermuir, some 2,000 strong, was largely a conventional one, and it was Montrose's aim throughout his operations to build up a respectably sized and armed regular force. One of the main causes of his eventual downfall was his failure to achieve this. The Irish Brigade, despite its undoubted fighting ability, remained a flawed weapon. Its strength fluctuated considerably. In part, this was caused by detachments constantly returning to their West Highlands base area to conduct semi-independent operations, but it was even more the inevitable result of attrition, especially disease and desertion. Soldiers with the reputation held by MacColla's Irish were in constant demand, and some of them would be encountered for many years in the service of various employers in the Highlands. The result was that the numbers of Montrose's Irish regulars sank steadily. At Auldearn in May 1645 he probably had about 800 Irish troops, and at Philliphaugh the following September, often regarded as the grave of the Irish Brigade, no more than about 500 of MacColla's men were actually present.[7]

Montrose attempted to build up a significant force of Scottish regular troops, but met with only limited success. To a great extent this was his own fault. As a politician Montrose had severe failings. He never seems fully to have grasped the need to establish good relations with the mercurial Marquess of Huntly, head of the powerful Gordons, the pro-Royalist clan that dominated north-east Scotland and whose support was essential if Montrose was ever to raise a field army strong enough to consolidate control of Scotland. As a result, the numbers of Scottish regulars remained small. Most significant among the foot was the Strathbogie Regiment, first raised by Huntly in 1639. A conventionally equipped unit, a detachment was described in April 1644 as 'about 60 musketieris and pikoniers, with twa cullouris, ane drum, and ane bag pipe'.[8] It is important to note that this unit, along with the other 'regular' foot regiment from the North-east serving with Montrose, commanded by Colonel Donald Farquerson of Monaltrie, were not clan units but fencible regiments raised on a territorial basis, and hence considerably more reliable. They also included a fair number of professional officers; the final commander of the Strathbogie Regiment, Colonel John Gordon of Kingsmill, had risen through the regiment from the rank of captain.

Famed in popular imagination among Montrose's men are the Highlanders, often credited with winning astounding victories over greatly superior numbers by virtue of the irresistible fury of the 'Highland Charge'. This is not supported by the evidence. In most of Montrose's battles, the Highlanders were in a minority in his forces. At Fyvie in October 1644 when, due to poor reconnaissance, Montrose narrowly escaped destruction at the hands of Baillie's army, his 1,500 men included no more than 500 Highlanders, and at Inverlochy the following February, in the defeat of the Campbells that is sometimes held up as a classic example of an inter-clan battle, Montrose's forces were less than half Highland in composition. Possibly only in his final victory at Kilsyth (15 August 1645) did Highlanders form the majority of the Royalist army.

Most of the clans that supported Montrose did so because they were Catholic and anti-Campbell rather than from deeply held allegiance to King Charles. Consequently, their participation tended to be highly conditional, and this, with the Highlanders' long-held custom of returning home after a major victory with their booty, made them militarily unreliable. The actual combat effectiveness of the Highlanders has frequently been exaggerated. The legendary 'Highland Charge' on closer examination was less formidable than sometimes suggested.

The popular concept of the 'Highland Charge' is that the clansmen, after disrupting the enemy with a volley of musketry, preferably falling on the ground to avoid counterfire, would then charge their unfortunate opponents while they were reloading and hack them apart with broadswords, axes and whatever else was available. This theory fails to carry conviction for a number of reasons. Firstly, the normally adopted tactic of regular infantry of firing in ranks 'by succession' meant that a fairly continuous fire could be kept up. Secondly, available evidence suggests that only about a quarter of the Highlanders in the Civil War period were equipped with muskets (although the proportion doubtless increased through battlefield captures). Indeed, apart from the Highland 'gentlemen' and their leading retainers who normally formed the front rank of a clan unit, the majority of its members were often extremely badly equipped, sometimes with little more than agricultural implements.

The fighting quality of many of the clansmen was often surprisingly poor. A unit was recruited from all sections and ages of a clan, ranging from young boys to greybeards sixty or more years old. As a result, a charge once launched would quickly lose any initial cohesion and would degenerate into a mob, with the majority of its members showing a healthy sense of self-preservation and hanging back unless the enemy routed. It would be noted during the 1745 Rebellion that the bulk of the actual fighting was carried out by the clan 'gentry' and by volunteers with a greater sense of commitment, and there is every reason to suppose that the same situation obtained a century earlier. Indeed, Highlanders were generally regarded as second rate and unreliable troops, whose famed 'charge', often a much more cautious and hesitant affair than the term suggests, worked only against a poorly trained or motivated opponent who lost his nerve and formation. Ironically, the well-attested reluctance of Montrose's men to take prisoners served on more than one occasion to cause opposing troops to hold together and fight more desperately than they might otherwise have done.

In short, the bulk of the real infantry fighting was done by Montrose's regular foot. The Highlanders were effective, if at all, only in pursuit, and, as with the Jacobite forces of 1745, the aim, never realised, was eventually to arm, train and use them as regulars.[9]

Montrose's greatest weakness, and one cause of his eventual failure, was lack of regular cavalry. This prevented him from building on his initial victories in the autumn of 1644 and establishing himself in the Scottish Lowlands a year earlier than actually happened. The situation was transformed early in 1645 by the sudden defection to Montrose of Lord George Gordon and his regular cavalry regiment. These, again contrary to the impression given by some biographers of Montrose, were fully trained and equipped in orthodox 'harquebusier' style. This unit, together with a small number of other horse, enabled Montrose to carry the war into the Lowlands and gain the initiative, rather than continue his rapid and dramatic-seeming marches, which had largely been to escape from enemy armies rather than to destroy them.

Though never numerically strong, his cavalry played a major role in Montrose's victories at Auldearn, Alford and Kilsyth. On the latter occasion, the 600 Royalist horse actually outnumbered their enemy counterparts and were the decisive factor in the Royalist victory.[10] Unfortunately, Montrose's notable lack of skill in the political sphere resulted, after Lord Gordon's death, in strained relations with his family which lost him the services of their horse at a critical phase of his operations. The 1,000 Border horse eventually recruited proved unreliable and fatally outmatched at Philliphaugh by David Lesley's experienced troopers.

THE REBELLION IN PERSPECTIVE

The course of Montrose's campaigns of 1644–6 have frequently been described,[11] and there is little purpose in retreading this well-worn path. However, it is worth looking in more detail at the impact of the rebellion both in Scotland and on the course of the Civil War as a whole.

Did Montrose ever have any realistic chance of success? Both the Marquess and his monarch, inveterate dreamers to the last, had high hopes of overthrowing the Covenanting regime north of the border. After his victory at Inverlochy in February 1645, at a time when virtually none of Scotland was under his indisputed control, Montrose wrote to the King: 'Through God's blessing I am in the fairest hopes of reducing this Kingdom to your Majestie's obedience, and, if the measures I have concerted with your loyal subjects fail me not, as they hardly can, I doubt not before the end of the summer I shall be able to come to your Majesty's assistance with a brave army.'[12] It was an unsubstantiated and wildly optimistic promise to which King Charles and his more deluded advisers such as Lord Digby clung ever more desperately long after its impossibility had been fatally exposed by Montrose's defeat at Philliphaugh.

It is unlikely that realistic military minds such as that of Prince Rupert ever subscribed to this view. The King's generals placed little store on help from the Scottish Royalists, but they may be criticised for not doing more to sustain a rebellion that could at least have diverted enemy resources. Montrose on more than one occasion pleaded for as few as 500 of the King's horse to be sent to support him, and such a reinforcement in the autumn of 1644 might have paid rich dividends. It was not until the spring of the following year that the Royalist high command began seriously to consider assisting Montrose, and not until after Naseby, with the English Royalist cause plunging towards defeat, that belated and unsuccessful attempts were made to send Montrose the reinforcements he had requested.[13]

Given that without English Royalist assistance, or a shift in Scottish support which was never realistically likely, Montrose could not have achieved the decisive success he hoped for, what impact did the rebellion actually have? Montrose was more fortunate than he perhaps deserved. He was aided initially by the attitude of the Covenanting authorities. For a long time the Scottish Committee of Estates discounted the threat presented by Montrose, and made few preparations to meet it until late August 1644. Even after the disaster at Tippermuir they proved unwilling to recall any of their experienced troops serving in England and Ulster, relying mainly upon raising new levies for the 'Home Army' to deal with the rebels.

This in itself frustrated the aim of the Scottish Royalists to take pressure off their English counterparts. There is a misconception that the relative lack of impact of the Army of the Covenant in England after Marston Moor was due to the preoccupation of its commanders with events at home. In fact, only in February 1645, after Inverlochy, were 1,500 men recalled from England and another 1,400 from Ireland. As late as May of the same year the Scottish authorities were still preparing to reinforce the army in England, and it was not until August 1645, when the victory of the New Model at Naseby had largely removed the need for Scottish assistance, that Leslie and most of the Scottish horse were called back home. The real reason that the Army of the Covenant failed to have the effect that its English allies had hoped for lay partly in the long-drawn-out sieges of Newcastle and Carlisle which absorbed most of its attention for over a year after Marston Moor, and partly also in its disgruntlement at what was regarded as the failure of the English Parliament to carry out its promises of financial support.[14]

Montrose also received unexpected benefits from the severe outbreak of plague that affected the towns of the Scottish Lowlands, in particular during 1644/5. This, together with growing war-weariness, disrupted government recruiting efforts and prevented it bringing its full potential resources to bear against the rebels. Ironically, these same factors would come into play against Montrose after his victory at Kilsyth. For a very brief time in late August 1645 it seemed that Royalist dreams were about to become reality. There was no major Covenanting army left in the field in Scotland, and many of Montrose's leading opponents were in flight. But the Royalist triumph was without substance. Montrose's army displayed all of the weaknesses that had dogged it throughout its brief career. Most of the

Highlanders and the vital Gordon units went home. MacColla and the bulk of his Irish Brigade departed to consolidate their hold in the Western Highlands. The same plague that had disrupted government preparations prevented Montrose from presenting the facade of a legitimate regime by occupying Edinburgh, while war-weary men who had proved unwilling to enlist under the banner of the Covenant proved equally reluctant to fight for King Charles.

Far from marching triumphantly over the Border at the head of 20,000 men, as he had rashly promised the King, Montrose found himself stranded in the Scottish Lowlands with about 500 remaining Irish and 100 horse. Pledged to hold a Parliament in Glasgow, and with increasingly desperate pleas for assistance from the King ringing in his ears, it would be political suicide for Montrose to retreat again to the Highlands. The result was his decision to rely upon uncertain promises of assistance from some of the Lowland gentry and push on south. It is hard to see what Montrose could realistically have hoped to achieve by this move for, although he did manage to recruit a numerically respectable force of Border horse, they proved no match for Lesley's relatively seasoned troopers at Philliphaugh. Even so, the defeat was equally a result of Montrose's fatal and several times repeated tendency to neglect adequate reconnaissance.

In strictly military terms, Philliphaugh was not fatal to Montrose. He had suffered higher casualties in his victory at Auldearn. But it was a body blow to his political credibility from which he never recovered. Always marginalised from the Scottish political mainstream and unable to establish a lasting rapprochement with Huntly and the Gordons, Montrose was largely confined to the Highlands with such Irish and clansmen he could persuade to follow him. The orders that, on 31 May 1646, Huntly and Montrose received from the King, a prisoner in Scottish hands, to lay down their arms merely drew a line under an increasingly hopeless military situation.

Montrose failed because he was unable to secure the support of enough of the Scottish magnates to field a properly balanced regular army. Credit is also due to the oft-maligned soldiers and generals of the Scottish government, who recovered from repeated defeats to contain and ultimately neutralise the

Royalists. As a battle commander, Montrose generally deserves the reputation that history has given him, as well as credit for his skill in holding together such a disparate army. His greatest weakness was a tendency to carelessness and haste, typified in his neglect of adequate scouting, which resulted in his being totally surprised on several occasions, and which, at Carbisdale in 1650, would ultimately prove fatal.

FIFTEEN

LANGDALE'S RIDE: THE NORTHERN HORSE AND THE RELIEF OF PONTEFRACT, 1645

'A Rabble of Gentility.'

> George Monck, *Observations upon*
> *Military and Political Affairs,*
> 1671, p. 92

By late evening on 2 July 1644, the Royalist armies under Prince Rupert had suffered a crushing defeat on the field of Marston Moor. Apart from a few stubbornly resisting garrisons, the North of England seemed lost to King Charles, and most of the Northern Royalist forces of the Marquess of Newcastle were broken beyond recovery. But a few thousand of his cavalry chose to fight on alongside the Royalist forces in the South and, under the title of the Northern Horse, during the next twelve months carved themselves a formidable reputation. Their relief of Pontefract, early in 1645, is one of history's classic, though little-known, cavalry operations.

The units later known as the Northern Horse were mainly raised in 1642–3.[1] We have already noted the high proportion of Roman Catholics in the ranks of some of the regiments of horse, and these religious bonds, along with the ties of kinship that existed in some units, helped give the Northern Horse its strong sense of identity. Especially after Marston Moor, a large proportion of the rank and file of the Northern Horse were minor gentry, yeomen and servants of the officers – all men with a personal stake in the restoration of Royalist fortunes in the North.

Many of the Northern Horse were relatively young – at the start of the war the cavalry colonels in Newcastle's army had an average age of thirty – and many older men abandoned the fight after Marston Moor. Those who remained were younger sons with few home ties, or men whose estates and livelihoods lay in enemy hands and whose recovery depended upon victory for the King. Yorkshire provided more recruits than any other county, followed by Northumberland, Durham, Cumbria, and a sprinkling of men from the rest of Newcastle's sprawling command.

The independence, and indiscipline off the field of battle, displayed by the Northern Horse was remarked upon by contemporaries. Their commanders seem to have been indifferent to the treatment meted out to civilians, disloyal or otherwise, but there were other reasons for this feature of the Northern Horse. Many of its members, with names like Carnaby, Fenwick, Errington and Wray, were grandsons of the infamous Border Reivers of Elizabeth's reign. They came from families where the tradition of freebooting ran deep, and it was perhaps inevitable that in the loosened social conditions of civil conflict they should revert to recent ancestral habits. After Marston Moor, the 'exiled' troopers encountered the traditional distrust of Northerners and Catholics displayed by many elsewhere, and they reciprocated with ruthless disregard for the civilian population. The Northern troopers were frequently accompanied by large herds of looted sheep and cattle, and resembled a tribe in exile. Observers noted disapprovingly their camp followers or 'leaguer ladies', and in January 1645 items looted in Salisbury included clothing for both women and children.[2]

Even before Marston Moor, the Northern Royalist cavalry were regarded unfavourably. In June 1644, when Newcastle's horse joined Prince Rupert in Lancashire, it was noted that they were 'not in good case either for horse or armes'[3] and were, according to another account, 'extreme barbarous'.[4] The Northern Royalist forces were perhaps never as well off for firearms as the King's forces elsewhere,[5] and there is some evidence that obsolescent items of armour and equipment may have been quite commonly utilised by the Northern cavalry. The quality of their mounts also tended to be inferior. In fact, some of the Northern Horse may have more nearly resembled the traditional Border 'moss-trooper' than the fully equipped harquebusier.[6]

SIR MARMADUKE LANGDALE

Such a force required a formidable leader. Fortunately, a man was available. Goring had been called south after Marston Moor and his replacement, Sir Marmaduke Langdale (born *c.* 1598), a Yorkshireman, was one of the outstanding cavalry commanders of the Civil Wars. In the 1620s, like many of his contemporaries, Langdale had gained military experience on the Continent. Never a very popular figure with some who knew him, Sir Marmaduke was hardbitten and forbidding, his character brought out in the anecdote that when he was dying, Langdale's son was still too afraid of his father to tell him so.[7]

Others took a different view. David Lloyd said:

He was a very lean and much mortified man, so that the enemy called him 'ghost' (and deservedly, they were so haunted by him); and carried that gravity in his converse, that integrity and generosity in his dealings, that strictness in his devotion, that experience, moderation and wariness in his counsel, and that weight in his discourse, as very much endeared strangers to his royal master's cause and to his own person.[8]

Langdale won the devotion of his own men, who increasingly placed their allegiance to him above anything else. Serving as a volunteer with the Northern Horse in the days before Naseby, Sir Henry Slingsby observed of his comrades:

they are not much inquisitive, and hitherto showed a mind indifferent what way they went, so they followed their General, and such an army had Caesar of whom they wrote that he would be so severe and precise in exacting discipline, as he would not give them warning of the time either of journey or battle, but kept them ready, intentive and prest to be led forth upon a sudden every minute of an hour, withersoever he would. And as Julius Caesar was severe in requiring an exact observance to strict discipline, so he would teach them to endure hardships by his own example, lighting from his horse and leading them on foot many times with the head bare, whether the sun did shine or the clouds did pour down rain.[9]

By the summer of 1644, Langdale was senior brigade commander with the Northern cavalry and had an able team of subordinates, including his second-in-command, Sir William Blakiston, and men such as Sir Gameliel Dudley and 'Sir Phillip Monckton, mostly young and noted for extreme gallantry in action – verging at times on insanity.[10]

At Marston Moor the Northern cavalry had totalled some 3,500 men, elements of over thirty weak regiments. To them was due most of the credit on the Royalist side and, after the defeat, Goring and his successor Langdale held together the core of their force, who did not regard the war in the North as yet lost. But by August 1644, with York fallen and prolonged Royalist resistance in Lancashire doomed, Langdale, whose men had begun to alienate the local population by their looting and widespread disorder,[11] resolved 'to advance to the Kinge, who if he get the better would be in a better condition to relieve these Northern Countries'.[12] Their increasingly desperate journey south almost proved to be the end for the Northerners. Though Langdale set off with over 2,000 men, numbers steadily dwindled both from losses in battle and desertion as the ordinary troopers, in particular, attempted to slip back home. Langdale was wounded in an action at Malpas in Cheshire, where many of his troopers displayed a reluctance to fight, and it was not until early in November, after peregrinations that had taken them into South Wales, that the Northerners, sadly reduced in numbers and effectiveness, eventually joined the King and his Oxford Army.

Pulled back to recuperate in winter quarters around Salisbury, it is a tribute to Langdale's leadership that within a few weeks he both re-animated and reorganised his troops. The personnel of the Northern Horse was constantly subject to change, serving as it did as a rallying point for Northern Royalist 'exiles', some of whom only remained in its ranks for a short time. By now, although it included the remnants of at least twenty-six regiments, the greatest proportion of its strength consisted of officers – in some cases 'reformadoes' – and their servants and personal retainers. The large number of field officers reduced to serving in the ranks must have caused command problems, and while potentially a formidable fighting force, morale seems to have been brittle. As Langdale's officers complained in February: 'Many of our soldiers are already wasted, and do daily moulder away, and . . . the main of our present strength consists of officers, gentlemen of quality, and their attendents, unmeet for those duties which are expected and required; and the loss of any of them is not small, but involves in it such multitudes as may, by their power and respect, be raised, if they once approach their own habitations. . . .'[13]

Langdale probably organised the Northern Horse into two brigades, each of about 800 men. His own consisted of men from Yorkshire, Lancashire and Derbyshire, while the second, under Sir William Blakiston, included troops from Northumberland, Durham, Cumberland and Westmorland. Each brigade was formed into two divisions, themselves made up of two squadrons of about 200 men, sometimes including the remains of several regiments.[14]

THE MARCH TO THE NORTH

As the New Year of 1645 dawned, the Northerners, their confidence raised by a successful skirmish at Salisbury on Christmas Day, had not lost sight of their intention to liberate their homeland. In February, with Langdale's knowledge if not at his instigation, a number of his senior officers submitted a petition to the King pointing out the value of the North to the Royalist cause and the need to relieve the dwindling number of garrisons still holding out there, principally Carlisle and Pontefract Castle, and asked leave 'to march to the North, where we are constantly resolved to adventure our dearest blood'.[15] Prince Rupert, anxious to avenge his defeat at Marston Moor, was sympathetic, especially as the alternative might be the disintegration of Langdale's force. But the Northern Horse would be needed when the Oxford Army took the field in the spring. In the end, a compromise was reached whereby Langdale was allowed to march to the relief of Pontefract, under increasing pressure from the Parliamentarian army of the Northern Association, under Ferdinando, Lord Fairfax, provided they rejoined Rupert immediately afterwards.

Pontefract Castle was of considerable strategic importance, guarding the crossing of the River Aire on the main route from the South into the Vale of York. The situation seemed ripe with potential for the Royalists, for the Parliamentarians felt that their hold on the North was far from secure and (with the dwindling Scots army still tied up with the siege of Carlisle) the only troops available were those under Lord Fairfax, currently being reorganised. But Sir Marmaduke faced a formidable task. Pontefract lay over 200 miles north of his quarters at Salisbury, and his small force of around 1,500 men would have to penetrate deep into enemy territory. Speed and secrecy were essential, and neither dependants nor baggage could be taken along. Langdale's troopers would have to forage for themselves and their horses along the line of march.

Langdale set off about 20 February. Initially, he passed through relatively secure Royalist territory but beyond Banbury, which he reached on 23 February, Sir Marmaduke had to be ready for action at any time. He was temporarily reinforced by 300 horse from the Banbury garrison, and the march resumed.

Contemporary military writers provided much advice on conducting an advance into enemy territory. John Cruso recommended that guides be employed from among the local population, 'which may be able to give certain and particular information concerning the high-wayes and cross wayes, how many there be of them, whether they be even, large and free, or streight [narrow], hilly, or impeached with difficult passages. Also concerning ditches, and rivers, whether there be bridges or not.'[16] Knowledge of enemy intentions and movements was vital:

Every good commander must have these two grounds for his actions: 1. The knowledge of his own forces, and wants (knowing that the enemie may have notice of thereof and therefore must be alwayes be studyinge for remedies, if the enemye should come suddainly upon him). 2. The assurance of the condition and estate of the enemie, his commodities and necessities, his counsels and designs, thereby begatting divers occasions, which afterwards may bring forth victories.[17]

For this reason Cruso advocated use of both spies and scouts, or 'discoverers', which must be sent out, 'not onely by the direct way, where the enemie is like to come, or you are to march, but to scoure all the by wayes on either side . . .'. These were to be 'choice men, valiant, vigilant and discreet'.[18] On the whole, Langdale was served well by his 'discoverers' during the following days.

An initial success came within hours of leaving Banbury, when the Royalists routed some local Parliamentarian horse near Flore in Northamptonshire. Langdale would have been encouraged had he known that the enemy remained ignorant of his true intentions. Not until 26 February was Sir Samuel Luke, Parliamentarian Governor of Newport Pagnell and principal orchestrator of intelligence operations in the area, able to report that 'Those forces which went from Banbury towards Newark prove to be the broken forces belonging to the Earl of Newcastle which have wintered near Salisbury [and] which are to recruit themselves in the North and relieve those places in danger by our forces.'[19] Luke had grasped the essentials of the Royalist plan, but very little time remained to counter it.

Detaching the Banbury forces, Langdale pressed on through Monday 24 February without sight of the enemy. That night the Northern Horse reached Market Harborough in Leicestershire, where Langdale received reports that the Parliamentarian East Midlands Horse under Colonel Edward Rossiter were preparing to contest his passage. Details remained unclear until the following evening when, as one of Langdale's commanders, Sir Gameliel Dudley, reported: 'Marching from Harborough towards Melton Mowbray, we were of full assured, for approaching neare the Towne we discovered some Horse and Dragoones in it, and upon another passe of the water in a faire Meade, about halfe a mile from the Towne, theire maine strengthe (as we judged them) beinge near 2000 in all, were drawne up to oppose us at the passage, being a place of very great advantage. . . .'[20] Accounts of the action that followed are contradictory; the Parliamentarians had some initial success before being overwhelmed by the Royalist reserves and driven back through the town in confusion. Rossiter withdrew to lick his wounds. He had failed to halt Langdale, and 'they are now on their march to Newark, and some think they intend for Pontefract, others think for the Association'.[21]

Even though they had already marched '15 long dirty miles' that day, Langdale urged his tired troopers on through the night. Next day they pushed on 4 miles beyond Newark, from where Langdale was reinforced by 400 horse and 400 foot. All this time the Northern Horse were living off the countryside, and Parliamentarian reports are filled with allegations of their atrocities, including torture, murder and rape.[22] Although doubtless exaggerated for propaganda purposes, it seems likely that they were founded on a basis of truth. Any civilian unfortunate enough to encounter Langdale's embittered followers could expect rough treatment.

The Parliamentarians remained in doubt as to the Royalist intentions and this hindered their countermoves. As late as 2 March Luke was writing to Sir William Brereton, Parliament's commander in Cheshire: 'Last week there passed by 2000 horse under Sir Marmaduke Langdale which must join those coming towards you, but whether they come to the enemyes' forces in your country or they in your country must go to them, I cannot yet determine.'[23] Among those anxiously sifting through reports of Langdale's progress were the Parliamentarian commanders besieging Pontefract Castle. For several days it seemed most likely that the Eastern Association was the Royalist objective, and although he took the precaution of pulling back his heavy siege guns, Lord Fairfax (himself in York) did not suspect immediate danger.

On the evening of the next day, Friday 28 February, Langdale arrived in Doncaster. Despite a slight advantage in numbers, the Parliamentarian forces at Pontefract, commanded by Commissary General John Lambert, were ordered by Lord Fairfax to stand on the defensive until reinforcements arrived. But Langdale was resolved to waste no time. Early on 1 March he resumed his advance, and prepared for action, warning his men 'of the difficulties they could expect this day to encounter with, and therefore to go armed with the constancy of undoubted resolution, it being a business that was at first no less dangerous to undertake than it was desperate to decline. The news was entertained by a welcome from the Soldiers that echoed aloud their joyful acclamation.'[24]

As the Royalists approached the crossing of the River Went, the last major barrier before Pontefract, at Wentbridge, they were briefly opposed by a 'forlorn hope' of enemy horse and dragoons, but after a confused engagement near the village of Darrington the enemy retired. Aiming to link up with the Pontefract garrison, Langdale left the main road at Darrington, and cut across country over the large open West and Carleton Fields, and some smaller enclosures known as the Upper Taythes.

THE RELIEF OF PONTEFRACT

Lambert's main force was drawn up on the south side of the Taythes, on an area of common land, the Chequerfields, with enclosures on its fringes, which lay between the townships of Carleton and Pontefract. The Parliamentarians had a small brook to their rear and rising ground to their front, and were probably deployed with their horse in the centre, and their foot (evidently mostly musketeers) and dragoons stationed in the hedgerows to their rear and right. Lambert's horse were still disordered by the fighting retreat that many of them had made from Wentbridge. It was probably about 5 p.m. when Langdale's leading troopers, in the words of Sir Gameliel Dudley 'gained the Top of the Hill over against the Castle, their [the Parliamentarians'] Army standing all drawne up at the bottom, and now me thought we viewed them with the fancy of that great Captaine when he first encountered Elephants: *Tandem par animis perculum video*'.[25]

There were two generally accepted ways to fight a cavalry action. The first was for a commander to deploy all of his troops fully before engaging in a 'united or grosse body'.[26] The alternative was a series of attacks by individual troops, a difficult operation to coordinate. As John Vernon explained, 'You must always appoint troops of Reserve, which are not by any meanes to engage themselves in fight till the first Troops have given the charge, and are reassembled behind them to make readie for the second charge.'[27] Langdale seems to have chosen the second method, mainly because he wanted to take advantage of the temporary confusion in the enemy ranks:

> A good advantage was it to us, that our Forlorn parties, seconded with severall divisions of our Horse, had beaten in that great body of their Van Curriers in such disorder into their Main Battaile as taking that opportunity with a continued charge they had not the time to recover themselves into any settled order, and though the suddainesses of the Action gave not leave for each Division of our Horse to observe its proper time and place for their severall orders to charge in, yet the whole of it was so fully done, as that there was not one body of them all, but did four or five severall times that day act their parts with very gallant Execution.[28]

Fighting continued for about three hours, the initial Royalist attack checked by heavy fire from the musketeers stationed in the hedges. The brunt of the action was borne on the Royalist side by about 400 horse, probably Langdale's 'reformado' unit, and his own regiment. Dudley added that by the end of the day 'no more than three small Bodies consisting of above 120 in each Bodie which with some Officers and Gentlemen together rally'd gave a seasonable Charge to the last of the Enemie's strength'.[29]

A vital role in breaking Parliamentarian resistance was played by about 100 musketeers from the Pontefract garrison who made a sally against the rear of the Parliamentarian foot who had been holding up Langdale's advance. Lambert's Regiment of Horse collapsed, probably after its commander was wounded, and was followed in rapid succession by the remainder of the Parliamentarian units. They fell back in increasing disorder towards Ferrybridge. Here the pursuit was temporarily checked by dragoons with an 'iron' gun, who attempted to hold the bridge, but they were quickly broken and the chase continued until nightfall.

Estimates of casualties differ widely. The Parliamentarians probably lost about 800 to 1,000 men, plus a large quantity of arms, ammunition and colours. Exact Royalist losses are unknown, but were relatively light. Langdale informed Prince Rupert in a despatch that night that the Pontefract operation had been 'prosperous beyond expectation'.[30] Not only had Lord Fairfax's army been dealt a severe blow, but enough supplies were brought into Pontefract Castle to enable it to hold out until July.

It is tempting to speculate on what the Northern Horse might have achieved if they had been allowed to consolidate their victory. While it is unlikely that Langdale could have reversed the decision of Marston Moor, a revitalised Royalist presence in the North might have transformed the summer's campaigning. In the event, Langdale had no option but to follow his orders and rejoin Rupert on the Welsh Border as quickly as possible. The Northern Horse had won their greatest victory. Henceforward, their story would be one of steadily increasing misfortune. Semi-mutinous as a result of the King's decision to abandon his proposed march North, they were overwhelmed, though fighting bravely, by Cromwell's superior numbers at Naseby in June and, after initial success, suffered another defeat in September at Rowton Heath.

The end of the Northern Horse as an effective fighting force came in October. Making a forlorn bid to join Montrose in Scotland, the last irreconcilable Northern troopers were broken in a fiercely contested action at Shirburn, ironically only 10 miles from the scene of their greatest triumph at Pontefract. A Parliamentarian officer, describing the prisoners taken on that occasion, captures the spirit of the Northern Horse:

> Some of the private soldiers I have taken into service, others that were pressed men I have discharged, and there remains about one hundred and fifty that I believe will never change their partie so long as they live. They are most of them troopers that have been in the same service formerly with the gentlemen that are prisoners. Whensoever they are sett at libertie it will be an addicion of so many stout desperate men to the enemies' strength.[31]

SIXTEEN

SIEGE: LORD JOHN BYRON AND THE DEFENCE OF CHESTER, 1645–6

'. . . for these poor means I have to maintain this place, you may be assured I shall improve them to the utmost, and how unfortunate soever I may be, you shall have an account of my charge befitting an honest man and one whom I hope you will not blush to own.'

Lord John Byron to Lord George Digby,
26 April 1645

Less well known than the great set-piece battles, the numerous sieges of the Civil War were equally far-reaching in their effects.

The main uses of garrisons were to deny key strategic points to an enemy and to control essential resources. They served as bases for intelligence, supply and revenue gathering, and to deny the same to the enemy. As the war went on, the garrison system grew more complex, with the development of 'fortified regions' such as that around Oxford, in which a number of smaller garrisons formed a fortified perimeter around a key strategic point. Garrisons could exert considerable influence. Even the smallest outpost with a troop of horse could make its presence felt over a 20-mile radius, and its demands on the local population could only be countered by the enemy setting up its own garrison as close as possible. The unfortunate local inhabitants frequently suffered from the exactions of both sides instead of just one. Garrisons were frequently criticised for eating up manpower. This was not a feature unique to the English Civil War. In 1632, for example, it has been estimated that 52 per cent of the army of Gustavus Adolphus was on garrison duty in Germany or the other Swedish possessions.

Although both sides maintained large numbers of garrisons, the Royalists made more use of them than the Parliamentarians. Parliament had largely undisputed control of London and much of eastern England, where garrisoning could be kept to a minimum. The Royalists were less fortunate. Very little of their territory was free from the threat of either attack or raids from isolated enemy bases such as Hull, Plymouth and Gloucester. As a result, the King was forced to maintain considerable numbers of garrisons in areas theoretically outside the main areas of fighting, such as Cornwall and Herefordshire, as well as in the great swathe of disputed land across the Midlands.

It is impossible to calculate how many garrisons the Royalists had at different stages of the war, still less how many troops they required. But figures for the spring of 1645, even after the King had lost control of much of the North, suggest that he still had upwards of 100 strong-points of all sizes, held by perhaps 20,000 men, a third of the military manpower theoretically available to him.[1] Yet, despite the criticisms sometimes levelled, it is difficult to see how these numbers could have been significantly reduced without threatening the whole of the Royalist war effort.

The destruction of the main Royalist field army at Naseby allowed the Parliamentarians to commence the long operation, lasting for over a year, of 'mopping up' the Royalist garrisons. Between Naseby and March 1647, some eighty-seven Royalist strongholds, containing over 20,000 men, surrendered or were captured.[2] These varied considerably both in their importance and their resistance. Some, such as Bristol, Bridgwater and Basing, were stormed with sometimes bloody consequences for their defenders. Others, like Lichfield and Raglan, were bombarded into submission or, like Beeston and Pendennis Castles, were starved into surrender. Particularly as the futility of further resistance became apparent, some yielded more or less tamely. Worcester put up a spirited resistance, mainly so that its Governor, the ruthless Henry Washington, could enhance his reputation in order to obtain employment abroad, but the greatest fortress of all, Oxford, fell surprisingly quickly. The longest and most fiercely maintained defence of any Royalist stronghold was at Chester, and exemplifies many of the features of siege warfare, its effect upon a civilian population under attack, and the influence of determined, ruthless and resolute leadership.

'A PLACE OF GREAT IMPORTANCE'

Chester's strategic location, on the main routes into North Wales and along the coast of north-west England, had been recognised since Roman times, and its fortifications had been developed further by medieval rulers. Chester had grown in importance as a port and, despite the silting up of the River Dee, its links with Ireland were of paramount importance to a King who increasingly hoped for military aid from that quarter.

In 1642 Chester was a compact city; the majority of its 8,000 inhabitants still lived within the confines of the medieval walls, though suburbs had grown up beyond them, especially to the north and east. Protected by its walls and the natural barriers of the Dee and its marshes, Chester was the ecclesiastical, economic and political centre for a wide area of Cheshire and North Wales. Its civic government, effectively in the hands of a small oligarchy of Aldermen known collectively as the 'Bretheren', had built up privileges and trading monopolies that they were determined to preserve. It has been claimed that Chester became Royalist primarily as a result of the manoeuvrings of this small group of Aldermen.[3] While there is some truth in this, feeling in Chester tended to favour the King, though there was, as elsewhere, a strongly neutralist element.[4] King Charles was quick to appreciate the importance of Chester and took prompt action in September 1642, visiting the town to ensure the election as mayor of the pro-Royalist William Ince.[5]

While initially having to tread carefully because of remaining neutralist feelings, the pro-Royalist faction in Chester, headed by the brothers William and Francis Gamull, leading merchants and employers in the city, and the influential Holme family, strengthened their hold. In March 1643 Francis Gamull was commissioned as colonel of a regiment of foot, intended for the defence of the city. Though in theory consisting of volunteers, the rank and file of the regiment were the employees of the Chester merchant families, and nearby gentry made up the bulk of the officers. The unit, eventually about 800 strong, was as much an instrument to ensure the 'Bretheren's' control of Chester as a defence force.[6]

The deterioration of the Royalist position in Cheshire in the opening months of 1643 increased the threat to Chester. Troops from North Wales strengthened the garrison, and an experienced soldier, Colonel Robert Ellice, was employed to lay out a system of outworks to protect the suburbs of the city. The defences, with earth ramparts and ditches linking a series of mounts or forts, followed the prevailing Dutch school of military engineering.[7] Their main weakness, never fully overcome despite several later revisions, was that, in deference to pressure from the citizens to protect their property, they were too extensive to man with the forces available.

In February Sir Nicholas Byron, a career soldier provided by the King at the request of the Chester Assembly, was appointed as Governor of the city. The role of Governor requires some explanation. Though many contemporary military manuals dealt in some detail with his responsibilities, in practice the powers of a Governor, particularly in a situation like Chester's where the civil authorities were fiercely jealous of their privileges, were neither well defined nor undisputed. All military units in a garrison, and measures relating to its defence, came under the control of its Governor. Most Governors acted to a greater or lesser extent through the civil authorities, without whose cooperation effective control was difficult. In practice, a great deal depended upon the personality of the individual Governor and the circumstances in which he was acting. Obviously, a town under actual or imminent threat of attack was under much tighter military control than it would have otherwise been. Chester had, in general, poor relations with its Governors, civilian and military interests coming into frequent conflict. Sir Nicholas Byron, partly no doubt because he was employed by the

Assembly, was initially less resented, though as military pressure mounted he eventually felt his anomalous situation untenable.[8]

Chester was regarded by the local Parliamentarian leader, Sir William Brereton, as too strong for his small forces to attack directly. In June he warned the Speaker of the House of Commons that 'The fortifications are as strong as the judgement and the art of those men that command there can contrive them. . . .'[9]

THE 'LEAGUER' BEGINS

Though Brereton overestimated Chester's strength, he was unable to mount a serious attack for almost eighteen months. A crisis occasioned by the Parliamentarian invasion of north-east Wales in November 1643 was averted by the arrival of the English forces from Ireland. However unwelcome their presence became to the citizens of Chester, the arrival of these troops meant that the city faced no serious danger of attack until the general deterioration of the Royalist position along the Welsh Border following their defeats at Marston Moor and Montgomery. In November 1644 Sir William Brereton made the first moves towards establishing a blockade of Chester by setting up several fortified outposts on the English side of the city.

In January 1645 the then Governor, Will Legge, was recalled to Oxford, and was soon afterwards replaced by Lord Byron. John, Lord Byron played the leading role in the defence of Chester for the remainder of the war, and has a strong claim to be the greatest of the King's Governors. The Byron family, of Newstead Abbey, Nottinghamshire, owed their original prosperity to coal-mining interests in that county and in Lancashire. Sir John (as he then was) appears to have been heavily in debt on the outbreak of war. Born in 1603, Byron had seen service on the Continent, and by 1642 was regarded as a committed supporter of the King. Clarendon described him as 'a person of a very ancient family, an honourable extraction, good fortune, and as unblemished a reputation as any gentleman in England'.[10] Given command of the first regiment of horse to be completed, Byron earned a respectable reputation as a cavalry commander, notably for his roles at Roundway Down and First Newbury, for which he was awarded his peerage.

Sent north to take charge of the forces from Ireland, Byron had a chequered record in higher command. Defeated at Nantwich, blamed by many for the disaster at Marston Moor, and suffering another crushing reverse at Montgomery,[11] Byron, a fiercely ambitious man, must have regarded the command at Chester as being his last opportunity to retrieve his fortunes. He would find there a stage ideally suited to his talents. Though quarrelsome, tactless, and at times heavy-handed, with all the intolerance for civilians of one who regarded himself first and foremost as a soldier, Byron had undeniable qualities of determination, resourcefulness, and ruthlessness, as well as an ability to win the loyalty of his soldiers, which would prove vital in the months to come.

Brereton's initial efforts to starve Chester into surrender were twice frustrated in the first half of 1645 by rescue operations mounted by the Royalist high command. The relief of the city was a major consideration in the planning of the Naseby Campaign. Though complaining bitterly that Prince Rupert (with whom, after Marston Moor, he was on increasingly bad terms) had drawn off most of his best men, forcing him to replace them with raw Welsh troops, Byron had not so far been seriously threatened.[12]

CHESTER SURPRISED

But the Royalist defeat at Naseby changed everything. With prospects of relief greatly reduced, the Cheshire Parliamentarians could at last concentrate their efforts against Chester. Initially, however, they received little encouragement from Parliament, and Byron spent the summer months in frantic attempts to secure further support from the King and the Commissioners of Array in North Wales. Despite many frustrations, he had some success,[13] but at considerable cost.

Under the terms of the Self-Denying Ordinance, Sir William Brereton had been removed from command of the Parliamentarian Cheshire forces and control was now vested in the County Committee and their professional officers, Michael Jones and James Lothian. They had been distracted by the King's movements for most of the summer and, in consequence, especially during Byron's absence, vigilance in Chester – for the moment almost entirely garrisoned by the City Regiment under the Deputy Governor, Sir Francis Gamull – had perhaps grown slack.[14] In the early hours of 20 September, under cover of darkness, a picked force of Parliamentarian troops were able to approach the over-extended and inadequately manned outworks of the city, seize one of the mounts and, amid growing panic among the defenders, occupy most of the suburbs, forcing the garrison back into the final redoubt of the old city within its medieval walls. Byron arrived back hot-foot to scenes of confusion and despair: 'I found all things in such confusion that had the Rebels attempted it, they might have carried the City as well as the Suburbs, For though all the City were in arms yet knew they not how to dispose of them or in what place to use them to best advantage, but ranged up and down the streets in promiscuous bodies, and would fain have done something, but knew not how to go about it. . . .'[15]

It was largely due to Byron's energy that the immediate crisis was overcome. He called together his officers, and the mayor, Charles Whalley, appointed commanders for the various posts and ordered Whalley to collect tools and equipment for work on strengthening the inner defences by backing the vulnerable sandstone walls with a rampart of earth to reduce the effects of bombardment. He also secured the services of 'three desperate fellows' (possibly soldiers from his own largely native Irish Regiment of Foot) to burn the buildings in the suburbs that offered cover to the besiegers. The latter had been surprised by the extent of their success, and had to bring up two or three heavy guns, as well as send out urgent pleas for reinforcements, before commencing their attack on the city proper. During the night of 20 September and throughout the following day 'the whole city, big with expectation of a sudden storm, stand armed for a brave resistance'.[16]

The Parliamentarian artillery commenced their bombardment at noon on 22 September. United by fear of the consequences of an assault as much as by loyalty to a cause, the citizens made feverish efforts to repair the breach in the friable sandstone walls caused by the bombardment. Byron related:

they fell to work, seeing the shot fall so fast. . . . I must not forget the diligence of one [Randle] Holme an alderman of the city, who brought woolpacks and featherbeds from all parts of the town to stop up the breach which with great industry and pains was made defensible against their battery. So that towards the town side it was very high and precipitous: but on the battery side towards the Enemy was made so flat by reason of the crumbling of the soft stone, and so wide, that six horses might have marcht up in ranck.[17]

The bombardment ceased at about 4 p.m., after thirty-two shots had been fired, when the breach created near the New Gate was some 25 feet in extent. Byron rejected a summons to surrender and, around 8 p.m., after dusk though with a 'faire moonshine', the Parliamentarian assault began. The attack was spearheaded by the firelock companies of Captains Gimbart and Finch, including a number of former Royalist soldiers from Ireland who had changed sides after being captured at Nantwich. Byron wrote that they advanced;

> with great boldnesse, but were received with as much courage by Sergeant Major Thropp's men [of Gamull's Regiment]. . . . Those in the Newgate and in the houses adjoining to the breach, annoyed the Enemy with their Shot, so did the granadoes and the firepikes, which were used by very stout men, and placed upon the flanks of the breach. Captain Crosby (who commanded the Chirk horse) did good service there, and the Rebels pressed on so resolutely that I caused more forces to be drawn down to assist Major Thropp's men. Thrice that night the Enemy was upon the top of the wall, but at last quite beaten off, seven of them were killed upon the top of the wall, who afterwards fell into the Street, and were the next day buried by us.[18]

The attackers, fortified by drinking a mixture of aqua vitae and gunpowder, pressed the garrison severely but were forced back by Crosby and his lieutenant, their dismounted troopers fighting with sword and pistol at the top of the breach. A secondary attack further along the walls failed because the Parliamentarians' scaling ladders were too short, and their assault troops did not receive proper support from their reserves, although the Parliamentarians admitted that 'if five hundred of them had entered, they had all been cut off, they were so ready and well-provided in the city'.[19]

By dawn the immediate crisis was over. At the cost of nine Royalist dead, and an unknown number of the enemy, the assault had been repulsed. But Byron had gained only a temporary respite, and it was with delight that he learnt that evening of the approach of King Charles and 3,500 horse. However, on 26 September the attempt by the Royalists to trap the besiegers ended in disaster at the Battle of Rowton Heath, when they were themselves caught between the Cheshire forces and the army under General Poyntz, and suffered heavy losses.

THE GREAT ASSAULT

Although the King had afforded Byron some temporary relief and had enabled him to bring into Chester another regiment of foot under Hugh Wynne, the long-term prospects were bleak. On his own estimate, Byron had to feed a population swollen by refugees to about 17,000, as well as his garrison, who were few enough. They consisted of about 800 of Gamull's men, of whose loyalty Byron harboured grave suspicions, 100 Irish soldiers of his own foot regiment, 200 of Roger Mostyn's and the 500 newcomers of Hugh Wynne's.

Byron resolved to hold out for as long as possible, for he reasoned that he was occupying enemy forces that would otherwise be used elsewhere and, bearing in mind George Monck's maxim that 'sieges ruin armies',[20] that he was inflicting severe losses on them in the process. He also hoped that either Sir William Vaughan's brigade, left by the King with orders to assist him, or the promised troops from Ireland would come to his relief. Byron called together the military and civilian leadership to concert defence measures, finance and the control of food supplies. He met with a mixed response. The mayor pointed out that most of the food stocks in the town were in private hands and could not be administered centrally without danger of a mutiny. Accommodation for the soldiers, in a city already packed with refugees, was scarce, and many of the Welsh troops had to be billeted in a large schoolhouse with 'hardly straw enough to lie on'.[21]

Temporarily reinforced by Poyntz, the besiegers were anxious to complete the reduction of Chester before relief could be organised. Probably they also hoped to gain the credit for its capture before the imminent resumption of command by Sir William Brereton, personally unpopular with a number of his colleagues. A desultory bombardment of the city was resumed the day after Rowton Heath, countered by frequent sallies by the garrison in attempts to disrupt construction of siege lines. The besiegers brought up four additional guns from Stafford and Shrewsbury, including 'a greate brasse piece of ordnance',[22] and in the early days of October intensified their bombardment, aiming both at the old breach near the New Gate and at a stretch of wall on the northern side of the city. The citizens' determination to resist was undoubtedly strengthened by fears of their fate at the hands of Poyntz's men in the event of a successful assault, for they were likely to be less merciful than the local Cheshire forces. Working alongside his officers and gentlemen, Byron set an example in efforts to shore up the walls with an earth rampart, 'which afterwards the Ladies and Gentlewomen gave in their own persons, by carrying earth themselves to the works'.[23] Stores of mattresses and woolpacks were prepared at strategic points to fill any breaches,[24] and on 9 October Byron rejected a final summons in which Poyntz threatened to submit Chester to 'the fury of enraged soldiers'.[25]

The Parliamentarians immediately opened a heavy bombardment, firing some 400 shots. An additional breach was made on the north side of the walls near the Goblin Tower and, a little before sunset, at about 4 p.m., the Parliamentarians;

> began to storm the Town at both Breaches, and to scale the walls on all parts (but upon the Rood-eye, where the river hindered them) with great resolution. At the breach (near the Goblin's Tower which afterwards went by the name of the new breach) Colonel George Vane[26] commanded, and Sir Edmund Verney[27] at the Newgate, which we called the old

breach . . . To Monsieur St Paul,[28] I [Byron] gave command of the horse that day, which he discharged with much honour and gallantry. Myself, with some Gentlemen with me, rode about the walls continually, from one guard to another, both to encourage the soldiers, and see such things supplied as were wanting in any place. The Enemy stormed the new breach with great disadvantage, having both a very steep bank to ascend, and when they were got up, a precipice to come down, and withall were flanked by two towers (the Goblin's Tower on the one hand and the New Tower on the other), from whence our musketeers were not sparing of their shot, besides they were to march over a plain ground without any shelter before they came to the breach. Notwithstanding all which disadvantages they both assaulted it and brought their ladders to the wall, and began to scale with a great fury. The line was filled with halberdiers where I had likewise caused heaps of stones to be laid in convenient distances, which when the Enemy came under the walls, did more execution than muskets could have done, the shot [musketeers] was placed upon the flankers of the wall, where it was most useful. Our men for a good space were at handy blows with them upon the top of the wall. The Enemy (as fast as their ladders were thrown down and their men knocked off) rearing up others in their stead, and bringing up fresh supplies.[29]

In the course of this bitter fighting 'my Lorde St Paule (almost as naked as his sword) ran rageinge in his shirt, up to the north breach, where the enemy prest extremely for an entrance, but were by him so bravely back't that sudden death denyes them tyme to call for quarter. Others who escaped the like condition were glad to use their heels.'[30] St Pol's state of undress has been the subject of speculation, but was probably the result of his stripping to his white shirt for ease of recognition by his men in the gathering darkness.

Byron resumes the story.

At the same time the Storm was begun in all other places, but at the Newgate (where Sir Edmund Verney commanded) continued not long, the breach there not being assaultable, and the wall too high for their ladders. So that (finding a few men would defend that place) I drew the greatest part of them to the Phoenix and Saddler's Towers, being but low and without any ditch, and the approach secured by walls and houses, within less than Carbine shot of the walls of the City, so that there the business was very hotly disputed. But at length, it pleased God that both here and in all places they were beaten off, and forced to leave their ladders behind them, whereof a great number with a good proportion of arms were brought into the Town. The days were then short and the darkness of the night saved many of their lives.[31]

Even Byron paid tribute to the efforts of the citizens:

I must not forget the great courage and gallantrye the Chester women expressed that day, who all the time the cannon played upon the new breach (whereof two were whole Culverin, and the other two pieces of 36 pound ball, besides these smaller pieces that flancked the breach from Brewer's Hall . . .), carried both Earth and feather beds, and other materials incessantly, and made up the breach in the very mouth of the cannon. And though eight or ten of them at the least, were killed and spoiled with great shot, yet the rest were nothing at all dismayed, but followed on their work, with as great alacrity and as little fear as if they had been going to milk their cows.[32]

Another eyewitness, Randle Holme, wrote more floridly: 'By this tyme our women are all on fire, striving through a gallant emulation to outdoe our men and will make good our yielding walls or loose their lives. Some are shot and three slain, yet they scorn to leave their undertaking, and this they continue for ten days space.'[33] The failure of the great assault, which arguably was an unnecessary gamble in the first place, was a serious setback for the Parliamentarians. It cost them over a hundred casualties, more than twice as many as the defenders, whose morale was greatly boosted by their success.

This was the last attempt to carry Chester by direct assault. The siege would obviously now be prolonged, as the Royalists, despite an ammunition shortage that Byron kept 'as a great and sad secret to myself' until he was able to improvise means of providing new supplies, made numerous and vigorous sallies to disrupt enemy activities. Intercepted letters from Welsh soldiers in Chester to friends and relatives at home suggest that morale remained high well into October. Buoyed by rumours of Royalist victories elsewhere (possibly deliberately 'planted' by Byron and his officers), Hugh Wynne reported '. . . we keep very good and constant guard, our men are very cheerful, and so be the townsmen, emulating one another who shall do the best service'.[34] But a common soldier, Rinald David, was less sanguine, complaining that 'I do stand in great want, for there is nothing to be had here without money, and God knows our allowance is very small.'[35]

Chester's most implacable foe, Sir William Brereton, now resumed command of the besiegers. Byron, scathingly but not inaccurately, summed up the situation that Brereton found: 'Matter of danger (which Sir Will. Brereton never greatly loved), was then pretty well past; and the King having no army in the field, nor likely to have any in haste: industry and patience he knew (wherein few excell him) must in time carry that City which had ever been his chiefest aim.'[36]

Royalist hopes were now pinned on the relief expedition that Sir William Vaughan had been charged with organising, using troops drawn from the garrisons along the Welsh Border. Despite some momentary alarm among the besiegers, there was never any real prospect of Vaughan succeeding, and on 1 November his forces were dispersed in an action near Denbigh.

FIRE AND FAMINE

Significantly, the first trickle of deserters from Chester had now begun. They painted a situation within the walls perhaps more gloomy than the reality yet was, with the Welsh 'who beg all their meat and are almost famished, and both soldiers and citizens in daily discontent'.[37] Brereton was facing problems of his own, with disruption from continuing Royalist sallies aggravated by mutinies among his unpaid men and 'the extreme foul weather – which is so violent that our men cannot endure out of doors . . .'.[38] But Sir William now brought a powerful new weapon into play. The Shropshire Parliamentarian Committee sent him their mortar and a small amount of ammunition. Firing incendiaries, the inaccuracy of mortar fire was more than compensated for by the damage it could inflict in the closely packed, mainly timber dwellings of the old city of Chester.

Byron organised countermeasures, placing watchers on key vantage points to report the fall of shells, and ordering each household to maintain a tub of water outside its door to extinguish fires. But the nightly bombardments, forcing the civilian population to take sleepless refuge in their cellars, steadily sapped their determination and will to resist. A further blow came on 25 November, with the failure of a major sortie intended to destroy a bridge of boats that the besiegers had erected linking their forces on either bank of the Dee.

In the meantime, using 'stick and carrot' methods Brereton sent occasional summons into the city, promising generous terms to the citizens if they surrendered and, suspecting that Byron and other diehard Royalists concealed his offers from the population at large, fired copies over the walls by means of arrows. Yet on 28 November Sir William was forced to report to the Speaker that 'The besieged remain still very obstinate, and do not seem inclinable to embrace any overtures made for their own preservation. . . .'[39] But by early December Brereton was reporting that 'the better sort eat beef and bacon, but little cheese, . . . the poorer sort of the city that are not soldiers are ready to starve, they are compelled to eat horseflesh'.[40] Tightening the screw, the mortar bombardment, which had faltered because of shortage of ammunition, was resumed with, on the night of 10 December, dramatic effects, as described by Randle Holme:

eleven huge granadoes like so many tumbling demi-phaetons threaten to set the city, if not the world, on fire. This was a terrible night indeed, our houses like as many splitt vessels crash their supporters and burst themselves insunder through the very violence of these descending firebrands. The Talbott, an house adjoining to the Eastgate flames outright; our hands are busied in quenching this whilst the law of nature bids us leave and seek our own security. Being thus distracted another Thunder-cracke invites our eyes to the most miserable spectacle that spite could possibly present us with – two houses in the Watergate slippes joynt from joynt and creates an earthquake, the main posts jostell each other, whilst the frighted casements fly for feare, in a word the whole fabrick is a perfect chaos lively set forth in this metamorphosis. The grandmother, mother and three children are struck dead and buried in the ruins of this humble edifice, a spulcher well worth the enemie's remembrance.[41]

On the five succeeding nights the mortar hurled twenty-nine more granadoes into Chester, destroying or damaging numerous houses in Eastgate and Watergate Streets, and proving 'the greatest terror' to the inhabitants. Both sides were suffering from the increasingly bitter winter weather, while deserters reported that some of the Welsh soldiers had died for want of food and the remainder were attempting to survive on a diet of 3d. a day's worth of bread boiled in beer.[42] Not surprisingly the soldiers were growing increasingly mutinous, despite Byron's assurances of imminent relief.

On 21 December, Lieutenant Philomen Mainwaring, a Parliamentarian prisoner in Chester, smuggled out a report to Brereton: 'The town is in great distress and the poor cry out daily in the streets for want of meat, desiring the Mayor and Lord Byron to turn them out of town. Thereupon Lord St Pol (on Saturday last) hearing them cry out so, found fault with them; their reply to him was; "thou French rogue, hold thy tongue. We must obey thy commands and be starved to death."'[43] A deserter added that the women, previously foremost in defying the enemy, 'gather themselves together every day crying out for relief to the governor and the rest of the commanders'.[44] The consensus was that Chester could not hold out above a fortnight.

On 26 December, with the enemy bridge of boats temporarily severed by ice on the Dee, a party of 100 horse under a Dutch professional soldier, Major Cornelius De Wit, managed to slip into Chester, each trooper carrying a bag of meal on his saddle. But this relief was largely symbolic. In the new year Brereton resumed his persuasions to the citizens to yield on generous terms, and by now was apparently in secret communication with the mayor, Charles Whalley.

Byron responded curtly to Brereton's summons: 'Keep your foolishly senseless paper to yourselves and know there are none in this city such knaves or fooles to be deluded thereby.'[45] He explained later: 'I thought it my duty to hold out the Town, as long as I could, though at the last I was sure to have the worse conditions, knowing that thereby I engaged an Army which (had it been at Liberty) was designed to pursue the King wheresoever he went, and therefore I turned a deaf ear to all notions of treaty though then I might have had almost any conditions I could demand.'[46] But, although a trickle of foodstuffs were still being smuggled into Chester for those able to afford the high prices demanded, the majority of the thousands of people crammed within its walls were facing growing hunger if not starvation. Brereton's notes described the reports he received. 'Cannot hold out a fortnight – so many will be starved. . . . Divers Welsh are dead from hunger. No drink to be bought nor any bread but what is got away by soldiers very early in the morning and all the day none can be bought. Five Welsh died last Saboth day, were starved, formerly there died twenty five in one week. . . .'[47] With time running out, Byron ordered a search for food to be made in every house in Chester.

SURRENDER

The results of Byron's search for food made grim reading; it was obvious that most households, some sheltering twenty or more people, had little or no corn left.[48] In an attempt to counter rumours by malcontents that 'the Governor and Commissioners were well provided for, Lord Byron and some of the Commissioners took opportunity severally to invite the Chief of the Malcontents to dine with them, and entertained them with boiled Wheat and gave 'em spring water to wash it down, solemnly assuring them that this and such like had been their Fare for some time past'.[49] It is unlikely this had any effect, for

Byron admitted that 'both citizens and soldiers now began to be very impatient and mutinous, and multitudes of women (who are ever first employed in seditious actions upon the privilege of their sex) daily flocked about my house with great clamours asking whether I intended they should eat their children since they had nothing else left to sustain themselves withall'.[50]

The citizens and most of the Assembly, apart from a few diehards such as Francis Gamull, were all now pressing him to seek terms, saying that 'he valued their lives less than a punctillo of honour'.[51] Byron had no option but to allow negotiations to begin on 15 January 1646, though, as he later admitted, 'Now that I was forced to begin a Treaty, all my study was how to spin it out as long as might be, to the end that if my Lord Astley really intended my relief, I might keep myself unengaged, until he had attempted it.'[52] There was in reality no sign of this happening. After the exchange of a good deal of fairly acrimonious correspondence between the two commanders, both well aware of the need to observe the formal niceties of surrendering a garrison, talks in earnest began on 29 January, and terms were agreed the following day, to take effect on 3 February.

Byron and his troops, including by tacit agreement the Irish soldiers of his own regiment, were allowed safe conduct to the garrisons still holding out in North Wales. Lord Byron felt that the conditions were 'for myself and the Officers with me . . . as good as in such an exigent I could expect, and those for the Citizens as ill as I could wish, their folly as well as knavery deserving no better'.[53] In fact, the city was spared from being plundered, and the rights and privileges of its inhabitants confirmed. Though Chester had suffered considerable damage to property and would shortly be struck by the ravages of plague, probably a consequence of the overcrowded conditions of the siege, its recovery during the following decade was surprisingly rapid.[54]

For Lord John Byron, dedicated Royalist, the by now hopeless fight went on in North Wales. He would eventually surrender at Caernarvon in June and, exempted from pardon, go into exile on the Continent. Though his career had ultimately ended in defeat, Byron, in his dogged defence of Chester in the longest 'leaguer' of the Civil Wars, had served his King well.

SEVENTEEN

ROYALIST WOMEN AT WAR

'Tell that insolent Rebell, he shall have neither persons, goodes
nor house . . . if the Providence of God prevent it not, my goodes
and house shall burne in his sight; myself, children and souldiers
will seale our religion and loyalty in the same flame . . .'

Charlotte la Tremoille, Countess of Derby in Edward
Seacombe, *History of the House of Stanley*, 1793, p. 242

The role of women in the mid-seventeenth century was a
subordinate one. They were still the 'Weaker Vessel', whose
primary duties were childbearing and obedience to their husband
or father. The events of 1642–60 brought no real change in
their status, but it was inevitable that in a civil war involving
virtually the whole of the British Isles women would be caught
up in a wide variety of ways.

Best known of the 'Royalist' women are, of course, Queen
Henrietta Maria, the 'grandee' wives such as Charlotte la
Tremoille, Countess of Derby and other well-publicised 'heroines'
like Lady Mary Banks, chatelaine of Corfe Castle, and Helen
Neale, defender of Hawarden Castle for her husband, Sir William.
Their exploits have been celebrated – and elaborated – in
contemporary propaganda and popular legend, and although
their roles are worthy of note, they unfairly overshadow the
many lesser-known women who found themselves caught up –
willingly or otherwise – in King Charles' war.[1]

216

'SHE-GENERALLISSIMA'

Henrietta Maria, the French-born wife of King Charles, is usually regarded as the epitome of Royalist womanhood. Following the death of the King's adored Duke of Buckingham in 1629, Henrietta Maria assumed a position of influence over her husband that soon extended into the political sphere. The Queen possessed considerable personal charisma, though hardly beauty in the orthodox sense. She was somewhat disloyally described in 1642 by her niece, Princess Sophia, as having 'long lean arms, crooked shoulders, and teeth protruding from her mouth like guns from a fort'.

As tensions rose between the King and his opponents, the Queen was a leading proponent of a 'hard-line' policy, urging her husband to stand firm and surrender none of his prerogatives. As a result of this, and her openly practised Roman Catholicism, she became increasingly a target of the Parliamentary opposition and it was partly with his wife's personal safety in mind that, in February 1642, King Charles despatched her to Holland with his daughter Mary, newly married to William of Orange.

However, of at least equal importance was Henrietta Maria's 'covert' role of marshalling foreign support for her husband, notably in the purchase of munitions and recruiting professional soldiers to serve in the Royalist armies. In order to finance this operation, the Queen had taken with her to Holland both her own considerable personal collection of jewellery and a number of items from the 'royal' collection.[2] By April 1642 she had begun selling or pawning them. Unsurprisingly, the Queen and her agents found it difficult to obtain advantageous rates from financiers eager to take advantage of her poor bargaining position but, as discussed more fully elsewhere,[3] it is clear that Henrietta's activities gave a vital boost to Royalist arms supplies, without which the King would probably have found it impossible to maintain the fight beyond the summer of 1643. Many valuable officers, such as George Goring, James King, and Princes Rupert and Maurice and their entourage, made their way to England in the opening months of the war in order to serve in the Royalist forces. It is usually said that Henrietta played a major part in their recruitment, though Rupert and Maurice were already bound to the King by filial ties, and most of the others would have in any case have entered Charles' service.

As well as seeking to stiffen her husband's resolve by a stream of entreaties, pleas and threats not to return, the Queen also had a considerable influence on Royalist strategy during her absence. It was the need to protect Henrietta and her vast munitions convoy that caused the Earl of Newcastle to follow a relatively passive strategy during the opening months of the war. After her perilous disembarkation at Bridlington on 22 February, Henrietta Maria continued to influence Newcastle's actions, whose forces she seems in some sense to have regarded as 'her' army. It is unclear how much the Earl fell under the Queen's spell, or whether he was, in fact, exasperated and frustrated by the demands and limitations that her presence imposed on him. Certainly, the Queen did nothing to reduce the feelings of resentment and neglect that Newcastle laboured under, and throughout her stay in England she would continue to nurture his suspicions and encourage his unwillingness to cooperate with the Royalist forces in the South.

Equally difficult to assess is the influence Henrietta had on Royalist policy following her eventual reunion with King Charles in July 1643. She is generally credited with frustrating many of the objectives of Prince Rupert and his supporters and nurturing the rise of the 'courtier' faction of Lords Digby and Percy, but the Prince was well able to make enemies on his own account, and the resentment she aroused among others of the King's councillors was only one more thread in the tangle of intrigue and web of conflicting interest groups that made up the Royalist Court and command structure.

There is little real evidence that the Queen had any major input into military decision-making, apart from whatever effect her urgings on Newcastle may have had.[4] In any case, Henrietta's effective presence lasted for little more than six months. By the autumn of 1643 she was pregnant and suffering from increasing ill health. Her departure in the spring, first for the supposed security of the West Country and, when this proved illusory, to France, meant the end of Henrietta's day-to-day involvement in events, although her views on political questions, expressed in her copious correspondence, continued to reach the

King, and the publication of their captured letters after Naseby proved a major propaganda victory for Parliament.

CASTLES AND CHATELAINES

The tale of the defence of Lathom House in the spring of 1644 by Charlotte la Tremoille, lion-hearted consort of James, 7th Earl of Derby, is an English Civil War epic. So well established in the popular imagination is it, that it seems almost sacrilegious to question some elements of the legend. Aged about forty-one at the time of the siege, Lady Derby was described as 'a well-built, almost fleshy woman, having large eyes, heavy eyebrows and a prominent nose'. In character she was 'at once haughty and humble. She was pious, and would, out of pride, stubbornly hold to a cause which she regarded as her duty . . . and would look with contempt upon anyone who offended her code'; Charlotte la Tremoille was a very formidable individual. A member of one of the most powerful Huguenot families in France, and granddaughter of William the Silent, she had been involved in the hurly-burly of European political life since her earliest years. Indeed, she probably found the relatively confined provincial life of consort to the somewhat diffident James Stanley rather irksome, and apparently relished the role presented by the siege of Lathom House.

Charlotte proved a skilled and formidable negotiator, who more than held her own against the embarrassed Sir Thomas Fairfax and his Lancastrian Parliamentarian associates, and her presence during what was admittedly an extremely ineptly conducted siege was no doubt a considerable factor in strengthening the resistance of the garrison. Military operations were largely under the control of a Scottish professional soldier, Captain William Farmer, and the national strategic importance of Lathom House was fairly slight. Like most of the Royalist chatelaines, Lady Derby found herself caught up in a siege more as a result of circumstances (she had initially been left in the apparent safety of her husband's principal seat while he was campaigning elsewhere in Lancashire) than from intent, and there is nothing to suggest that she objected when Prince Rupert, on relieving Lathom in June 1644, required Lady Derby and her daughters to leave for the security of the Isle of Man, handing over the governorship of Lathom to a soldier.[5]

The situation at Lathom is closely paralleled by the story of Lady Mary Banks at Corfe Castle in Dorset. As with the other chatelaines, she had been left on the family estates while her husband was absent serving the King, and like them she recognised that her duty to her lord lay in protecting his interests by ensuring that the members of his household and garrison carried out his wishes. Also assisted by a professional soldier, a Captain Bond, Lady Banks held out with relative ease against an ineffectual assault and, like Lady Derby, when Corfe was again under threat later in the war she successfully applied for a pass to retire to London.[6]

Less well known is the case of Lady Helen Neale, defender of Hawarden Castle in 1645. Unusually among the chatelaines, Lady Helen was not protecting her husband's estates. Sir William Neale, younger son of a relatively minor Northamptonshire gentry family, had been scoutmaster to Prince Rupert before the Prince appointed him Governor of Hawarden, probably in February 1644. Like other 'landless' Royalist commanders, his charge provided accommodation for his wife and family and, as a result, in her husband's absence Lady Helen found herself nominally in charge of operations (with the assistance of the Deputy Governor, Captain Thomas Whitley) when Parliamentarian forces under Sir William Brereton unexpectedly laid siege to Hawarden in April 1645. Despite threats of mining, Lady Helen assured Sir William that 'though my mind is upon the rack betwixt hope and despair, I am purposed (God blessing me) to hold out as long as there is meat for man, for none of those eminent dangers shall ever frighten me from my loyalty, but in life and death I will be the king's faithful subject and thy constant loving wife'.[7] Lady Helen's ordeal was soon over when the mine failed to explode, and Hawarden was relieved by the approach of the main Royalist field army.

THE 'OTHER ARMY'

Though they have received by far the greatest attention, the chatelaines had among the easiest of the trials encountered by Royalist women. They generally continued to live in conditions of relative comfort, except in periods of intense attack, and could usually be sure of reasonable treatment even if they fell into enemy hands.[8] Far different were the experiences of the women of humbler origin who, in a wide range of roles and situations, followed the King's armies.

Easiest perhaps, in the sense of merely being in cramped quarters and threatened chiefly by disease rather than enemy action, were the lives of the wives and daughters of the King's officers and officials in Oxford and the other Royalist garrison towns. Eighteen-year-old Ann Fanshawe came to Oxford from a life that had hitherto been both privileged and secure:

> From as good houses as any gentlemen in England had we come to a baker's house in a narrow street, and from roomes well furnisht to lye in a very bad bed in a garrett, to one dish of meat and that not the best ordered; no money for we were as poor as Job, nor clothes more than a man or two brought in their cloak bags. We had the perpetual discourse of losing and gaining of towns and men; at the windows the sad spectacle of war, sometimes plague, sometimes sickness of other kind, by reason of so many people beeing packt together. . . .'[9]

A number of officers of the King's Lifeguard of Foot had their wives and families quartered with them in Oxford. When Lieutenant Abrie was killed, probably at the First Battle of Newbury, his wife was left as a widow in Oxford with two young children. Others lived in slightly more style; the wife of Captain Frank Windebanke, whose surrender of Bletchingdon House to Cromwell in April 1645 was partly occasioned by his concern for her safety, had two servants in their quarters at Oxford.[10] The wives of NCOs and common soldiers sometimes received official recognition. The Irish wives of some of the King's Lifeguard (very possibly of some of the Cheshiremen who had previously served with the forces in Ireland) were quartered in Oxford in 1643.[11]

It was quite unusual for those wives, particularly of officers, with permanent quarters to accompany their husbands in the field. Nevertheless, an army on the march could acquire a considerable number of women followers of one kind or another. Great trains of non-combatant followers were frowned upon by authority, which made spasmodic attempts to reduce their numbers, though with limited success. The problem seems to have afflicted the Royalists more than their opponents, partly perhaps because so many of their men were serving far from homes that might anyway be in enemy hands.

The exact status of many women camp followers is often in doubt. In August 1644 a Parliamentarian wrote of the Northern Horse as it marched south through Lancashire after Marston Moor that 'They carried along with them many strumpets, which they termed "Leaguer Ladies".[12] These they made use of in places where they lay in a very uncivill and unbecoming way . . .', while in 1642 Bulstrode Whitelocke said of Sir John Byron's Regiment of Horse that they 'had their whores with them'.[13] Yet the fact that in December 1644 items looted by the Northern Horse in Salisbury included clothing for both women and children perhaps suggests that at least some of these females were enjoying more regularised relationships.[14]

Similarly unclear is the standing of the Irishwomen captured by Sir Thomas Fairfax after his victory at Nantwich in January 1644. The Parliamentarian newsletters wrote in lurid terms of the 'Irish' having a 'Female Regiment . . . these were weaponed too; and when these degenerate into cruelty, there are none more bloody'. Among the prisoners were reported to be 120 Irishwomen 'of whom many had long knives with which they were said to have done much mischief'. The *True Informer* went so far as to claim that they were armed with 'great knives half a yard long', with which to cut the throats of prisoners and wounded, with a hook at the end 'made not only to stab but tear the flesh from the very bones'. The writer urged that the unfortunate women should be 'put to the sword or tied back to back and cast into the sea'.[15] Most of this was arrant nonsense, and Fairfax seems to have quietly released them.

Some women following the armies may have been legally married to their menfolk and accompanied them either from loyalty or because they and their husbands had been unemployed or homeless at the time of enlistment. Others may have followed a lover or, in the case of the Irishwomen, because the army was the only place in which they could find a precarious safety. But the army provided towards the upkeep of neither dependants nor widows. As a result, the latter in particular had to survive as best they could, usually by the time-honoured expedients of cooking, nursing, whoring or a quick remarriage. The Parliamentarians employed widows of their soldiers as nurses in their military hospitals, and it may be assumed that the Royalists followed the same practice. Others survived by looting the dead after a battle or by a variety of trades, including whoring (though this carried a range of penalties from being whipped and driven out of camp to mutilation, probably rarely imposed in the Royalist forces), as well as acting as victuallers, sutlers and laundresses.

The life of the women who followed the armies was at least as hard as that of the soldiers. They shared the same shortages of food and ravages of disease. Though documented instances of rape or other sexual assaults are surprisingly few (possibly because they were rarely reported), women were in particular danger in the aftermath of battle. The most notorious example was the fate of the women who fell into Parliamentarian hands during the pursuit after Naseby. About 500 'common Vermin' were captured attempting to flee on foot, including many 'Irish women, of cruel countenance some of them were cut by our soldiers when they took them . . .'. This was evidently at least in part revenge for the treatment meted out to Essex's foot after Lostwithiel, for a near-contemporary account relates that the Parliamentarian horse 'cut and slashed the women, with this sarcasm at every stroke, "Remember Cornwall, you whores!"', while the Parliamentarians themselves admitted that 'The Irish women Prince Rupert brought on the field (wives of the bloody Rebels in Ireland, his Majesties dearly beloved subjects) our soldiers would grant no quarter to, about 100 slain of them, and most of the rest of the whores that attended that wicked Army are marked in the face or nose, with a slash or cut. . . .'[16]

Various attempts have been made to explain this incident, a popular suggestion being that the women were in fact Welsh, whose cries for mercy in their own language the troopers of the New Model mistook for Irish.[17] In fact, there is every possibility that the unfortunate women were indeed Irish, perhaps the wives of soldiers of the King's Lifeguard mentioned earlier. The most likely explanation is that the Parliamentarian soldiers had been so fired up by tales of rebel atrocities in Ireland and by reports that the King was preparing to bring those same men over to England that, further inflamed by the effects of battle, they were overcome by bloodlust.

Probably receiving no more than rough handling and robbery were the occupants of 'wagons carrying the middle sort of Ammunition Whores, who were full of money and rich apparell'.

WOMEN IN BATTLE

There were many occasions when women found themselves actively involved in combat. The majority of these incidents occurred in besieged towns or garrisons under attack, and women's and indeed civilian involvement in general does not necessarily denote any fervent attachment to a particular side. The women of Royalist Chester and Parliamentarian Gloucester were equally prominent in the defence of their homes, largely motivated by fear of their fate if the town fell to the enemy, particularly by storming.

The women's involvement might take various forms. At Chester on 29 September 1645 it was recorded that the bantering and insults shouted by the besiegers 'almost chide us out of patience, in so much that our very women possesses the lyne and in behalf of the men accept of the encounter . . .'.[18] They played a much more active and dangerous role in repelling the great Parliamentarian assault of 10 October.[19] Later, when Brereton's Parliamentarians commenced a nightly mortar bombardment of the city, women played an important role in fire-watching precautions: 'Our women like soe many she-astronomers have so glued their eyes to heaven in expectation of a second thunder that they cannot be got to bed lest they dream of a granado.'[20]

A similar picture emerges of the part played by women in the defence of Worcester in 1646. About 400 of the 'ordinary sort' of women worked daily on strengthening and repairing the defences, often under enemy bombardment, and reportedly, armed with muskets, took a more active part in the fighting. At Basing House, during Waller's unsuccessful attacks in 1644, the women in the garrison hurled tiles and other missiles from the rooftop and battlements at the attackers.

Finally, there were the unknown, though probably small, number of women who managed to pass themselves off as men and actually served with the Royalist forces. Most cases are so poorly documented as to be impossible to verify. A number of women with the armies may have dressed as men in the belief that this would afford them greater safety, and incurred in the process the displeasure of King Charles who forbade the practice, saying that any woman found wearing male attire would be liable to 'the severest punishment which law and our displeasure shall inflict'.[21] However, this did not prevent Lord Percy from dressing his mistress as one of his troopers early in 1645. She was captured near Andover by no less a person than Oliver Cromwell, who noticing 'a youth with so fair a countenance', ordered her to sing, which she did 'with such a daintiness' that Percy was forced to confirm his captor's suspicions.[22]

Actual cases of women serving as soldiers involved in combat are few. At the storm of Shelford House in November 1645, Sydenham Poyntz reported a Royalist woman corporal among his prisoners, while there is an unconfirmed tradition of Jane Ingleby, the daughter of a Yorkshire yeoman, fighting as a trooper of horse and returning home wounded from Marston Moor.

However, the most formidable and surprising of Royalist Amazons was one Captain Frances Dalzeil, said to have been an illegitimate daughter of the Earl of Carnwath. She apparently led a troop of horse in the Earl of Crawford's Regiment in the Oxford Army and later served in the 1644 campaign in north-east England. Her cornet is said to have depicted a hanged man.[23] An encounter between this redoubtable lady and King Charles would have been interesting to witness!

EIGHTEEN

THE SCOURGE OF WAR

'From the plundering of soldiers, their insolence, cruelty, atheism, blasphemy, and rule over us, Lord Deliver us.'

Henry Townsend, *Diary*,
vol. I, p. lxxx

Agreat fear of ordinary Englishmen faced with the threat of Civil War was that all the reputed horrors of the Thirty Years' War on the Continent and the ongoing rebellion in Ireland would be repeated in their own homeland. They had been fed a stream of terrifying tales, both from returning soldiers and by lurid descriptions in pamphlets such as *The Lamentations of Germany*, published in 1638, containing chapters with titles such as 'of Tortures and Torments', 'of Rape and Ravishing' and filled with horrific illustrations captioned 'Croats eat children', 'noses and eares cut off to make hatbands' and the like.[1]

The rebellion in Ireland that broke out with terrifying suddenness in the autumn of 1641 brought the threat dramatically nearer home. Again there were blood-chilling tales of widespread massacre, rape, torture, and butchery of babies by the Catholic rebels, lent apparent authenticity by refugees arriving at English ports such as Chester, which led to ferocious reprisals by government forces in Ireland and the expectation of a papist uprising in England with similar consequences.

It is often assumed that the reality of Civil War, at least as it affected England and Wales, was relatively mild in comparison with the Continental experience. However, modern research casts doubts on this. The impact of the Thirty Years' War in Germany, it has been persuasively argued,[2] was less all-destructive than sometimes claimed. Large areas of the country remained relatively unscathed, while elsewhere, fighting, and its impact on civilians, was sporadic, and its damage sustainable. However, the methods used by the warring Continental armies, albeit employing different terminology, were quickly adopted by the contending forces in England and Wales, and still more in Ireland and Scotland. So, while no more children were eaten by Croats or anyone else than in Germany, and the articles of war at least partially observed by both sides also limited some of the worse excesses, many of the other unpleasant features of the war there became only too familiar to the peoples of the British Isles.[3] Disorder and harassment of civilians and prisoners, ranging from looting and rough handling to killing, was common to both sides. The Royalist forces have gained, with some justification, the worse reputation, but their opponents behaved in a similar fashion, although sometimes from different motives.

As with the conflict in Europe, the greatest deviation from the accepted conduct of war and the worst impact on the lives of the civilian community tended to occur in areas of contested control, where neither side was able to establish an undisrupted administration. One reason for the apparent greater degree of indiscipline and extortionism of the Royalists was that much of their territory remained insecure and subject to attack, so that no settled quasi-civilian government could be established, as was possible, for example, in the Parliamentarian-held South-east and much of the Eastern Association. It is no coincidence that the Welsh Border and West Midlands, which were always under threat, witnessed many cases of Royalist excesses. The Welsh Border was the scene of operations for many of the professional soldiers who had previously served in the savage war in Ireland, and also for some foreign mercenaries. Their example seems to have been one that militarily inexperienced gentry in the King's service sought to emulate, and on occasion to outdo. It is equally unsurprising that a region which had seen so many examples of military (in this case Royalist) misbehaviour should also witness the genesis of the armed anti-war 'Clubman' movement, involving many of the lesser local gentry who were the bedrock of the social and economic system threatened by the excesses of war.

PLUNDER

The greatest impact of the war on the lives of ordinary people came from the demands of the opposing forces for money, men, supplies and horses. In theory at least, this was formalised by the 'contribution' system.[4] But that process, frequently barely camouflaged extortion, often degenerated into open violence.

While the war on the Continent had seen the development, by such military entrepreneurs as Wallenstein, of complex and at times highly effective means of maintaining very large armies, the threat and use of force remained an inevitable adjunct to the military economy. Nevertheless, it was generally recognised by commanders that uncontrolled plundering by their men not only alienated the local population, but eventually undermined the economic structure on which the continued existence of their forces depended. The result was the evolution of the system known in England as 'contribution', in which payments in cash or kind by a community were theoretically agreed between military commanders and the local civilian authorities. In practice, however, either because of reluctance or inability to pay, unauthorised additional demands by local commanders, or the arrival in a district of major field forces from elsewhere, arrangements frequently broke down and were replaced by actual or threatened violence. On the Continent, this at its simplest took the form of the *Brandeschatzung* or 'fire raid', in which a community would be threatened with burning unless it supplied a given quantity of cash or commodities. In return, it might receive the dubious assurance of a letter of protection.

Although not always stated so baldly, this procedure was quickly adopted by Royalist troops. Unsurprisingly, with his previous military experience confined to the Continent, Prince Rupert was the first practitioner. On 9 August 1642 he demanded £2,000 from the Mayor of Leicester warning that 'If any disaffected persons with you shall refuse themselves, or persuade you to neglect the command, I shall tomorrow appear before your town in such a posture, with horse, foot and cannon, as shall make you know it is more safe to obey than to resist his Majesty's demands.'[5] The result was £500 for the Prince and an outcry that caused the King to disown his nephew's actions. Yet Rupert proved reluctant to abandon what were accepted military methods in Europe. In February 1643 his forces sacked Cirencester, and a more notorious example followed on 3 April at Birmingham. The small Midlands manufacturing town was strongly Parliamentarian in its sympathies, and its citizens could expect rough treatment when it fell to Rupert's forces. Just how severe their experience was is, as usual, the subject of dispute. A widely circulated Parliamentarian account describes it in graphic terms:

Having thus possessed themselves of the town, they ran into every house, cursing and damning threatening and terrifying the poore Women most terribly, setting naked Swords and Pistols to their breasts, they fell to plundering all the Towne before them, as well Malignants as others, picking purses, and pockets, seeking in holes and corners, Tiles of houses, Walls, Pooles, Vaults, gardens and every other place they could suspect for money or goods, forcing people to deliver all the money they had. . . . They beastly assaulted many Women's chastity, and impudently made their brags of it afterwards, how many they had ravished; glorying in their shame especially the French among them were outrageously lacivious and lecherous. . . . That night few or none went to Bed, but sate up revelling robbing, and Tryanising over the poor affrighted Women and Prisoners, drinking drinke, healthing upon theire knees, yea, drinking Healths to Prince Rupert's Dog. . . .'[6]

Much of the detail is unspecific and unprovable, and in any case does not greatly exceed the treatment meted out in any town taken by assault. The cause of greatest horror occurred next day when, on the Royalist departure,

they used every possible dilligence to set fire in all the streets, . . . and stood with drawn swords about the burning houses, endeavouring to kill every one that appeared endeavouring to quench the flames. The houses burned were about eighty-seven, besides multitudes of barns, stables and other outbuildings. People unfurnished and fallen into extreme distress by this fire, three hundred and forty upwards. They have made Birmingham a woeful spectacle to behold, a thoroughfare for thieves and plunderers.[7]

The Royalist response was defensive. While forced to admit to a fire whose effects were plain to see, they claimed that it had been started in defiance of the Prince's direct orders, that Rupert had given the inhabitants permission to extinguish the flames, but that this had been prevented by high winds.[8] It was an unconvincing explanation, seemingly not accepted even by King Charles, who wrote to Rupert in embarrassed and convoluted terms, urging him to 'mingle severity with mercy, that your carriage and behaviour towards our subjects may gain upon their opinions, and take their affections rather than their towns . . . have a care of spilling innocent blood . . . but spare where you may destroy . . .'.[9] Rupert apparently took the King's words to heart, and no other town stormed by him during the war suffered the same amount of material destruction. At Bristol in July 1643, for example, though looting both of civilians and of the surrendered garrison did occur, Rupert tried to limit its effects.

The King's known opposition seems to have limited further incidents of *Brandeschatzung*, though not its threat, but more generalised plundering was an eradicable feature of the Royalist forces. It happened everywhere, carried out by the main field armies through to the smallest garrison with its roaming troop of horse. King Charles, in his spasmodic and ineffectual fashion, regretted it and issued a number of proclamations forbidding unauthorised looting.[10] In November 1642, after the sack of Brentford had stiffened resistance by the defenders of London, he went so far as to decree the death penalty for the 'unjust and unlawfull actions by divers Soldiers of our Army'.[11]

In reality, looting was impossible to eradicate. It was sometimes the result of desperation or necessity, but the property of the enemy, actual, suspected or pretended, and the booty of a captured town were regarded as 'the soldiers' right for their hard service'. Rupert promised his men the plunder of Bolton and Liverpool in the campaign of 1644. Even at Leicester in May 1645, when the King himself was present, the town was thoroughly sacked by his victorious army. Many officers increasingly used plunder to maintain their troops, particularly in contested areas where less forceful methods proved ineffective. The Midlands and Welsh Border saw a number of Royalist practitioners of these methods, including Sir Michael Woodhouse, Governor of Ludlow, and Thomas Leveson at Dudley. But the most successful and consequently most notorious of all was Sir William Vaughan, 'the Devil of Shrawardine'.[12]

William Vaughan was probably a member of a Welsh Border family. Aged about sixty on the outbreak of war, he was a professional soldier for most of his life, fighting on the Continent before serving as a captain in the Scots War of 1639.[13] In 1641 he went to Ireland. Here, on 7 February 1643, he commanded the horse in Richard Grenville's victory at Rathconnell and was knighted by the Earl of Ormonde. In December 1643, commanding four troops of horse totalling 300 men, Vaughan landed near Chester with the soldiers from Ireland sent over to serve the King. His force quickly became a regiment of horse in its own right. Its officers were mainly professional soldiers, including Captain John Devalier, a Florentine,[14] and there were a number of native Irish among its troopers.[15] Vaughan quickly earned a reputation both as a cavalry commander and for his success in maintaining and indeed expanding the strength of his regiment. He performed the latter feat by establishing a number of small garrisons across North Shropshire, recruiting foot to hold them and quartering a troop of horse in each, and then exacting contributions from the surrounding communities.

Vaughan's officers showed all the customary ruthlessness of professional soldiers in enforcing their demands. Captain John Devalier, Governor of Caus Castle, in October 1644 required from the Constable of Stockton the agreed weekly contribution of 1 quarter of beef, 1 side of mutton, 3 strikes of oats, 2 of rye, 14 lb of cheese, 7 lb of butter, 1 couple of poultry, and 5s. in money, 'which if you refuse you may expect my coming to fetch it'. By 26 November he was warning that if arrears in contributions were not made up within one week 'I will forbear no longer, and if any mischiefe befalle you by my soldiers in going forth, you must blame yourselves for itt, and stand your perill'. On 29 May 1645 he openly threatened to burn any townships that defied his commands.[16] As the Royalist position on the Welsh Border deteriorated, Vaughan's raiders spread their activities ever further afield. On 27 November 1644 Sir William is recorded as robbing the drapers of Dolgellau of '£140 in money and commodities',[17] while in February 1646 his troopers were pillaging around Clun and Presteigne. At Gladestry they robbed Michael Jones of between £400 and £500, his writings and the rings from his wife's fingers.[18] So notorious had the depredations of Vaughan's troopers now become that the Governor of Ludlow, Sir Michael Woodhouse, himself no respecter of civilian rights, refused them entry to the town.

Yet, in narrowly military terms, the methods of 'the Devil' and his ilk were effective. If Sir William terrorised his Shropshire satrapy, he also proved a formidable opponent to the Parliamentarians, winning several locally important victories, and as late as May 1645, accompanied by his wife and her ladies in a coach and six, he was able to lead 400 horse to reinforce the King in the Naseby Campaign.[19] It was the success of such commanders in maintaining their units, however unscrupulous the methods they employed, that forced the Royalist high command, especially in relatively remote areas where their writ ran weakly if at all, to acquiesce in their activities whatever the price paid in loss of local support.

Particularly after Naseby, with the destruction of the main field army and the steady loss of Royalist territory that followed, military operations were increasingly motivated by the need to sustain the remaining troops than by any coherent strategy. This resulted in the loss of what little popular support the King's men still retained.

ATROCITIES

If barely legitimised looting was commonly employed by troops on both sides, and tacitly accepted by senior officers, 'atrocities' (defined here mainly as incidents in which soldiers or civilians were killed in relatively cold blood rather than actual combat) were rarer, if more common than sometimes suggested. We are usually dependent for details on enemy accounts produced largely for propaganda purposes, so there can be considerable difficulty in establishing the exact circumstances of each incident, and sometimes indeed whether they actually happened at all. However, closer examination does reveal a clear pattern. Most Parliamentarian 'atrocities', such as the execution of 'Irish' prisoners discussed elsewhere, occurred in the later stages of the war, and in the former case could be held to be legitimised by an Ordinance of Parliament. Other occurrences, like the massacre of women in the Royalist baggage train at Naseby and the sack of Basing House in October 1645, were partly the consequence of the stress of combat and storm, and also the result of inflammatory sermons and propaganda aimed at whipping up hatred among the attackers.[20]

Here we are concerned primarily with Royalist actions. Despite Parliamentarian claims, no clear evidence of Royalist 'atrocities', as defined above, occurs before late 1643. The change coincided with the arrival of English troops from Ireland, hardened soldiers accustomed to a harsher style of war than had so far generally been seen in England. An indication of their attitude came with the threats issued to the defenders of Hawarden Castle by Captain of Firelocks Thomas Sandford. Yet it is also true that there is no evidence that Sandford, described by his opponents as a man of 'big words', actually carried out his threats on this or any other occasion in his brief English career.[21] Ironically, the first clearly documented Royalist 'atrocity', although carried out by troops of Lord Byron's 'Anglo-Irish' army, was in fact the work of locally raised men, not troops from Ireland. On 23 December 1643:

The Kinge's ptie coming to Bartholmley Churche, did set upon the same; wherein about xxtie Neighbours where gonne for theire safegarde. But major Connaught, major to Collonell Sneyde, . . . wth his forces by wyelcome entred the Churche. The people within gatt up into the Steeple; But the Enymy burnyinge formes, pewes, Rushes and the lyke, did smother theim in the Steeple that they weire Enforced to call for Quarter, and yelde theim selves; wch was granted them by the said Connaught; But when hee had theim in his power, he caused theim all to be stripped starke Naked; And most barbarouslie and contry to the Lawes of armes, murthered, stabbed and cutt the Throates of xii of theim; and wounded all the reste, leavinge many of theim for Dead.[22]

Thus was the Parliamentarian account, given added weight by its local authorship and supported by an alleged letter from Lord Byron to the Marquess of Newcastle but surviving only in a version published in a Parliamentarian newsletter, in which the Royalist commander purportedly boasts that 'the rebels possessed themselves of a Church at Bartumley, but wee presently beat them forth of it, and put them all to the sword; which I find to be the best way to proceed with these kind of people, for mercy to them is cruelty'.[23]

Puzzling features remain. Malbon's account suggests that a number of unarmed civilians had been savagely murdered but (contrary to his alleged words) there is no record of Lord Byron ever carrying out such actions, despite his well-attested dislike of civilians. The actual circumstances may have been less clear-cut. By 9 January, Byron's brother Robert, with reports of Bartholmley stiffening local resistance, was claiming to Ormonde that a summons to surrender had been rejected, after which the Royalists had fought their way into the church. Although it was usual even then to give quarter to any prisoners taken, there was no obligation under the laws of war to do so.[24]

The man held responsible for the 'massacre', Major John Connock, was probably a professional soldier[25] with Snead's Staffordshire-based regiment, an undistinguished regional cavalry unit. The most probable explanation for his action is either that Royalist forces were fired on after a surrender had supposedly been agreed or that Connock 'misread' what was acceptable to Byron, based perhaps on the major's desire to make a reputation among seemingly bloodthirsty officers from Ireland such as Sandford. In addition, the outcome may have been inflamed by local enmities long since obscured. In the event, Byron found the 'massacre' a considerable embarrassment and it received no publicity from the Royalists. For Connock, the consequences would ultimately be fatal. He was brought to trial eleven years later, at Chester Assizes in October 1654. Accused of murdering 'several persons' at Barthomley, he was actually found guilty on one charge, that of killing John Fowler with a battleaxe. Connock, protesting his innocence though offering no defence, was found guilty and executed on 17 October.[26]

The next incident, also on the Welsh Border, was equally

notorious and, once again, linked to forces from Ireland. Sir Michael Woodhouse, Colonel of the Prince of Wales' Regiment of Foot and Governor of Ludlow, had previously been a soldier in Ireland, where he had served with Sir Richard Grenville at Trim, a garrison noted for the harsh treatment meted out to actual or suspected rebels.[27] Arriving in England in the summer of 1643 and evidently bringing several of his officers with him, Woodhouse quickly transferred 'Irish' methods to the Welsh Border. In February 1644 he led his men against Hopton Castle in Herefordshire, held by a small Parliamentarian garrison under Colonel Samuel Moore. The defenders put up unexpectedly prolonged resistance, repulsing four assaults, inflicting, according to Moore's own claim, several hundred casualties on the attackers, and angering them considerably in the process, with reports current of the garrison using poisoned bullets and killing the wounded.

The Parliamentarians had rejected several summons to surrender before agreeing, on 13 March and with their ammunition running short, to yield on 'mercy only', a vague term that might be taken to mean that their lives would be spared, though at the discretion of the besiegers. The most detailed account of what happened next is that of Samuel Moore. According to Moore, his twenty-seven men piled their arms, and left the castle, 'expecting mercy'. But;

> command was given that they should be tied two and three then they were stripped naked as ever they were born, it being about the beginning of March, very cold and many of them sore wounded in defending their own workes, there they remained about an hour till the word was given that they should be left to the mercy of the common soldiers, who presently fell upon them, wounding them grievously, and drove them into a cellar unfinished, wherein was stinking water the house being on fire above them, when they were there every man of them presently massacred.[28]

Apparently not suspecting what was about to happen, Moore had been separated from his men and taken into a house, where he was harangued and threatened for some time by Woodhouse himself, and later informed by another Royalist officer of the fate of his soldiers. Writing later, he added that his second-in-command, Major Phillips, had been stabbed to death despite offering £200 for his life, and 'all the rest, being twenty-five, were killed with clubs or such things after they were stripped naked. Two maids they stripped to their smocks and cut them, but some helped them to escape.[29]

The massacre at Hopton Castle, one of the worst atrocities of the war, was apparently a premeditated action by Woodhouse, he and his officers remaining out of the way while their men were allowed to vent their anger on the prisoners. It may be that what began as a 'roughing up' quickly degenerated into something worse, but as an experienced soldier Woodhouse must have been aware of the likely course of events, which he probably saw as a salutary example to other enemy garrisons, notably nearby Brampton Bryan Castle, of the consequence of defiance. It has been plausibly suggested that Moore himself was spared mainly because he was a friend of Sir Edward Nicholas, the Royalist Secretary of State.

The Royalist newspaper *Mercurius Aulicus*, normally so expansive, is noticeably reticent in its account of the affair, making no mention of the fate of the defenders. The reaction of the Royalist high command, notably Prince Rupert at Shrewsbury, is unrecorded but it may be significant that when Brampton Bryan surrendered to Woodhouse on 17 April, again on 'mercy only', the sixty-seven men of its garrison were spared and treated as normal prisoners of war.

Perhaps the best-known claimed 'atrocity' involving Royalist forces was the infamous 'Bolton Massacre' of 28 May 1644, again partly involving troops from Ireland, this time commanded by Rupert himself. As the Prince and his forces crossed the Mersey, bent on restoring Royalist fortunes in West Lancashire, local Parliamentarian troops under Alexander Rigby, who had been laying siege to Lathom House, beat a hasty retreat to Bolton. This town, 'the Geneva of the North', was noted for the Puritanism of many of its inhabitants and its hostility to the King. Its defences were fairly weak, and the decision by Rigby and his officers, reinforced by about 500 armed townsmen, to make a stand was probably ill considered. They nonetheless threw back the first Royalist assault, and hanged a captured 'Irish' soldier in full view of the attackers.[30]

Rupert, 'highly provoked', ordered a renewed attack, and in vicious street fighting the Parliamentarians were driven back through the streets towards the centre of Bolton. According to Parliamentarian accounts there now followed massacre and atrocity likened to the great sack of Magdeburg in the Thirty Years' War:

> at theire entrance, before, behinde, to the right, and lefte, nothing heard but kill dead, kill dead, was the word in the Towne, killing all before them without any respect, . . . pursuing the poore amazed people, killing stripping and spoiling all they could meet with, nothing regarding the doleful cries of women and children; but some they slashed as they were calling for quarter, others when they had given quarter, many hailed out of their houses to have their brains dasht out in the strettes . . .[31]

Closer examination modifies this picture. Even the lurid account quoted above only actually names one woman as being among those killed, and there was ample evidence that, for example, 700 of the defenders of Bolton who had taken refuge in the church were granted quarter. Prince Rupert's actual orders prior to the second assault appear to have been to give no quarter to 'any Person then in Armes',[32] a definition that would have included any of the armed townsmen (or indeed women) not able to jettison their weapons in time. Ill treatment there certainly was, but for the most part it seems to have consisted of rough handling, insults and widespread looting rather than systematic slaughter. The most publicised incident was the alleged killing in cold blood by the Royalist Earl of Derby of his former servant now Parliamentarian officer, Captain William Bootle.[33] It was one of the charges leading to the Earl's execution in 1651, but Derby himself always strenuously denied the accusation and Bootle is equally likely to have met his death in combat. The contemporary Bolton Parish Registers list seventy-eight dead townsmen and four women, who together with several hundred of Rigby's men seem a more probable tally of fatalities than the thousands claimed in Parliamentarian propaganda.

A similar if less-well-publicised episode occurred a few days later on Rupert's capture of Liverpool after an equally fiercely contested siege. Learning on the night of 11 June that Liverpool's Governor, Colonel John Moore, and most of his regular soldiers had abandoned the town to its fate, the Royalists scaled the deserted defences and poured into Liverpool. As usual, Rupert had promised his men the sack of the town and remained outside, possibly for several hours, before restoring order. There seems in the interim to have been considerable confusion, with panic and uncoordinated resistance by the surprised townsfolk, and it is clear that a considerable number were killed. Lord Byron, in a private and therefore presumably reliable letter to Ormonde, wrote that the Royalists 'entered the Towne with little or noe resistance, found about 400 of the meaner sort of menne, whereof most were killed, some had quarter . . .'.[34] Once again killing of confused, half-asleep citizens unwisely attempting to protect their property, rather than systematic massacre, seems the most likely explanation.

At neither Bolton nor Liverpool is there any reference to the burning of property as had occurred at Birmingham in the previous year. Although those who suffered in these towns would have gained little comfort from it, it seems that Rupert and his commanders had slightly moderated their behaviour, whether at the behest of the King or from a realisation of what was at present politically counterproductive in England.[35] The noticeable increase of savagery in Royalist operations that had been a feature of the winter and spring of 1643/4 was clearly linked to the arrival of hard-bitten professional soldiers from Ireland, accustomed to a different style of warfare than was so far acceptable in England. By the summer of 1644, they had mostly realised, or been made to accept, that such methods were too costly in terms of popular support to be continued, as well as being possibly repugnant to King Charles himself.[36] With the exception of Grenville's capture of Saltash in September 1644, there would be no more incidents like the massacre at Hopton Castle. For the remainder of the war most such killings would be the work of the Royalists' opponents.

NINETEEN

THE LAST BATTLE:
STOW-ON-THE-WOLD, 1646

'You have done your work, boys, and may go play, unless you fall out among yourselves.'

Jacob, Lord Astley,
21 March 1646

By the end of 1645, the Royalist cause was desperate: the Oxford Army foot were broken at Naseby; plans for new recruitment from Wales and the Marches had been shattered by the defeat of the Western forces at Langport and the loss of Bristol; the King's remaining horse were broken at Rowton Heath and Sherburn; and Montrose was fatally worsted at Philliphaugh. Clarendon summed up the position:

There were yet some garrisons which remained in his obedience, and which were like, during the winter season, to be preserved from any attempt of the enemy; but upon the approach of the spring, if the King should be without an army in the field, the fate of those few places was easy to be discerned: And which way an army could possibly be brought together, or where it should be raised, was not within the compass of the wisest man's comprehension. However, the more difficult it was, the more vigour was to be applied to the attempt.[1]

Apart from the far South-west, only in the southern Marches of Wales did the King still possess a significant foothold. The city of Worcester retained links with the remaining Royalist garrisons of Wales and the West Midlands. Its proximity to Wales, from where there was still a faint hope of new levies and where more sanguine Royalists such as Digby and the Earl of Glamorgan promised that Irish Confederate troops would land, also made it vital.

Various desperate schemes were aired in Oxford. In December a plan put forward earlier by Sir Richard Willys, former Governor of Newark, was revived when it was proposed to concentrate the garrisons of Worcester, Exeter, Newark, Chester and Oxford at Worcester on 20 February. By this means it was hoped to raise a force of 3,000 foot and 2,500 horse, to be reinforced by 2,000 recruits levied along the Welsh Border during the winter. This army could either march into the West to link up with the remaining Royalist forces there, advance into Kent and Sussex in the faint hope of triggering a Royalist uprising, or support the landing of the oft-promised but almost entirely imaginary foreign mercenaries supposedly being raised in France by the Queen.[2] Such a plan, whatever chance it might have had a few months previously, was by early 1646 verging on the realms of fantasy. By February, with resistance in the West on the point of collapse after Hopton's defeat at Torrington, Charles was thinking instead of a dash into Kent at the head of 2,000 horse and dragoons in an attempt to secure the port of Rochester.[3]

In reality, what little hope remained rested in the hands of one man, that under-rated Royalist commander, the 67-year-old Jacob, Lord Astley. It had been almost entirely thanks to the tireless efforts of Astley that the chaotic forces raised for the Scots Wars of 1639 and 1640 had materialised,[4] and his services as Major General of the Oxford Army foot and adviser to the King and Prince Rupert had been rewarded in November 1644 by a well-deserved peerage. A year later, with his cause on the edge of ruin, King Charles turned once again to the old veteran. On 6 December 1645 Astley was effectively placed in command of all the remaining Royalist forces outside the West of England, with the title of Lieutenant General of Worcestershire, Staffordshire, Herefordshire and Shropshire. The post of Lieutenant General of Horse was given to a man who could have exercised it more effectively at the beginning of the year. Sir

Charles Lucas, an excellent fighting commander who had shown his worth at Marston Moor, formerly a supporter of Rupert but estranged from him for some time, was given the unenviable task of attempting to reorganise the disorderly remnants of the Royalist horse.[5]

By the end of 1645, the Royalist forces on the Welsh Border, comprising the fragments of Gerrard's South Wales army,[6] Sir William Vaughan's notorious horse, and the remainder of foot units from a variety of sources, were more of a threat to unfortunate civilians who crossed their path than to the enemy. Vaughan's depredations had become so blatant that even Sir Michael Woodhouse, himself not known for moderation, refused his cavalry entry to Ludlow. A Parliamentarian writer described some of Gerrard's former troopers as 'the most rude, ravenous, and ill-governed horse that I believe ever trod the earth'.[7]

Even before assuming command, Astley's already slim hopes of success received a severe blow when, on 16 December, the important garrison of Hereford fell to a surprise Parliamentarian attack. This effectively ended Vaughan's half-hearted attempts to ease pressure on Chester, and his small force dispersed to protect their respective home garrisons. In these unpropitious circumstances Astley and Lucas arrived at Worcester on Christmas Day. The immediate plan was for them to lead 2,200 men to join the 1,500 horse and foot under Vaughan's command at High Ercall, and then attempt the relief of Chester with the aid of troops promised by the North Wales Royalists and non-existent forces from Ireland.[8] For a time the Parliamentarians took the threat seriously, using a network of spies, including a woman who secured personal interviews with Vaughan, the Governor of Worcester and even Prince Maurice,[9] to report on Royalist plans. But as Archbishop Williams had already warned Astley, there was 'no real relying' on the promises from Ireland, while a small and unenthusiastic North Wales Royalist force was easily dispersed on 25 January at Ruthin by Brereton's forces. A rumoured 1,500 horse from Banbury, reportedly marching to join Astley, proved to be a small raiding party and it turned back near Evesham, leaving the Royalists, as the Parliamentarian Worcestershire Committee assured Brereton, to 'draw out and march back again, stagger to and fro as if they knew not whither to betake themselves'.[10] Snow followed by a sudden thaw rendered rivers uncrossable and roads impassable, and in effect ended any chance of Astley marching to Byron's aid.

By the time that Chester fell on 3 February 1646 Astley was concentrating on his primary mission of raising a field army for the spring. An essential prelude was the reorganisation of Royalist administration in the area, fallen into a state of near-anarchy following Maurice's resignation in September. Astley's success in this was not least among his largely unrecognised achievements during the war. In order to win support from the local community, and check the burgeoning anti-war movement ominously headed by members of the local gentry, Astley took a firm hand with his unruly garrison commanders. Sir Samuel Sandys, Governor of Worcester, resigned in protest and was replaced by Henry Washington, a tough and resolute career soldier who, though hated by the citizens, defended his charge with tigerish determination in the last days of the war.[11] Commanders of proven ability – Sir Thomas Tyldesley, a leading Lancashire Royalist, and Sir William Blakiston, the redoubtable deputy of Langdale in the Northern Horse – were made Governors of Lichfield and Tutbury Castle, while Vaughan's men were taken in hand by Sir Charles Lucas.

Astley had less success with the civilian authorities. They proved unwilling or unable to collect £2,000 arrears in contributions, so that Astley was forced to retain free quarter.[12] Nevertheless, by early March, he had restored a reasonably efficient administration in his command, and had even begun to regain some measure of civilian confidence. But these achievements, however welcome in themselves, were secondary to Astley's primary task. His efforts to gather troops were, paradoxically, assisted by the steady erosion of the remaining Royalist garrisons. The fall of such strongholds as Chester served to release more hardened veterans to serve in Astley's field army. And, as spring approached, he began to call in every man who could be spared from the outlying garrisons. In Oxford, however, King Charles was continuing to hesitate over his next move. He lacked any coherent strategy, and his desperation early in 1646 is summarised by Clarendon: 'If he could by all possible endeavours have drawn out of all his garrisons a force of 5,000 horse and foot (which at that time seemed a thing not to be despaired of) he did more desire to have lost his life in some signal attempt upon any part of the enemy's army than to have enjoyed any conditions which he foresaw he was ever like to obtain by treaty.'[13]

Though he had virtually no foot at his disposal, the King had in the course of the winter succeeded in collecting about 1,200 horse from his garrisons around Oxford, and these, under the capable leadership of Sir John Cansfield, former Colonel of the Queen's Regiment of Horse, had been raiding widely over the surrounding countryside. A plan was under active consideration for them, possibly accompanied by the King, to march to join Astley. According to Sir Edward Walker, it was expectation of this that prevented Astley from assisting a brief Royalist uprising in South Wales in February and caused him to limit his military operations to the relief of the garrison of Madresfield near Worcester and some raids into Warwickshire.[14]

The Royalist position around Oxford deteriorated further after the failure in January to retake Abingdon, and 'thereupon his Majesty resolved to joyne himself with the Lord Astley, and either endeavour to relieve Banbury, or to retire to Worcester, and there take new Resolutions. To this end Lord Astley had Order to march with all his Horse and Foot out of Worcestershire and over Avon to come to Stow, and so to Chipping Norton; where his Majesty with about 1,500 Horse and Foot drawn out of Oxford and other Garrisons intended to meet him.'[15] It was a similar opening gambit to that of the Naseby Campaign, but undertaken in far less favourable circumstances.

Astley collected together detachments from all available garrisons, in some cases abandoning them. At Chirk Castle the Governor, Sir John Watts, was ordered at the end of February to bring his 100 firelocks and 50 horse south to Ludlow on the first stage of their march to join Astley. But on 1 March they were trapped in Churchstoke Church by Parliamentarian troops from Montgomery and, after a fierce two-hour fight, they were forced to surrender. Others were more successful, and Astley held a general rendezvous at Bridgnorth prior to commencing his hazardous march. His army included many reminders of the great days of the Cavaliers. Among his 700 horse were the remaining fragments of such once redoubtable regiments as those of Lord Byron and Prince Maurice, the remnants of Gerrard's and Vaughan's forces, and many reformadoes, including the colourful Lorraine mercenary, the Comte de St Pol, formerly Major General of Horse to Lord Byron. The foot were drawn from an equally wide range of sources, including in their ranks the survivors of Prince Rupert's Lifeguard of Firelocks, many of them red-coated Irishmen, those of his brother Prince Maurice, the last of Sir Michael Earnley's Regiment of Foot from the army in Ireland, (veterans of Nantwich), and sixty men of Sir Charles Lloyd's Montgomeryshire Regiment that had first seen action at Edgehill and had made their way back to Bridgnorth after their gallant defence of Devizes. These veterans were joined by other experienced troops from the garrisons of Worcester, Bridgnorth and Ludlow, though apparently by very few of the hoped-for new levies.[16] It was a band of unpaid and desperate men, for the most part diehard Royalists, who were staking their all on a last throw.

Astley's task was a formidable one. Thanks to captured letters and despatches, the enemy were aware of his intentions and already moving to thwart him. The army of Sir William Brereton, having taken Chester, was now besieging Lichfield but was ready to detach horse in pursuit of Astley, while troops from Hereford and Gloucester, under Colonel John Birch and Major General Thomas Morgan, a 'diminutive, fiery, resolute Welshman', were also poised to intercept the Royalist march. Nearer to Oxford, the horse of Colonel John Fleetwood were ready to block any juncture with the King.

From Bridgnorth Astley marched his 700 horse and 2,300 foot via Kidderminster to Worcester, where he halted for a few days to make final preparations. The passage of the River Avon at Evesham was in enemy hands, so the Royalists would have to find other means to cross the river. Then they must deal with Birch and Morgan, who, with a force slightly smaller than their own, lay across the likely Royalist line of march at Broadway on the edge of the Cotswolds. Fortunately moving with some lack of haste, Sir William Brereton and about 1,000 Cheshire, Shropshire and Warwickshire horse were heading south from Lichfield.

Morgan and Birch had rendezvoused at Gloucester on 15 March, and then marched to Evesham, where they were reinforced by 600 of the garrison, placing a force of about 2,300 Parliamentarians across Astley's likely path. The Royalist commander's hopes of beginning his march undetected, and being well on his way to join the King before the enemy reacted, had been dashed. Nevertheless, the old general's first moves were both skilful and successful. Leaving Worcester on 19 March, Astley sent Lucas and some of the horse in a feint towards Evesham, while his main body marched north along the Droitwich road. The Parliamentarians were left in doubt whether Astley's objective was Oxford, or if after all he planned to attempt the relief of Lichfield, and the ever-cautious Brereton reacted by abandoning his intended rendezvous with Birch and Morgan and falling back towards Birmingham in order to keep between Astley and Lichfield. Having thus temporarily disposed of one of his opponents, early on 20 March Astley swung south-east in a night march across country via Feckenham and Inkberrow, and reached the Avon at Bidford. Here he sprang another surprise. The Royalists had with them a bridge of boats, and so crossed the river before marching on along the old Roman Buckle Street through Honeybourne and Chipping Campden up into the Cotswolds, brushing past the flank of Morgan and Birch at Broadway.

Neither side was anxious to bring on an immediate battle; the Parliamentarians wanted to await Brereton, while Astley saw joining the King as his priority. By late afternoon on the 20th, the Royalists had reached the crest of the Cotswolds near Broadway and were pushing on across the downlands towards Stow-on-the-Wold, their rearguard skirmishing with parties of Morgan's horse who were attempting to slow down the Royalists until Brereton came up. As dusk fell, with still no sign of Sir William, Morgan called off his men, though he continued to follow Astley at a distance.

It may be that the Royalist commander assumed that he had deterred Morgan from attacking, or simply that his own men were exhausted after marching without respite since the previous night, covering in some cases as many as 25 miles. Whatever the reason, he 'early begins to draw into quarters' around the village of Donnington, about 2 miles from Stow. Astley might have been wiser to have occupied the town itself, which afforded better defensive possibilities.

The Parliamentarians, meanwhile, were recovering from being outmanoeuvred. Brereton had still been hesitating in the Stratford area when, on the morning of the 20th, he received news that the Royalists were laying a bridge of boats across the Avon. Morgan reported that he intended to engage Astley in the Cotswolds and asked for urgent assistance. Even now Brereton does not seem to have reacted with any particular haste, and he only reached Stratford 'about the going down of the sun', when another messenger arrived from Morgan reporting him to be within 3 miles of the enemy, with the forlorn hopes already engaged, 'and if Sir William made not hast they would be gone, for he himself should be too weak to engage all their Forces'.[17] Brereton was further delayed by the bridge at Stratford having been damaged, so that his men could only cross one at a time, and it was about midnight before his leading troopers were approaching the Cotswolds.

THE BATTLE

It was between 1 and 2 a.m. on 21 March that Brereton's horse, totalling about 800 men, eventually linked up with Morgan. Realising that he could not avoid battle, and possibly still hoping to be reinforced by troops from Oxford, for the last time Astley drew up a Royalist army in battle array, taking up position on a steep hillside about ¼ of a mile west of Donnington, now partially occupied by Horsington Plantation.

Both sides seem to have formed up in conventional fashion. Astley and his foot were in the Royalist centre, with about 350 horse under Lucas on the right, and the remainder, probably led by Sir William Vaughan, on the left. Brereton commanded the Parliamentarian right, with Birch in the centre and Morgan on the left. Deployment complete, a pause followed as the Parliamentarians awaited daylight before launching their attack. It may have been about 6 a.m. when the final battle of the First Civil War began. It was fiercely contested, the Parliamentarians shouting their watchword of 'God be our Guide', the Royalists replying with 'Patrick and George'.

The initial Parliamentarian attack on the left, made by Morgan with 400 horse and 200 firelocks, was twice thrown back by the counter-attacks of Sir Charles Lucas and his horse, during which Lucas was unhorsed and briefly captured but rescued by a party of Royalist firelocks. In the centre the struggle was equally intense, Birch having his horse killed under him and, as his secretary wrote, 'Hard it was for a while, their reformadoes standing stoutly to it.' However, on the Parliamentarian right, Brereton, 'most bravely going on with the Right Wing of Horse, and, at least, 200 Firelocks, fiercely charged the [Royalist] Left, both of Horse and Foot, and totally routed them'. Vaughan's horse were no doubt inferior in quality to Brereton's men, as well as being outnumbered two to one, and Vaughan himself 'hardly escaped but not without some wounds'.

Brereton's success was decisive. He turned his horse against the flank of Astley's stubbornly resisting foot, while Lucas's cavalry were either routed or made off. Sir Charles himself took refuge in a nearby wood, where at daylight he was captured by Parliamentarian troops searching for stragglers. Astley attempted to pull his foot back into Stow-on-the-Wold for a final stand. Here some were cut down in the streets, while the remainder were surrounded in the market place. Astley was taken prisoner by a trooper of Birch's cavalry. The old soldier accepted the inevitable philosophically. He ordered his men to surrender and, himself 'being somewhat wearied from the fight' was given a drum to sit on by his captors, to whom he remarked wryly, 'you have done your work, boys, and may go play, unless you fall out among yourselves'.[18]

The battle had cost the Royalists about 100 dead, with 67 officers and 1,630 men taken prisoner. They were confined for the night in St Edward's Church, and then taken to Gloucester. Astley's words were accurate. The King had lost his last field army and, apart from the long epilogue of reducing the many remaining Royalist garrisons maintaining an increasingly futile resistance, the First Civil War was over.

TWENTY

AFTERMATH

For these four years of discord have so changed
The gentleness, already of this Nation.
And men and women are so far estranged
From civil to barbarous inclination.
They are so prone to mutinous disorders,
So forward in all mischievous projections
So little moved with robberies and murders.

George Wither, *Vox Pacifica*,
1647

The disbandment of the King's armies was long-drawn-out. Almost two years passed between the defeat of the Oxford Army at Naseby in June 1645 and the surrender of Harlech Castle, the last Royalist garrison in mainland England and Wales, in March 1647. The time involved made it easier to absorb the rank and file of the Cavalier forces back into society.

As the King's garrisons surrendered in increasing numbers from the summer of 1645 onwards, more and more of their defenders, recognising that the cause was lost or that their officers no longer had the authority to keep them in the ranks, took the opportunity to end their military careers. A dwindling hard core of officers and men, dedicated Royalists, professional soldiers, or individuals with nothing to lose, took advantage of surrender terms to make their way to the nearest Royalist garrison still holding out. But increasing numbers wanted only to return home and pick up as best they could the threads of their former lives. Wise Parliamentarian commanders made this as easy as possible. When Exeter and Oxford surrendered in 1646, Sir Thomas Fairfax agreed that the Royalist soldiers should be allowed free quarter and easy marches during their journeys home, while cavalry troopers should keep their horses (often essential for their civilian livelihood) or receive compensation. Those opting to go overseas, usually professional soldiers, were allowed their personal weapons.[1]

Though little documentary evidence survives, the average Royalist soldier probably returned to civilian life fairly easily. Although it was true that the economic fabric of the country had suffered grievous damage, with towns, villages and estates the length and breadth of the kingdom reeling from the effects of war,[2] the massive task of reconstruction meant that skills and labour were at a premium, and those who had been in a settled occupation prior to the war generally found little difficulty in returning to it, albeit sometimes in more straightened circumstances. Those recruits drawn from the 'underclass' of the vagrant, criminal and unemployed probably sank back into the condition from whence they had come. Some, including former soldiers of both sides, found their reluctantly acquired military skills of use in pursuing criminal careers. Highway robbery certainly increased. In May 1647 Bulstrode Whitelocke noted a letter from the Sheriff of Oxfordshire, saying that 'many troopers, Irish and others, who had been in arms against the Parliament, robbed all passengers, and that he had raised the "posse comitatus" and apprehended about one hundred of them'.[3] A particular problem were the organised gangs of former cavalrymen who, under the leadership of actual or pretended ex-officers such as the notorious 'Captain' Jemmy Hinde, preyed on travellers,[4] becoming the origin of the 'gentleman' highwayman of popular legend.

Of more concern to the Parliamentarian authorities were the large numbers of former Royalist officers. Many of those from the gentry and grandee classes would, it was hoped, be sufficiently deterred by the impact of sequestration and the heavy fines they were required to pay as 'delinquents' to 'compound' for their estates not to have any desire to take up arms again. More worrying were the large numbers of rootless, unemployed, professional soldiers hanging around the streets and taverns of large towns, especially London, ripe for potential mischief. Some were rounded up and returned to their native parishes under the vagrancy laws, while others were recruited for foreign service by agents of the European powers. Nearer to home, the war in Ireland was continuing. Some of the soldiers who had come over to England to serve the King in the earlier years of the war, among them Fulke Hunckes, who had commanded a regiment at Nantwich, and that able cavalry officer Marcus Trevor, now joined Parliament's forces against the Irish Confederates and their English Royalist allies. They found themselves in arms against old comrades such as Sir William Vaughan, who had joined Ormonde and was killed at Rathmines in 1649, and Sir Arthur Aston and Sir Edmund Verney, butchered in Cromwell's storming of Drogheda in the same year.

Some of King Charles' most prominent commanders had fought their last battle in his service. Jacob, Lord Astley, though under frequent suspicion, did not take up arms again and died in 1652. Even such Royalist stalwarts as Henry Washington, though regarded by the authorities with grave distrust, did not actually take the field in the Second Civil War of 1648 or any later uprisings. But the vast majority of the King's old officers remained remarkably steadfast. While fear of further crippling financial penalties deterred many of the 'grandees' from rash actions,[5] they mostly continued to offer more tacit support, and there was a constant supply of younger sons and men with little to lose ready for action. Through the long years of conspiracy and occasional resort to arms which continued until the Restoration of 1660, the main weakness that doomed Royalist efforts would be lack of organisation rather than shortage of potential manpower.

The series of risings in 1648 known as the Second Civil War, in conjunction with the Scottish invasion of England (now in support of the King), demonstrated the continuing potential of the King's old soldiers. Although prompt Parliamentarian countermeasures crushed most of the risings before the Royalists could begin to re-form any organised military structure, Sir Marmaduke Langdale in the North raised a useful little army, about 7,000 strong, including in its ranks many veterans of his Northern Horse and the Marquess of Newcastle's foot.[6] In the South-east, former Royalist commanders Sir Charles Lucas and Sir George Lisle took up arms, raised recruits and acted as a rallying point for other Royalist irreconcilables from across England, paying for their 'treason' with their lives after the capture of Colchester by Fairfax.[7]

Other diehard supporters of the Stuarts, while avoiding the supreme penalty, went into exile abroad, either voluntarily or by virtue of being excluded from pardon. Men such as John Byron, Ralph Hopton, Marmaduke Langdale and Richard Grenville, with the saturnine figure of Prince Rupert serving as a rallying point for Royalist activity on land and sea, though they were frequently as much absorbed by internal rivalry and enmities as by their opposition to the regime in England, provided the exiled Stuart Court with a hard core of determined and experienced activists who could have provided the command structure for a new Royalist army.

ARMY IN EXILE

It was not until 1656 that King Charles II, who had been eking out a poverty-stricken existence on the Continent awaiting some twist in European politics which would lend him foreign assistance against the Cromwellian regime in England, found means to raise a Royalist army in exile. The defeat of the Irish Confederates in 1652 had resulted in an agreement with the English government, anxious to remove potential sources of disaffection, by which Irish commanders and their troops could take service with any European power not currently hostile to England. Upwards of 20,000 men joined the large numbers of Irish, as well as some English and Scottish Royalists, who were already serving in the armies of France and Spain. By 1656 Irish troops in the French army formed eight regiments of foot.

In April 1656 Charles II signed the Treaty of Bruges with Spain, which was now involved in war with both England and France. The King's brother, James, Duke of York, serving as a volunteer with the French, was charged with the tricky task of extricating the Irish troops from France to serve King Charles and Spain. The results were mixed, for many of the Irish preferred the 'very good conditions' they enjoyed in France to the uncertainties of the King's service in Flanders.[8] Charles was probably never able to muster more than about 3,000 men, formed into five regiments. One, the King's Regiment of Guards, was mainly English (and provided employment for some of the numerous 'reformadoes' seeking subsistence), one Scottish and three Irish. The army was completed by the Duke of York's Lifeguard of Horse, fifty strong, mostly English Royalist gentry and, unlike most of the foot, well equipped.

Cromwell's agents were unimpressed by the new army:

> Those English that are among them follow their old wont of vapouring and carousing, bragging to be their own carvers of other men's estates and fortunes, if ever they get but foot in England . . . at present there is a great feud betwixt them and the Irish, because they are the best treated here, as being . . . likliest to be most true to the Spaniard, and the most keen instrument against the Puritan Roundhead rebels.

But even they were 'better versed in the art of begging than fighting', while in April 1657 it was reported that 'of all the armies in Europe there is none wherein so much debauchery is to be seen as in these few forces which the King hath gotten together, being so extraordinarily profane from the highest to the lowest . . .'.[9]

Despite these strictures, the small Royalist army, commanded by the Duke of York, fought alongside the Spanish Army of Flanders in the campaigns of 1657 and 1658, climaxing in the Battle of the Dunes (14 June 1658). Here the English Civil War was transported to the sand dunes of Flanders when the Royalist troops clashed with Cromwellian forces under Sir William Lockhart serving with the French Army. But the outcome of the battle was a resounding defeat for the Spanish and their Royalist allies.[10] This was a major setback for King Charles, and raised serious doubts as to the likely fate of his troops at the hands of the Cromwellian army in any invasion of England. To make matters worse, the truce that the Spaniards reached with the French in the summer of 1659 meant that they no longer had any interest in supporting Charles' schemes to recover the English throne, or in maintaining his army.

Although Charles managed to preserve the structure of his force, by the summer of 1659 his understrength regiments mustered no more than 2,000 men in all.

RESTORATION

In the event the Restoration of 1660 was achieved without a shot being fired. Although their King 'enjoyed his own again', the outcome was far from being the unallayed Royalist triumph hoped for by his supporters, many of whom, including Byron, Hopton and Sir Richard Grenville, did not in any case live long enough to enjoy its fruits.

For the Cavalier veterans, the compromise nature of the political settlement limited opportunities for reward, revenge and self-aggrandisement. First to be disappointed were King Charles' loyal army in exile. With the possible exception of his Regiment of Guards, a force that consisted mainly of unpopular Scotsmen and former Irish Catholic rebels was a political embarrassment which the King thought better than to parade before his uneasily reconciled English subjects. For months to come, the remnants were left in Flanders to survive as best they could.

In theory, the Royalist forces were to be absorbed into the garrison of Dunkirk, and the more acceptable of them, such as the Duke of York's Regiment, quickly were.[11] The fate of the remainder was less happy. A largely unheeding government in London was bombarded by petitions from their desperate officers. The King's Regiment hoped for assistance from their Colonel, Lord Wentworth, who had returned to the fleshpots of England. In August 1660 his officers petitioned him:

> We are scarcely left one part of four who at Dunkirk battle entirely devoted themselves to be sacrificed for our King's sake, rather than deceive his reposed confidence in the resolve of his too few [at the time] loyal subjects. But having escaped the worst, beyond our hope, as to be prisoners, three parts of us perished with a tedious imprisonment and want of bread, and the few remainder here languish as having no allowance to live.[12]

They received no reply, and spent a bitter winter in the Spanish garrison of Nivelles, the officers 'obliged to sell their clothes, some even to their last shirt',[13] grudgingly granted quarters by the Governor, but told to 'expect their own subsistence from their own King, being restored to three Kingdoms'. Captain John Gwynne wrote that the mutinous men were forced to 'beg, steale or starve', and lovingly recollected a Christmas dinner for himself and his fellow officers of 'a well-grown young fat dog, as cleanly drest, and as finely roasted, as any man need put into his belly'.[14] The worst deprivations of the King's Guards came to an end early in 1661, when they were ordered to Dunkirk and recruited, reorganised and re-equipped. In November 1665, when Dunkirk was handed back to France, the regiment was returned to England to be amalgamated with the King's Regiment of Foot Guards.

Their Scottish and Irish comrades suffered a harsher fate. Partly because of fears of disputes with the ex-Cromwellian members of its garrison, they were not admitted to Dunkirk but left to subsist as best they could in nearby Mardyke. Some of the Irish soldiers built huts of earth sods for themselves and their wives and children, whom, the Governor of Dunkirk complained, 'take up much room', while their officers bemoaned that they had 'pawned or sold all they had, even their very clothes and arms, to maintain themselves'.[15] The Irish (and to a lesser extent, the Scots) were in a worse state than the English troops; as former rebels, the Irish officers 'in spite of their fidelity, fear that if they return to Ireland, their arms will be taken from them, and they will be thrown into gaol, on pretence of dangerousness'.[16]

Some of the Irish eventually returned to French service; the lack of concern that the English government felt towards them is illustrated by the fact that they completely forgot about the 380 men of the Duke of Gloucester's Regiment, until reminded by its commander, who was then sent orders to disband it.[17] The solution to disposing of the remaining troops (Royalist and Cromwellian) around Dunkirk was provided by the King's marriage acquisition of Tangier. They were incorporated in the garrison sent to defend this new outpost. Most of the 'forgotten army' of King Charles II would leave their bones in the

African sand, another testimony to the ingratitude of the Stuarts to their most loyal servants.

THE OLD CAVALIERS

Not least among the problems facing Charles II on his restoration to the English throne was the need to recompense and reward the thousands of veterans of his father's armies of the First Civil War. With limited means at his disposal, and mindful of the need to tread carefully in his as yet insecure new domain, Charles inevitably failed to meet all expectations.

One solution, particularly for the professional and career soldiers, were postings in the regular army. However, with the military establishment considerably reduced by a 'Cavalier' Parliament with bitter memories of the New Model, scope was limited. In May 1660 Charles II had two armies. In Flanders were the remnants of his 'Royalist army', while in England he inherited the Cromwellian forces. Both were in poor condition. While the regular army had not opposed the Restoration, it was divided and demoralised, its pay badly in arrears. Charles felt unable to trust it, and for the moment relied upon George Monck as Commander-in-Chief to keep the troops in line. He quickly became convinced of the need to disband most of them, while placing command of those regiments retained in reliable hands. The disbandment went smoothly, partly because Parliament ensured that funds were available to pay off the men, and by early 1661, hastened by security scares, the formation of the new army, which never exceeded about 6,000 men, had begun.[18] As well as military considerations, one of the King's motives in forming his new army was to reward and employ some of the horde of impoverished former officers of his own and his father's old Royalist armies. As a result, many old Cavaliers resumed their military careers, though often in a more subordinate role than they had previously enjoyed.

Thus, in November 1660, John Russell, former Lieutenant Colonel of Prince Rupert's Regiment of Foot and a professional soldier, became Colonel of the First Foot Guards. At the age of forty-eight, Russell, like many of the Cavalier appointees, was well past his military prime and such appointments, while politically and personally understandable, did little for military efficiency. Henry Washington, the ferocious ex-Governor of Worcester, was Russell's Major. Others had to be content with lesser rank. Lord Charles Gerrard received a captaincy, albeit in the prestigious Lifeguard of Horse, with his Major General of the First Civil War, Randolph Egerton, as his Lieutenant. That other noted cavalry commander, the Earl of Northampton, was also a Captain of Horse, while Sir William Leighton, former Lieutenant Colonel of the King's Lifeguard of Foot, was a Captain in his Majesty's Own Regiment of Foot.[19] Prince Rupert's old protégé, Will Legge, was made Captain of the Tower of London, and Bernard de Gomme became Surveyor General.[20]

Some, particularly career soldiers of more plebeian status, took up appointments with the English forces serving overseas. Sir Abraham Shipman, former Governor of Chester, and Sir Gervase Lucas, who had held Belvoir Castle, both impoverished, were even prepared to serve as Governors of far-off Bombay.[21] The elderly Lord Belasyse, who had served under Newcastle and then as Governor of Newark, finished his undistinguished military career as a mediocre Governor of Tangier.[22]

There was no way that commissions could be found in the greatly reduced English military establishment for all the old Cavaliers seeking employment, and many were reduced to serving in the ranks. Captain John Gwynne, for example, became a trooper in the Lifeguard.[23] Most of those obtaining military employment were men who had held senior rank during the Civil Wars, or were in a position to exert political or personal influence. The King was still faced with a flood of petitions for assistance and compensation from old Royalists of lesser standing. In an effort to ameliorate the situation, in 1662 Parliament passed an Act for the relief 'of many Worthy Persons brought into great Distress for their Service to the Crown'.[24] The sum of £60,000 was to be raised from a Poll Bill and distributed among former officers of the Royalist armies without means of support. Claimants were verified by commissioners in the regions, appointed from men of local standing, and payments awarded on a graduated scale, based on arrears of pay outstanding from the war. The exact definition of hardship is unclear, as well as the efficiency with which the claims were assessed.[25] The published *List of Claimants*, or 'Indigent Officers',[26] contained the names of 5,353 men, mostly below field officer rank. It is unsurprising that this attempt failed to solve the problem. In 1663, for example, it was felt necessary to organise a plate lottery for the benefit of impoverished Cavaliers.[27]

Often suffering even greater hardship were many of the former rank and file of the old Royalist armies. Though some of the wounded had, in theory at least, been granted pensions during the war,[28] these, even if ever paid, ceased with the King's defeat. During the Interregnum, veteran Royalist soldiers or their families in need would have had to rely on the support of their parish or local almshouse. The Restoration resulted in a flood of petitions for relief to county Quarter Sessions throughout the country. In 1662 Parliament passed an Act authorising the payment of small pensions to maimed or indigent former Royalist soldiers or their widows.[29] Applicants had to produce a certificate from an officer under whom he (or the husband of a widow) had served, or be otherwise vouched for by persons of local standing. In addition to a pension, the Justices could order parish relief. The total numbers of claimants are impossible to estimate. The records for many counties have not survived, and there seems to have been considerable regional variation in both the degree of generosity with which local justices interpreted the Act, and in the energy of former officers, squires and local parsons in supporting the petitioners. In Dorset, for example, 815 petitioners are recorded, while in neighbouring Wiltshire the number is only 327.[30]

Petitioners' claims varied widely. In Cheshire, Robert Warburton of Warburton, a labourer, had been a trooper under Richard Massie in Sir Robert Byron's Regiment. During the war he had lost his horse, saddle, bridle and pistols, worth £7, and never received any pay. Richard Heyes, also of Warburton, had served under Lord Byron at Montgomery, where he lost a mare that had cost him £7 and was shot in the thigh and shoulder. Anne Beckwith, a widow, petitioned that her husband had been a soldier for over three years in Henry Mainwaring's company of Gamull's foot. He was wounded and taken prisoner at Chrisleton in January 1645, and then imprisoned at Nantwich where he died.[31]

Many soldiers had fought and suffered the length of England in the service of King Charles. One such was Rowland Humphrey, a Welsh soldier of Sir Charles Lloyd's Regiment, who petitioned from Devizes where the regiment had been in garrison for much of the war and where Humphrey had evidently settled. He:

> was long before the Battaile att Edgehill a foote Souldier in the service of the late Kings Matie Charles the first in the late Warrs in a Regt under the command of the then Coll. Sr Thomas Salusbury until his Deathe . . . & afterwards in the same Regiment under Sr Charles Lloyd where yor peticonr was made a Corporall & was sometymes in the foote Company of Capt. Robert Chaloner and sometymes of Capt. John Edwards in the same Regimt & so continued in the same service for the space of three yeares and upwards & untill after the Devizes Garrison was taken from the said Sr Charles Lloyd shortly after wch yor petr was forced to leave the same by reason of the Great Losse of bloud wch he had susteyned to the greate weakninge of his body through ye meanes of seaven sev'all woundes & wch yor petr had before that tyme received in the said service vidcet:- one wound wth a sword in the head in ye fight at Newbery; one shott through the hand in the same ffight; one shott through the Legg at Kidlington Greene betweene Oxford & Woodstocke, one wound wth a sword in the knee att Banbury, one wounde in the left Arme in Cornwall whereby he hath allmost lost the use of it; one great Cutt wth a sword in the handrist at the taking Bristoll for King Charles and alsoe a great blow with a muskett in the mouth wch beate out allmost all his teeth before besides the cutting of his Lippes, at the sidge att Readinge. All wch said woundes and blowes hath soe decayed yor petrs body that he is thereby made almost unfitt for any bodily Labor & so unable to worke to gayne a Livelihood for himselfe & wife & two children, yor petr beinge growne poore & lost his estate he then had by reason of his being in the said service.[32]

He was awarded £3 a year, to be paid quarterly.

During the following decades, King Charles' old soldiers gradually faded from the scene. Few had received any great material reward for their services, and most of those who had resumed military careers were dead or finally retired within a decade. Some remained active for longer. Charles Gerrard was a supporter of William of Orange in the Revolution of 1688, while Richard Grace, sometime captain in Prince Rupert's Regiment of Horse and colonel of a regiment of Irish foot in Charles II's army in exile, defended Athlone for King James against the Williamite forces in 1691. Perhaps the last-surviving field officers of the Royalist army were Sir Henry Newton, Lieutenant Colonel to the Prince of Wales' Regiment of Horse, who died in 1701, and Major William Beaw, who became a bishop and lived until 1705.

The date of death of the last soldier of King Charles I is unknown, but some evidently reached a great age. William Hasland, who claimed to have fought at Edgehill and then for William III in Flanders, was granted a Chelsea pension of 1s. a day in 1731 at the reputed age of 111. Even more remarkably, the London press of 1736 reported the survival in Ribchester, Lancashire, of William Walker, an old Cavalier aged 123 who had had two horses shot from under him at Edgehill.[33] If, incredibly, this contained some element of truth, Walker must certainly have been the last Cavalier.

CONCLUSION

Within four years of the defeat at Naseby, King Charles was dead, executed by a victorious Parliament, and his son and heir a penurious Continental exile. Repeated Royalist insurrection and intrigue never seriously threatened the grip of the new regime in England and when Charles II was restored to his British thrones in 1660, he came back not as a result of military triumph but in consequence of the internal collapse of the regime and the unwillingness of the bulk of the army to continue to maintain it. A restored monarchy was seen by most Englishmen as the only alternative to anarchy. Viewed in this context, the failure of the Royalist armies of the First Civil War seems absolute. Yet to view the Cavalier war effort purely with hindsight ignores its considerable achievements, not to mention the fact that, if events on more than one occasion had turned out but a little differently, King Charles might have been victorious.

The first considerable Cavalier achievement was their success in fielding a viable fighting force in 1642. At a time when Parliament had most of the material advantages, there was a real possibility during the opening weeks of the war that the Royalists might be crushed, and King Charles captured, before his field army could be formed. Such an outcome was avoided partly through the hesitancy of Parliament's Lord General, the Earl of Essex, and partly because of the strenuous efforts and improvisation of the King's commanders.

Yet the army that fought at Edgehill, though respectable in numbers, was seriously deficient in equipment. It was these continuing shortages, particularly in munitions, that prevented the Oxford Army from taking the offensive during the first half of 1643. It was probably only Essex's lethargy, and the disease that ravaged his army during the early summer of 1643, which prevented the Parliamentarians from taking the Royalist capital of Oxford, with incalculable results for the progress of the war.

The Royalist success in overcoming their material disadvantages was considerable, and is frequently underestimated. Beginning the war with very limited arms production, by the summer of 1643, despite almost total Parliamentarian supremacy at sea, they were able to equip three major field armies, largely by means of imports from abroad, and to carry through the major offensive operations that brought about two-thirds of the total area of England and Wales, including England's second city of Bristol, under their control. From this point onwards, the creation of a munitions industry, virtually from scratch, at Oxford, Bristol and elsewhere, meant that the Royalists were generally adequately equipped; shortages at critical moments were frequently caused by distribution problems rather than a lack of munitions.

The Royalists made little permanent imprint on English military development. Prince Rupert's oft-cited 'innovations' in cavalry tactics, though they may have differed slightly initially from the Continental practices on which they were based, rapidly came to reflect them closely. Though there is evidence that Royalist commanders continued to introduce European innovations, the same process may be observed among their opponents, and indeed the English Civil War as a whole led to no significant new military development beyond the creation of a standing army. England remained backward in the art of war compared with Continental powers such as France, and even Cromwell's New Model Army was, on the whole, traditional in its organisation and tactics.

Other Royalist disadvantages were never mastered. From the start of the war Parliament benefited not only from possession of London and its resources, but also from largely undisputed control of most of south-east and eastern England. This gave it the advantage of interior lines, and also the ability to develop a stable and efficient local administration. The position of the Royalists was much less satisfactory. Their main recruiting areas in Wales, the North and the West were a considerable distance from the ultimately decisive theatre of war in southern England, and regionalism, the demands of local commanders, long and insecure lines of communication and increasing reluctance to serve made it very difficult to utilise their resources effectively. The larger reservoir of manpower available to the Parliamentarians not only made it easier for them to recruit, but also left them less vulnerable to defeat than were the Royalists. As both Marston Moor and Naseby were to demonstrate, a major reverse for the main Royalist field armies was a disaster of potentially fatal proportions, while after a similar defeat at Lostwithiel in September 1644, Essex was able to rebuild his army within weeks.

These inherent weaknesses were among the factors limiting the development of a coherent Royalist grand strategy. In 1642 the King felt that the occupation of London would be sufficient to end the war in his favour. Whether he was correct in this supposition is debatable, but even if Essex's army had been substantially defeated at Edgehill it is questionable if the Royalist forces, especially with the approach of winter, would have been capable of taking London in the face of continued determined resistance. It is still more unlikely, with the fortifications of the capital steadily strengthened, that any later assault would have succeeded, so long as any viable Parliamentarian armies remained in the field to prevent a complete blockade being imposed, and so long as the Parliamentarian fleet retained command of the sea.

It could indeed be argued that the failure to end the war quickly in 1642 left the Royalists not only at an increasing disadvantage as time went on, but also lacking a feasible war-winning strategy. For the King, 1643 was a year of consolidation, aimed at securing control of the provinces and clearing supply lines to the temporary Royalist capital of Oxford, and gaining support from Ireland and overseas, prior to a renewed assault on the Parliamentarian 'heartland' of south-east England by all available forces.

It was a strategy which met with some, but not enough, success. Though the King's failure to take Gloucester in September has been held to be the turning point of the war, more damaging was the inability of the Oxford Army to destroy Essex's forces soon afterwards at the First Battle of Newbury. A Royalist victory there would have so threatened London as to force Parliament to attempt to divert the army of the Eastern Association southwards to protect the capital, considerably easing the task of Newcastle's Northern Royalists in countering the imminent Scots invasion.

By 1644 the material superiority of Parliament was being felt increasingly. Although the Scots alliance never bore all of its hoped-for benefits to the English Parliament, the Scots army tilted the balance of the war in the North. More and more the Royalists found themselves encountering numerically superior enemy forces, so that hopes of victory depended upon isolating individual enemy armies and bringing them to battle in situations of disadvantage. There is no doubt that, from the strictly military viewpoint, the decision to maintain Oxford as the Royalist capital, rather than switching to a more secure location such as Bristol or Exeter, was a serious mistake. Rather like the choice of the Confederate government in the American Civil War to shift their capital to Richmond, dangerously close to the main theatre of war, the safety of Oxford, itself of limited military value except as a jumping-off point for an advance on London, and after the rise of Bristol of less importance as a munitions centre, became a factor that seriously distorted Royalist strategy. The 1644 campaign focused on using the forces built up along the Welsh Border by Prince Rupert to join Newcastle in crushing the Scots invasion as quickly as possible before the King, with the now clearly inferior Oxford Army, could be overwhelmed by the Parliamentarian armies in the South. It was a high-risk option, but the only one now open to the Royalists. In fact, it came closer to succeeding than is often realised. Given greater cooperation between Rupert and Newcastle, the result of Marston Moor could easily have been different, and Royalist victory in the North, coupled with the King's success in isolating and defeating Essex at Lostwithiel, might have been enough to win for the Royalists at least a favourable compromise peace.

Marston Moor was the decisive battle of the English Civil Wars. After it, Royalist strategy displayed increasing desperation, with the Oxford Army the only major effective field army remaining to the King. Only the ineptitude of its opponents, and the skill of some of its commanders, preserved it from destruction at the Second Battle of Newbury in October 1644. By the opening of the 1645 campaign, it is hard to accept that Prince Rupert was being realistic in his purported belief in the possibility of winning a compromise peace. If the Royalists had accepted the strategy proposed by, among others, Lord Digby and George Goring, in preference to Rupert's Northern projects, they might well have inflicted a serious defeat on the New Model Army but, without a major failure of nerve by the King's opponents, this could have done little more than delay the inevitable.

In assessing the causes of Royalist defeat, much of the blame is inevitably placed upon King Charles and various of his advisers and senior commanders. Certainly, there was considerable disunity in the Royalist high command, and lack of a firm guiding central authority. Yet for much of the war the Royalists were at no more of a disadvantage in this respect than their opponents. Parliament had its own insubordinate generals, and its direction of the war was equally at the mercy of the intrigues of competing political factions. So far as military matters were concerned, King Charles seems generally to have taken the advice of his Lord General, the Earl of Forth, and until the autumn of 1644 the operations of the Oxford Army were on the whole coherent and reasonably successful.

The decisive change came in the winter of 1644/5, and the opening weeks of the new campaigning season. With the formation of the New Model Army, Parliament, its determination to win revitalised by the rise of the Independents, at last obtained a unified fighting force under capable commanders. More importantly, the war's directing body, the Committee of Both Kingdoms, which was handling administrative matters with increasing effectiveness, finally delegated operational control of the new army to its commanders. None of these reforms were matched, or perhaps even possible, on the Royalist side. The shrinkage of territory under the King's control not only reduced the dwindling resources available to him, but exacerbated the breakdown of local administration, bringing with it increasing military anarchy and civilian discontent. Prince Rupert was clearly an unfortunate choice to succeed Forth in command of the Royalist armies. His authority, incomplete from the start, was further undercut by his uncle's wavering support. Rupert's own limitations of character, youth, foreign birth, and relative inexperience helped make his appointment an overall disaster for the Royalist cause. The defeat at Naseby, with the King unable, as usual, to exert his authority over rival subordinate factions, Rupert effectively opting out as Commander-in-Chief on the day of battle, and the best of the King's troops absent in the West, displayed the failings of the Royalists at their worst.

Yet it is hard to see how, in the circumstances obtaining by early 1645, anyone else could have fared better. The Royalist armies collapsed as much because of the failings of their own administrative system, and the exhaustion and war-weariness of the areas from which the King had drawn most of his support, as from military defeat. In the end, it was not material shortages, or even lack of potential manpower, which doomed the Cavalier armies but the refusal of the bedrock of the King's support, the rural gentry and their dependants, to support any longer what they deemed to be a lost cause.

NOTES

1. Background to War

1. C.H. Firth, *Cromwell's Army*, 4th edn, London, 1962, p. 1.
2. For example, Sir Edward Cecil in 1628 (quoted Firth, *Cromwell's Army*, pp. 5–6).
3. See Edward M. Furgol, *A Regimental History of the Covenanting Armies, 1639–51*, Edinburgh, 1990, p. 2.
4. Philipp Eliot-Wright, *The English Civil War*, London, 1997, pp.12–13.
5. Mark Charles Fissel, *The Bishops' Wars: Charles I's Campaigns against Scotland, 1638–40*, Cambridge, 1994, p. 195.
6. R.H. Morris and P.H. Lawson, *The Siege of Chester*, Chester, 1923, p. 18.
7. Robert Ward, *Animadiversions of War*, London, 1635, p. 30.
8. Morris and Lawson, *Siege of Chester*, p. 18.
9. Fissel, *The Bishops' Wars*, p. 270.
10. *Ibid.*, p. 100.
11. *Ibid.*, *passim*.
12. Peter Newman, 'The Royalist Officer Corps, 1642–46: army command as a reflection of the social structure', in *Historical Journal* 26, 1983, pp. 945–58.
13. For example, Joyce Lee Malcolm, *Caesar's Due: Loyalty and King Charles 1642–46*, London, 1983, esp. Chap. 3.
14. Edward, Earl of Clarendon, *History of the Great Rebellion*, edited by W.D. Macray, 6 vols, Oxford, 1888, Vol. II, p. 335.
15. Peter Young, *Edgehill 1642*, Kineton, 1967, pp. 214–34.
16. Malcolm, *Caesar's Due*, p. 81.
17. See Chap. 11 of the present work, p. 11.
18. Malcolm, *Caesar's Due*, p. 80.

2. The Officers

1. Young, *Edgehill*, p. 5.
2. F. Benfield (ed.), *A Royalist's Notebook: the Commonplace Book of Sir John Oglander*, New York, 1971, p. 109.

3. The (very limited) change in social status of the officer corps of the New Model Army would not be apparent until 1647 onwards.

4. Quoted Peter Newman, *The Old Service: Royalist Regimental Colonels and the Civil War, 1642–46*, Manchester, 1993, p. 29.

5. For our purposes this may be broadly defined as a member of the peerage.

6. Examples of the former are the units of Gilbert Gerrard and Lord Molyneux raised in Lancashire, mainly from tenants and retainers of the Earl of Derby. Of the family-orientated units, Sir John Byron's Regiment of Horse, which included among its officers three of his five brothers, is one example. The regional character of regiments should not be exaggerated. Many raised only a cadre in their 'home' territory, and then recruited throughout the King's march through the West Midlands.

7. Examples include Sir John Byron and Sir Charles Gerrard, both with extensive pre-war military service in the Low Countries, who had not, however, been so employed for some time prior to 1642.

8. An extreme example of the latter was the Scottish professional soldier Sir James Turner, who claimed that his choice of side was determined solely by the destination of the first ship to leave the port of Hamburg! (Sir James Turner, *Memoirs*, edited by J. Thompson, Edinburgh, 1829, p. 45.)

9. Sir Richard Bulstrode, *Memoirs . . .*, London, 1721, p. 75.

10. *Ibid.*

11. Young, *Edgehill*, pp. 207–8.

12. *Ibid.*, p. 216.

13. *Ibid.*, p. 219.

14. *Ibid.*, pp. 219–20.

15. *Ibid.*, p. 224.

16. Sir Edmund Duncombe, a man of 'mean extraction', was unable to maintain the regiment of horse that he raised in 1643.

17. Stuart Reid, *Officers and Regiments of the Royalist Army*, Southend-on-Sea, nd, pp. 27–8.

18. See Newman, 'Royalist Officer Corps', pp. 945–58.

19. Reid, *Officers*, pp. 151–2.

20. The same characteristics, if not as strongly marked, may be found among the 'old' foot regiments of the Oxford Army. Lord Astley's had officers from at least seven counties, and the King's Lifeguard from six (*Ibid.*, pp. 5–6; 105–6).

21. Newman, *Old Service*, p. 128.

22. *Ibid.*, pp. 127–9.

23. The term 'swordsmen' is used to cover the various categories of officer who, generally speaking, depended on his military career for his livelihood.

24. Crawford is an example of the difficulty often encountered in determining whether an officer served the King primarily out of mercenary motives or from conviction. Most of the foreigners with the Royalists probably served from the latter motive.

25. He was eventually hanged by the Royalists for rape, among other crimes.

26. Reid, *Officers*, p. 147.

27. *Ibid.*, p. 110.

28. Lord Byron evidently had doubts regarding the authenticity of the title, remarking that he 'gave himself the title of Lord St Pol' (Lord John Byron, 'Account of the Siege of Chester', in *Cheshire Sheaf*, 4th series, No. 6, 1971, p. 10).

29. For these and others see Peter Newman, *Biographical Dictionary of Royalist Officers in England and Wales, 1642–1660*, New York, 1981, *passim*.

30. There is no detailed treatment of this enigmatic character. See DNB for life and sources.

31. Newman, *Old Service*, p. 138. The word 'cavalier' was derived from 'cabellero', referring in this case to the Spanish light cavalry who earned an unsavoury reputation in Europe.

32. *Ibid.*

33. Sir Henry Slingsby, *Diary*, edited by D. Parsons, Edinburgh, 1836, p. 139.

34. Newman, *Old Service*, pp. 207–8. Significantly, Newman quotes figures which suggest that officers believed to be Catholic had a much higher chance of being denied quarter.

35. Quoted in John Lewis (ed.), *May It Please Your Highness*, Newtown, 1996, p. 37.

3. The Horse

1. John Vernon, *The Young Horseman*, London, 1644 (reprinted Southend-on-Sea, 1995), pp. 34–5.

2. *Ibid.*, p. 35.

3. Quoted in Basil Reckitt, *Charles I and Hull*, London, 1951, p. 20.

4. Young, *Edgehill*, p. 209.

5. Clarendon, *Great Rebellion*, Vol. VI, p. 73.

6. W.C. Abbott, *Writings and Speeches of Oliver Cromwell*, 4 vols, Oxford, 1939, Vol. I, p. 204.

7. Young, *Edgehill*, pp. 208–9; Newman, *Biographical Dictionary*, item 985.

8. CCRO, QSR 1/643, 743.

9. Bulstrode, *Memoirs*, quoted in Young, *Edgehill*, pp. 269–70.

10. B.P. von Chemnitz, *Koniglichen Schwedischen in Teustschland, 1648*, Vol. I, quoted in Richard Brzezinski and Richard Hook, *The Army of Gustavus Adolphus: Cavalry*, London, 1993, p. 23.

11. Stuart Reid, personal communication.

12. Brzezinski and Hook, *Cavalry*, p. 24.

13. Clarendon, *Great Rebellion*, Vol. VI, p. 85.

14. Anon [Bernard de Gomme?], *His Highnesse Prince Rupert's Late Beating up of the Rebel's Quarters . . . and his Victory at Chalgrove Field*, Oxford, 1643, p. 8.

15. Peter Young (ed.), 'Sir John Byron's Relation to the Secretary of State of the Last Western Action between the Lord Wilmot and Sir William Waller', in *Journal of the Society for Army Historical Research*, Vol. XXXI, No. 127, 1953, p. 23.

16. Peter Young (ed.), *Military Memoirs of the Civil War*, London, 1963, p. 23.

17. *Ibid.*, pp. 7–8.

18. Ian Roy (ed.), *The Royalist Ordnance Papers*, Parts I and II, Oxfordshire Record Society, 1964 and 1974, Part I, item B 41.

19. *Ibid.*, item B 193.

20. *Mercurius Aulicus*, 16 November 1644, p. 1,258.

21. Stuart Peachey and Alan Turton, *The Chief Strength of the Army*, Southend-on-Sea, 1991, p. 76.

22. Staffs. RO, *Denbigh Letterbooks*, CR2017/C9, f. 126.

23. F. Redlich, *The German Military Entrepreneur and his Workforce*, New York, 1964, quoted in *English Civil War Notes and Queries*, No. 44.

24. Edward Robinson, *Discourse of the Warr in Lancashire*, edited by William Beaumont, Chetham Society, Vol. LXII, 1864, pp. 56–7. Information supplied by Alan Turton.

25. John Cruso, *Militarie Instructions for the Cavall'rie*, London, 1632, p. 64.

26. R.N. Dore (ed.), *Letterbooks of Sir William Brereton, Vol. II*, Record Society of Lancashire and Cheshire, Vol. 128, 1990, items 770 and 801.

27. Eliot Warburton, *Memoirs of Prince Rupert and the Cavaliers*, 3 vols, London, 1849, Vol. II, p. 69.

28. *Ibid.*, pp. 70–1.

29. Vernon, *Young Horseman*, p. 86.

30. Lord Saye and Sele, *Vindiciae Veritatis*, quoted in Peter Newman, *Marston Moor*, Chichester, 1981, p. 79. It is unlikely that more than about 25 per cent of the Royalist troopers could have been classified as 'gentlemen'.

31. Quoted Newman, *Marston Moor*.
32. The most detailed study of Naseby is Glenn Foard, *Naseby: The Decisive Campaign*, Whitstable, 1995.
33. BL, Harleian MS 986, ff. 83–90.
34. For Marrow and his officers see Newman, *Biographical Dictionary*, items 432, 943 and 1,546; Reid, *Officers*, pp. 123–4.
35. Bulstrode, *Memoirs*, p. 134.
36. Thomas Carte, *Original Letters*, 2 vols, London, 1739, pp. 109–10.
37. Clarendon, *Great Rebellion*, Vol. IX, p. 135.
38. Dore, *Letterbooks, Vol. II*, item 770.
39. Quoted in J. Fortescue, *History of the British Army*, 13 vols, London, 1910–13, Vol. II, p. 282.

4. The Foot

1. See Keith Roberts, *Soldiers of the English Civil War: 1. Infantry*, London, 1989, p. 15.
2. Apart from the colonel's, which was commanded by a 'captain-lieutenant'.
3. Young, *Edgehill*, p. 233.
4. *Ibid.*, p. 16.
5. Clarendon, *Great Rebellion*, Vol. VIII, p. 32.
6. *Ibid.*
7. Newman, *Biographical Dictionary*, item 895.
8. Matthew Carter, *True relation of that Unfortunate as Gallant Expedition to Kent and Colchester 1648*, 2nd edn, London, 1759, p. 190.
9. Peter Young, *Naseby 1645*, London, 1985, p. 34.
10. Eliot-Wright, *English Civil War*, p. 94.
11. Clarendon, *Great Rebellion*, Vol. VI, p. 83.
12. Eliot-Wright, *English Civil War*, p. 96.
13. *Ibid.*
14. Apart perhaps for a few pot helmets, the Oxford Army pikemen were dressed identically to the musketeers.
15. Roy, *Royalist Ordnance Papers*, Part II, item B 71.
16. Eliot-Wright, *English Civil War*, p. 105.
17. CSPD, 1644, p. 204
18. Eliot-Wright, *English Civil War*, pp. 95–6.
19. BL, Harleian MS 8502, f. 89.
20. See John Barratt, 'The King's Lifeguard of Foot', in *Military Illustrated*, No. 54, November 1992, pp. 24–9.
21. BL, Harleian MS 6851, f. 219.
22. BL, Harleian MS 6802, f. 95.

23. Red was becoming the standard coat colour in the Parliamentarian forces, although the New Model Army was not, as often stated, an all-redcoat force from the start.

24. Som. RO, Phelips MSS, DD/PH/27, f. 77.

25. For the increasing significance of the musketeer see Stuart Reid, *Gunpowder Triumphant*, 2nd edn, Southend-on-Sea, 1989.

26. *Ibid.*, pp. 35–6. The availability of muskets, both from the Bristol manufacturers and imported from the Continent via Weymouth, was a key factor in this.

27. See Young, *Edgehill*, p. 233.

28. See Barratt, 'The King's Lifeguard of Foot', pp. 24–9.

29. See (with caution) Joyce Lee Malcolm, 'A King in Search of Soldiers: Charles I in 1642', in *Historical Journal* 21, 1978, pp. 251–73, and M.D.G. Wanklyn and Peter Young, 'King in Search of Soldiers: a Rejoinder', in *Historical Journal* 24, 1981, pp. 47–54.

30. Richard Gough, *The History of Myddle*, London, 1981 edn, p. 5.

31. *Ibid.*

32. *Ibid.*, p. 51

33. CCRO, QSR 1/641.

34. *Ibid.*

35. John Barratt, *For Chester and King Charles: Francis Gamull's Regiment and the Defence of Chester*, Birkenhead, 1995.

36. Charles Carlton, *Going to the Wars*, London, 1992, p. 261.

37. John Lynch, *For King and Parliament: Bristol in the English Civil War*, Stroud, 1999, p. 69.

38. BL, Harleian MS 6852, f. 193; Ian Roy, 'The Royalist Army in the First Civil War', pp. 186–7. Cornwall was for a time excused impressment, as well as a few other places such as Oxford and Chester, provided they raised regiments for their own defence.

39. HMC, 15th Report, App. II, p. 104.

40. Clive Holmes, *The Eastern Association in the English Civil War*, London, 1974, p. 166.

41. Malcolm, *Caesar's Due*, p. 110.

42. G.N. Godwin, *The Civil War in Hampshire*, London, 1904, p. 127.

43. Young, *Naseby*, p. 99.

44. Even if captured, until the latter stages of the war such men were normally exchanged. Then Parliament greatly reduced its participation in this practice, possibly because few of its own men were being taken prisoner.

45. A sample of petitions in the CCRO shows over fifty men who claimed two or more years' continuous service, in many cases extending for the duration of the war.

46. Clarendon, *Great Rebellion*, Vol. VIII, p. 145.

47. BL, Harleian MS 986.
48. *Ibid.*
49. Eliot-Wright, *English Civil War*, p. 124.
50. Official rates of pay varied widely in different Royalist armies at various stages of the war. In any case, the reality rarely matched the theory, but the relative proportions of pay for officers and other ranks remained roughly the same.
51. Stuart Peachey and Alan Turton, *Old Robin's Foot*, Southend-on-Sea, 1987, p. 58.
52. Young, *Naseby*, pp. 78–107.
53. Quoted Reid, *Gunpowder Triumphant*, p. 28.
54. Norman Tucker (ed.), *Military Memoirs: The Civil War: Memoirs of John Gwynn*, London, 1967, p. 46.
55. Sir Edward Walker, *Historical Discourses upon Several Occasions . . .*, London, 1705, p. 130.
56. For a detailed analysis of the infantry action see Foard, *Naseby*, Chap. 5.
57. Bodleian Library, Clarendon MS 23.
58. Tucker, *John Gwynn*, p. 53.
59. BL, Harleian MS 6804, f. 92.
60. Richard Elton, *Compleat Body of the Art Militarie*, London, 1650, p. 73.
61. 'Relation of Colonel Walter Slingsby', in Ralph, Lord Hopton, *Bellum Civile*, edited by C.E.H. Chadwyck-Healey, *Transactions of the Somerset Record Society*, Vol. 18, 1902, p. 54.
62. *Kingdom's Weekly Intelligencer*, 10–17 June 1645.
63. Bulstrode Whitelocke, *Memorials of English Affairs*, London, 1682, p. 145.
64. See Minutes of the Royalist Council of War at Hereford, 23 June 1645, quoted in Warburton, *Memoirs*, Vol. III, pp. 119–20; BL, Harleian MS 6852, ff. 273, 277. Lieutenant Colonel Leighton of the King's Lifeguard was in Hereford as late as December 1645, still attempting to re-form his regiment. Only about two regiments of foot, commanded by professional soldiers, seem actually to have been completed in South Wales and despatched across the Bristol Channel to serve with the Royalist forces in the West.

5. *Dragoons and Firelocks*

1. Gervase Markham, *The Souldier's Accidence*, London, 1625, p. 42.
2. Duc de Rohan, *Complete Captain*, London, 1631, p. 10.
3. Markham, *Souldier's Accidence*, p. 42.

4. Sir James Turner, *Pallas Armata: Militarie Essayes of the Ancient Grecian, Roman and Modern Art of War*, London, 1683, p. 236.

5. Cruso, *Militarie Instructions*, p. 31.

6. Vernon, *Young Horseman*, p. 8.

7. Roy, *Royalist Ordnance Papers*, Part II, item B 125.

8. *Ibid.*, item B 193.

9. For example, on 16 June 1643 Henry Washington's Dragoons were issued with 36 muskets and 36 bags with girdles and hangers (*Ibid.*, item B 127). In December 1642 the Royalist Council of War ordered the manufacture of 3-ft long muskets specifically for the dragoons, but it is unclear if these were ever issued.

10. See Newman, *Biographical Dictionary*, items 458, 1,470 and 1,545.

11. The same characteristics may be observed in the Parliamentarian army of the Earl of Essex, suggesting a deliberate policy adopted by both sides.

12. Young, *Edgehill*, p. 110. They also outnumbered the Parliamentarian dragoons by two to one.

13. *Ibid.*, pp. 182–3.

14. Howard Clayton, *Loyal and Ancient City*, Lichfield, nd, p. 45.

15. Holmes, *Eastern Association*, p. 169.

16. Roy, *Royalist Ordnance Papers*, Part II, item B 136. In the event the supplies were actually despatched by wagon, and captured.

17. Bulstrode, *Memoirs*, p. 100.

18. Roy, *Royalist Ordnance Papers*, Part II, item B 289.

19. John Barratt, *For Duty Alone: Hopton's Account of the Last Campaign in the West*, Birkenhead, 1995, p. 38.

20. Newman, *Biographical Dictionary*, item 458.

21. See Peter Young, 'The Royalist Army at the Relief of Newark', in *Journal of the Society for Army Historical Research*, Vol. XXX, 1952, pp. 145–8.

22. Richard Symonds, *Diary of the Marches of the Royal Army*, edited by C.E. Long, Camden Society, 1859, p. 73.

23. See Peter F. Wemyss, 'The Shropshire Dragoons', in *Intelligencer*, Vol. 1, No. 1, August 1993.

24. *Mercurius Aulicus*, 23 November 1643, p. 671.

25. See Eliot-Wright, *English Civil War*, p. 30. In October 1645 the garrison of Chester consumed a hundredweight of match every three days.

26. Elton, *Compleat Body*, p. 145.

27. BL, T.T.E. 12.2.5, *A Full Relation of our Good Successe*, 1642.

28. Quoted in John Rowland Phillips, *Memoirs of the Civil War in Wales and the Marches*, 2 vols, London, 1874, Vol. II, pp. 107–8. Hawarden surrendered after a short siege, though there is no

evidence that Sandford's threats, which were not carried out, had any influence.

29. Traditionally, the firelocks climbed up the precipitous northern face of Beeston Crag under cover of darkness. It has to be said that no strictly contemporary account specifies this route, although the writer has been informed that, at least until recently, retracing Sandford's climb was a popular pastime among young men of the neighbourhood (see John Barratt, *Civil War Stronghold: Beeston Castle at War, 1642–45*, Birkenhead, 1995, pp. 3–5).

30. Thomas Malbon, *Memorials of the Civil War in Cheshire*, edited by James Hall, Record Society of Lancashire and Cheshire, Vol. 19, 1889, pp. 105–6.

31. Dore, *Letterbooks of Sir William Brereton, Vol. I*, Record Society of Lancashire and Cheshire,
    Vol. 123, 1983–4, item 610.

32. See John Barratt, 'What Sandford's Firelocks Did Next', in *English Civil War Notes and Queries*, No. 50.

33. CSPD, 1641–3, pp. 500–2.

34. They may have included veterans from Wentworth's 'New Army' of 1640, including a number of officers (Reid, *Officers*, p. 156).

35. Quoted Lynch, *For King and Parliament*, p. 161.

36. Philipp Eliot-Wright, 'The Royalist Firelocks', in *English Civil War Notes and Queries*, Nos 49 and 50, and 'Firelock Forces', in *Military Illustrated*, No. 75, August 1994.

6. Ordnance and Munitions

1. Ward, *Animadiversions of War*, ii, p. 26.

2. See Stuart Reid, *Scots Armies of the 17th Century: 1. The Army of the Covenant*, Southend-on-Sea, 1988, p. 26.

3. Young, *Edgehill*, p. 31.

4. Clarendon, *Great Rebellion*, Vol. VI. p. 62.

5. Young, *Edgehill*, p. 92.

6. See Roy, *Royalist Ordnance Papers*, Part I, pp. 16–17.

7. *Ibid.*

8. *Ibid.*, pp. 26–7.

9. Bernard de Gomme, *Journal of the Siege of Bristol*, reprinted in Warburton, *Memoirs*, Vol. II., pp. 233–64.

10. BL, Add. MS 18981, f. 212.

11. Roy, *Royalist Ordnance Papers*, Part II, n. 1, p. 431.

12. *Ibid.*, n. 21, p. 435.

13. *Ibid.*, n. 73, p. 444.

14. *Ibid.*, n. 82, p. 446.

15. *Ibid.*, item B 115.
16. *Ibid.*, item B 118.
17. *Ibid.*, Part I, p. 23.
18. *Ibid.*
19. Clarendon, *Great Rebellion*, Vol. VII, p. 201.
20. Ronald Hutton and Wyllie Reeves, 'Sieges and Fortifications', in John Kenyon and Jane Ohlmeyer (eds), *The Civil Wars*, Oxford, 1998, p. 219.
21. See Newman, *Biographical Dictionary*, item 542.
22. Ronald Hutton, *The Royalist War Effort*, London, 1981, p. 76.
23. See Roy, *Royalist Ordnance Papers*, *passim* and esp. Introduction, Part I, pp.7–57.
24. *Ibid.*, p. 48.
25. Clarendon, *Great Rebellion*, Vol. VIII, p. 94.
26. F.J. Varley, *The Siege of Oxford*, Oxford, 1932, p. 94.
27. Peter Edwards, 'Logistics and Supply', in Kenyon and Ohlmeyer, *The Civil Wars*, pp. 243–4.
28. Lynch, *For King and Parliament*, pp. 122–32.
29. Eliot-Wright, *English Civil War*, p. 107.
30. Lynch, *For King and Parliament*, p. 128.
31. Edwards, 'Logistics and Supply', pp. 254–5.
32. *Ibid.*, p. 252.
33. Roy, *Royalist Ordnance Papers*, Part II, item C 62.
34. Eliot-Wright, *English Civil War*, p. 108.

7. Logistics

1. See J. Engberg, 'Royalist Finances during the English Civil War 1642–1646', in *Scandinavian Economic History Review* 19, 1966, p. 91.
2. For instance the £5,000 'mounting money' provided to Sir John Byron by the Marquess of Worcester and the contributions towards the Lifeguard of Foot from Thomas Bushell.
3. Morris and Lawson, *Siege of Chester*, pp. 32–3.
4. Ashburnham was not formally appointed until November 1643.
5. Engberg, 'Royalist Finances', p. 83.
6. *Ibid.*
7. See Edwards, 'Logistics and Supply', p. 264.
8. Engberg, 'Royalist Finances', p. 85.
9. Parliament was rather more successful, as Royalist estates tended to be more valuable, its territory was more economically valuable, and its administrative machinery more effective.
10. David Eddishaw, *Civil War in Oxfordshire*, Stroud and Oxford, 1995, p. 79.

11. See, for example, Edwards, 'Logistics and Supply', pp. 269–70; Hutton, *Royalist War Effort*, pp. 179–82.
12. Whitelocke, *Memorials*, Vol. I, p. 540.
13. Lynch, *For King and Parliament*, p. 131.
14. Hutton, *Royalist War Effort*, esp. Chap. 16.
15. See Geoffrey Parker (ed.), *The Thirty Years War*, 2nd edn, London, 1997, pp. 90–1.
16. Clarendon, *Great Rebellion*, Vol. IX, p. 32.
17. Malcolm Atkin, *The Civil War in Worcestershire*, Stroud, 1995, p. 84.
18. J.W. Willis-Bund (ed.), *Diaries of Henry Townshend of Elmley Lovett, 1640–1663*, 3 vols, Worcestershire Historical Society, 1915–20, Vol. I, p. 160.
19. Margaret Toynbee (ed.), *Papers of Henry Stevens*, Oxfordshire Record Society, Vol. XLII (1962), pp. 15–16.
20. See Chap. 4 of the present work, p. 33.
21. Firth, *Cromwell's Army*, p. 24.
22. *Ibid.*
23. Quoted in Carlton, *Going to the Wars*, p. 226.
24. Quoted Warburton, *Memoirs*, Vol. II, p. 259.
25. Quoted in Carlton, *Going to the Wars*, p. 222.
26. Sir Thomas Conrad, *Richard Wiseman*, London, 1891, pp. 46–7.
27. Sir Henry Ellis (ed.), *Letters Illustrative of English History*, 3rd series, 4 vols, 1819, Vol. IV, p. 226.
28. Varley, *Siege of Oxford*, pp. 97–8.
29. BL, Harleian MS 6804, f. 92.
30. *Transactions of the Oxfordshire Historical Society*, 1893, Vol. XXIV, p. 251.
31. Toynbee, *Henry Stevens*, Letter XIX.
32. BL, Harleian MS 6804 ff. 204–204v.
33. *Mercurius Aulicus*, 3 May 1643, pp. 226–7.
34. *Ibid.*, 9 June 1644, p. 1,012.

8. The High Command

1. See Chap. 12 of the present work, p. 121.
2. He had served with the Cadiz expedition of 1597, and the ill-fated La Rochelle operation of 1629.
3. David Lloyd, *Memoirs of the Lives, Actions etc of those Excellent Personages . . .*, London, 1668, p. 674.
4. Quoted Geoffrey Ridsdell-Smith, *Leaders of the Civil Wars*, Kineton, 1967.
5. He did not necessarily have to heed their advice. Sir Thomas

Fairfax, for example, when commanding the New Model Army, frequently disregarded the advice of his.

6. See Ian Roy, 'The Royalist Council of War, 1642–6', in *Bulletin of the Institute of Historical Research* 35, 1962, pp. 150–68. Most of the surviving contemporary material consists of half a dozen notebooks of Sir Edward Walker, the King's Secretary at War. The full Minute Books of the Council were evidently among the records destroyed prior to the surrender of Oxford in 1646.

7. An exception was the Ordnance Office (see Chap. 6 of the present work, p. 57).

8. In November 1642 Rupert had wanted to follow up the partial victory at Edgehill with a rapid thrust on London by a mobile column. The objections of a majority of the Council, concerned both by the operation's feasibility and the civilian casualties likely to be incurred, carried the day.

9. See Pete Darren, 'Prince Rupert and the "Swordsmen"', in *English Civil War Notes and Queries*, Nos 36 and 38.

10. The title of 'Colonel General', like that of 'Field Marshal', could vary in its responsibilities. Normally it involved command of a specific geographical area, or an arm of the service, such as dragoons.

11. See Hutton, *Royalist War Effort*, pp. 50–1.

12. *Ibid.*, p. 49.

13. Quoted in Warburton, *Memoirs*, Vol. II, pp. 387–8.

14. *Ibid.*

15. See M.D.G. Wanklyn, 'Royalist Strategy in Southern England', in *Southern History*, V, 1985, pp. 65–6.

16. *Ibid.*, pp. 68–9.

17. Clarendon, *Great Rebellion*, Vol. VIII, p. 3.

18. Forth and Hopton probably lost about 500 men, while Waller was crippled by financial problems and mutiny among his troops.

19. Wanklyn, 'Royalist Strategy', p. 69.

20. Clarendon, *Great Rebellion*, Vol. VIII, pp. 26–33.

21. Warburton, *Memoirs*, Vol. II, p. 415.

22. BL. Add. MS 18981, f. 182.

23. Walker, *Historical Discourses*, p. 107.

24. For example, in A.H. Burne and Peter Young, *The Great Civil War: a Military History*, London, 1959, p. 179.

25. Warburton, *Memoirs*, Vol. II, p. 436.

26. See Ronald Hutton, 'The Structure of the Royalist Party, 1642–46', in *Historical Journal* 24, 1981, pp. 553–69.

27. Largely based on a letter purportedly written by Arthur Trevor on

23 October 1644. However, there are a number of difficulties in accepting the authenticity of this document.

28. Warburton, *Memoirs*, Vol. III, pp. 27–8.

29. See Chap. 3 of the present work.

30. Warburton, *Memoirs*, Vol. II, p. 408 (wrongly assigned to 1644).

31. *Ibid.*, Vol. III, p. 28.

32. See Foard, *Naseby* and John Barratt, *The Last Blow in the Business: Royalist Strategy in the Naseby Campaign*, Southend-on-Sea, 1995.

33. Prince Maurice would have been a possible choice, however, see Foard, *Naseby*, pp. 337–8, for a fuller discussion of Rupert's actions at Naseby.

34. Warburton, *Memoirs*, Vol. III, pp. 119–21.

9. Daily Life

1. George Monck, *Observations upon Military and Political Affairs*, London, 1671, p. 31.

2. Stuart Peachey and Alan Turton, *The Fall of the West*, 5 vols, Bristol, 1992, Vol. 5, p. 231.

3. William Barriffe, *Militarie Discipline: or the younge artillerieman*, London, 1635, p. 181.

4. Anon., *Orders and Institutions of War*, London, 1642.

5. Anthony Wood quoted in Varley, *Siege of Oxford*, p. 105.

6. BL, Harleian MS 2125, f. 320.

7. CCRO, MC/1/3/34.

8. Symonds, *Diary*, pp. 30, 41. The King was making strenuous efforts to win support from among the generally apathetic population of Somerset and Devon.

9. *Ibid.*, p. 56.

10. Quoted in Carlton, *Going to the Wars*, p. 285.

11. Newman, *Biographical Dictionary*, item 372.

12. Symonds, *Diary*, p. 36.

13. *Ibid.*, p. 30.

14. *Ibid.*, p. 76.

15. Quoted in Carlton, *Going to the Wars*, p. 81.

16. George Ormerod (ed.), *Military Proceedings in Lancashire*, Chetham Society, II, Manchester, 1844, pp. 66–7; Young, *Edgehill*, pp. 41–5.

17. See Lynch, *For King and Parliament*, p. 111, for rates in the Bristol garrison in November 1644.

18. Carlton, *Going to the Wars*, p. 94.

19. See Chap. 7 of the present work, p. 70.

20. Letter from Sir John Mennes to Prince Rupert of 6 February 1644, quoted in Warburton, *Memoirs*, Vol. II, pp. 371–2.

21. Quoted in Carlton, *Going to the Wars*, p. 280.
22. Warburton, *Memoirs*, Vol. II, p. 262.
23. Carlton, *Going to the Wars*, p. 94.
24. Clarendon, *Great Rebellion*, Vol. III, p. 121.
25. Tucker, *John Gwynn*, p. 52.
26. HMC, 12th Report, Beaufort Papers, p. 39.
27. Symonds, *Diary*, p. 57.
28. *Ibid.*, p. 65.
29. Richard Atkyns, 'The Vindication of Richard Atkyns', in Peter Young (ed.), *Military Memoirs: the Civil War*, London, 1967, p. 22.
30. Quoted in Carlton, *Going to the Wars*, p. 219.
31. Byron, 'Account of the Siege of Chester', p. 14.
32. Carlton, *Going to the Wars*, p. 87.
33. Lynch, *For King and Parliament*, p. 91.
34. Carlton, *Going to the Wars*, p. 250.
35. The Royalist garrison defended by Sir Stephen Hawkins' Regiment of Foot, which had surrendered in June.
36. Symonds, *Diary*, p. 67.
37. Walker, *Historical Discourses*, p. 80.
38. Quoted in Carlton, *Going to the Wars*, p. 255.

10. 'Western Wonder'

1. William Scawen, *Observations*, 1777, quoted in Mary Coate, *Cornwall in the Great Civil War and Interregnum*, Oxford, 1933, p. 2.
2. Atkyns, 'Vindication', p. 12.
3. Walker, *Historical Discourses*, p. 50.
4. Mary Coate, 'The Duchy of Cornwall: its History and Administration 1640–60', in *Transactions of the Royal Historical Society*, 4th series, Vol. 10, 1927, pp. 135–69.
5. See Mark Stoyle, 'Last Refuge of a Scoundrel: Sir Richard Grenville and Cornish Particularism', in *Historical Research* 71, No. 144, 1998, pp. 31–51.
6. Roger Granville, *History of the Granville Family*, Exeter, 1895, p. 213.
7. BL, T.T.E. 10.3.2, *True Proceedings of the Severall Counties of Yorke, Coventery, Portsmouth, Cornewall . . .*, London, 1642.
8. Amos Miller (ed.), 'Joseph Jane's Account of Cornwall during the Civil War', in *English Historical Review*, Vol. 90, 1975, p. 98.
9. Newman, *Biographical Dictionary*, item 1,317
10. *Ibid.*, item 908; Reid, *Officers*, *passim*.
11. Stuart Peachey, *The Battle of Modbury, 1643*, Bristol, 1993, p. 24.
12. BL, T.T.E. 93.6, *True Intelligence from Cornwall . . .*, London, 1642.

13. Quoted in Warburton, *Memoirs*, Vol. I, n. 1, pp. 420–1.
14. *Ibid.*
15. Ralph, Lord Hopton, *Bellum Civile*, edited by C.E.H. Chadwyck-Healey, *Transactions of the Somerset Record Society*, Vol. 18, 1902, p. 24.
16. *Ibid.*, p. 23.
17. Coate, *Cornwall*, p. 39.
18. Peachey, *Modbury*, p. 25.
19. Francis Basset gave the men of one regiment £5 (Coate, *Cornwall*, p. 40).
20. Clarendon, *Great Rebellion*, Vol. VIII, p. 31.
21. Lloyd, *Memoirs of the Lives*, p. 343.
22. These may have been members of the *posse comitatus*.
23. Hopton, *Bellum Civile*, pp. 27–8.
24. Quoted in John Stucley, *Sir Bevill Grenvile and his Times*, Chichester, 1983, p. 122.
25. Hopton, *Bellum Civile*, p. 30.
26. Quoted in Stucley, *Sir Bevill Grenvile*, p.123. Enemy casualties were light partly because the Cornish troops were reluctant to fire on their fleeing opponents.
27. Quoted *Ibid.*, p. 128.
28. See F.T.R. Edgar, *Sir Ralph Hopton: The King's Man in the West, 1642–52*, Oxford, 1968 pp. 119–20.
29. Hopton, *Bellum Civile*, p. 37.
30. Quoted in Coate, *Cornwall*, p. 64.
31. Clarendon, *Great Rebellion*, Vol. VII, p. 89.
32. Quoted in Coate, *Cornwall*, p. 69.
33. Hopton, *Bellum Civile*, p. 47.
34. Atkyns, 'Vindication', p. 12.
35. Estimates in Edgar, *Sir Ralph Hopton*, p. 120.
36. Bodleian Library, Clarendon MS 1738(2).
37. *Ibid.*
38. Atkyns, 'Vindication', p. 19.
39. Clarendon, *Great Rebellion*, Vol. VII, p. 127.
40. *Ibid.*, Vol. VII, p. 132.
41. *Ibid.*
42. *Ibid.*
43. Coate, *Cornwall*, p. 100.
44. Mark Stoyle, 'Sir Richard Grenville's Creatures: the New Cornish Tertia, 1644–46', in *Cornish Studies* 4, 1996, pp. 26–44.
45. Stoyle, 'Last Refuge', pp. 49–51.
46. John Rushworth, *Historical Collections*, 8 vols, London, 1688–1701, Vol. V, p. 360.

11. 'Nursery of the King's Infantry'

1. See, for example, BL, T.T.E. 89.3, *The Welsh-Mans Postures*, a satirical pamphlet of 1642.
2. BL, T.T.E. 11.6, *Special Passages*, No. 5, 13 September 1642.
3. Glanmor Williams, *Renewal and Reformation in Wales*, Oxford, 1987, p. 368.
4. For example, C.V. Wedgwood, *The King's War*, London, 1958, esp. pp. 447–8, and Malcolm, *Caesar's Due*.
5. Quoted in Peter Gaunt, *A Nation Under Siege: Wales in the Civil War*, London, 1991, p. 9.
6. *Ibid.*, p. 16.
7. A lengthy extract of Salusbury's letter of June 1642 to his sister is quoted in Norman Tucker, *Denbighshire Officers of the Civil War*, Colwyn Bay, nd, pp. 116–18.
8. Reid, *Officers*, *passim*.
9. Newman, *Biographical Dictionary*, items 207 and 1,233.
10. Richard Herbert's Regiment.
11. NLW, Wynne of Gwydir Papers, No. 1,711.
12. Quoted in Phillips, *Civil War in Wales*, Vol. I, p. 128.
13. See Young, *Edgehill*, pp. 107–34.
14. *Ibid.*, pp. 223–4.
15. See Neil Chippendale, *Brentford 1642*, Southend-on-Sea, 1992, *passim*.
16. Hutton, *Royalist War Effort*, p. 268.
17. Norman Tucker, *North Wales in the Civil War*, Colwyn Bay, 1957, p. 14.
18. *Ibid.*, p. 15.
19. *Ibid.*, pp. 32–3.
20. Tucker, *Denbighshire Officers*, pp. 149–51.
21. Lloyd, *Memoirs of the Lives*, p. 661.
22. Included were Richard Herbert's and John Price's Regiments.
23. See John Adair, *Roundhead General*, 2nd edn, Stroud, 1997, Chap. 7.
24. John Corbet, *Military Government of Gloucester*, London, 1647, p. 27.
25. John Stradling had assumed command after his brother's capture at Edgehill.
26. Tucker, *Denbighshire Officers*, pp. 110–11.
27. Some sources say August.
28. Roy, *Royalist Ordnance Papers*, Part II, item B 117.
29. BL, Harleian MS 6804, f. 92.
30. Tucker, *John Gwynn*, p. 53.
31. Newman, *Old Service*, pp. 268–70.

32. See Chap. 12 of the present work, p. 111.
33. Hutton, *Royalist War Effort*, p. 137; Warburton, *Memoirs*, Vol. II, pp. 401–2.
34. Hutton, *Royalist War Effort*, pp. 136–7.
35. *Ibid.*, pp. 139–40.
36. For example, Marcus Trevor's Regiment, only 30 strong in February, probably mustered 300 men at Marston Moor. Lord Byron's Regiment of Foot certainly included a number of Welsh recruits, as did Sir Michael Woodhouse's at Ludlow. On 3 May 100 newly pressed recruits were captured on their way to Rupert at Shrewsbury (John Lewis (ed.), *Fire and Sword Along the Marches*, Newtown, 1996, p. 12).
37. Hutton, *Royalist War Effort*, p. 148.
38. See John Barratt, 'The Battle for Oswestry', in *English Civil War Times*, No. 53, nd, pp. 4–9.
39. Brereton's Despatch, quoted in Andrew Abrahams, *The Battle of Montgomery, 1644*, Bristol, 1994, p. 17.
40. Hutton, *Royalist War Effort*, p. 151.
41. Abrahams, *Battle of Montgomery*, p. 21.
42. Quoted in Phillips, *Civil War in Wales*, Vol. II, p. 246.
43. BL, Egerton MS 787, f. 83. A further general levy was also ordered, although it is unclear how successful it was.
44. Perhaps 1,000 of the existing foot may also have been Welsh.
45. Wedgwood, *King's War*, p. 457.
46. Minutes of the Royalist Council of War, 25 June 1645, quoted in Warburton, *Memoirs*, Vol. III, pp. 119–21.
47. *Ibid.*, p. 135.
48. *Ibid.*, pp. 385–6.
49. The two foot regiments, under Colonels William Slaughter and Matthew Wise, fought at Langport and continued to serve in the West until the end of the war. They are probably the Welsh troops noted in Bodmin on St David's Day 1646, wearing leeks in their hats.
50. Hutton, *Royalist War Effort*, p. 186.
51. Quoted in A.H. Dodd, *Studies in Stuart Wales*, Cardiff, 1971, p. 133.

12. 'The Popish Army'

1. The best survey, used extensively here, is Peter Newman's unpublished PhD thesis 'The Royalist Armies in the North of England', University of York, 1978.
2. Sir Phillip Warwick, *Memoirs of the Reign of Charles I*, Edinburgh, 1825, p. 235.
3. Margaret Cavendish, Duchess of Newcastle, *Life of William Cavendish*,

NOTES

Duke of Newcastle [1886], edited by C.H. Firth, London, nd, p. 13. See also Stuart Reid, *All the King's Armies: a Military History of the English Civil War 1642–1651*, Staplehurst, 1998, p. 70.

4. Stuart Reid (ed.), *Declaration of the Earl of Newcastle* [1642], Southend-on-Sea, 1983.
5. Reprinted Firth, *Newcastle*, App. IV, p. 190.
6. *Ibid.*, p. 191.
7. Rushworth, *Historical Collections*, Vol. III, p. 92.
8. Sir James Turner, *Memoirs*, edited by J. Thomson, Edinburgh, 1829, p. 45.
9. See Chap. 6 of the present work.
10. Firth, *Newcastle*, p. 23. Newman, *Old Service*, p. 265.
11. Holmes, *Eastern Association*, p. 84.
12. The fullest account of Adwalton Moor is Dave Cooke, *The Forgotten Battle*, Heckmondwyke, 1996.
13. Newman, *Old Service, passim.*
14. *Ibid.*, p. 234.
15. Newman, 'Royalist Armies', *passim*, and (with caution) Young, *Marston Moor*, pp. 55–60.
16. Firth, *Newcastle*, p. 122.
17. See Reid, *Officers, passim.*
18. Newman, *Old Service*, pp. 261–3.
19. Eliot-Wright, *English Civil War*, p. 107.
20. Jack Binns, *'A Place of Great Importance': Scarborough in the Civil Wars*, Preston, 1996, p. 104.
21. Reid, *Declaration*.
22. Firth, *Newcastle*, p. 29.
23. M.A.E. Green (ed.), *Letters of Queen Henrietta Maria*, London, 1857, p. 225.
24. Wedgwood, *King's War*, p. 364.
25. Newman, *Old Service*, p. 215.
26. Quoted in Firth, *Newcastle*, p. 29.
27. Warwick, *Memoirs*, p. 265.
28. Warburton, *Memoirs*, Vol. II, p. 360.
29. *Ibid.*, p. 481.
30. *Ibid.*, p. 397.
31. *Ibid.*, p. 399.
32. Firth, *Newcastle*, p. 29.
33. *James Somerville's Account*, reprinted in Young, *Marston Moor*, p. 261.
34. William Lilly, *His Life and Times*, London, 1826, pp. 77–8.
35. Sir Hugh Cholmley, *Memoirs*, edited by C.H. Firth, in *English Historical Review*, V, 1890, p. 352.
36. Clarendon, *Great Rebellion*, Vol. VIII, p. 82.

13. An Army from Ireland

1. See C.V. Wedgwood, *The King's Peace*, London, 1955, pp. 350, 400–6.
2. Notably Joyce Lee Malcolm, 'All the King's Men: the Impact of the Crown's Irish Soldiers in the English Civil War', in *Irish Historical Studies*, Vol. XXI, 1975, pp. 239–64.
3. See Keith Lindley, 'Impact of the 1641 Rebellion upon England and Wales, 1641–45', in *Irish Historical Studies*, Vol. XVIII, 1972, esp. p. 146.
4. Eventually they would be increased to 10,000 foot.
5. Ian Ryder, *An English Army for Ireland*, Southend-on-Sea, 1987, p. 5.
6. *Ibid.*, p. 14.
7. There were in fact two armies. The Scots forces in Ulster operated largely independently of the authorities in Dublin.
8. Thomas Carte, *History of the Life of James, First Duke of Ormonde*, 6 vols, Oxford, 1853, Vol. V, p. 5.
9. *Ibid.*, p. 321.
10. Warburton, *Memoirs*, Vol. II, p. 402.
11. Carte, *Ormonde*, p. 511.
12. *Ibid.*, pp. 505–6.
13. *Ibid.*, p. 521.
14. See John Lowe, 'The Campaign of the Irish-Royalist Army in Cheshire, November 1643–January 1644', in *Transactions of the Historic Society of Lancashire and Cheshire*, 1959, Vol. 111.
15. See R.N. Dore, 'The Sea Approaches: the Importance of the Dee and the Mersey in the Civil War in the North-West', in *Transactions of the Historic Society of Lancashire and Cheshire*, 1986, Vol. 138, pp. 136–58.
16. HMC, Report 20, pp. xi–41.
17. For troop strengths see Ryder *English Army*, p. 31.
18. See Chap. 17 of the present work, p. 178.
19. *Chester Assembly Book* (AB1/2, f. 64v).
20. Thomas Carte, *Original Letters*, 2 vols, London, 1739, Vol. I, p. 29.; Lowe, 'Irish-Royalist Army', pp. 51, 59–60.
21. See John Barratt, *A Happy Victory: the Siege and Battle of Nantwich, 1644*, Birkenhead, 1996, pp. 31–2. The Royalist officer actually responsible appears to have been Major John Connock of Ralph Snead's Staffordshire Regiment of Horse. He was executed in 1651 for his role in the massacre.
22. Possibly 300 were killed.
23. Sir Thomas Fairfax, *A Brief Memorial of the Northern Actions in which I was Engaged*, London, 1985 edn, p. 25.

24. See Barratt, *Happy Victory*. A great deal of ammunition had been expended in the unsuccessful assault of 17 January, and a major munitions convoy en route to Byron had recently been captured.

25. Carte, *Ormonde*, Vol. VI, p. 33.

26. *Ibid.*, p. 56.

27. Warburton, *Memoirs*, Vol. II, p. 371.

28. See Dore, *Letterbooks*, Vol. II, App. XI, pp. 595–6; Lewis, *May It Please Your Highness*, p. 5.

29. Reid, *Officers*, *passim*.

30. Warburton, *Memoirs*, Vol. II, p. 402.

31. See John Barratt, *The Siege of Liverpool and Prince Rupert's Campaign in Lancashire, 1644*, Bristol, 1994.

32. Symonds, *Diary*, pp. 254–5.

33. See Chap. 11 of the present work, p. 111.

34. Quoted in Andrew Abrahams, *Battle of Montgomery*.

35. See Young, *Naseby*, p. 107.

36. A number of officers from Ireland were among the prisoners. See Chap. 19 of the present work, p. 206.

37. Hopton, *Bellum Civile*, pp. 62–3.

38. *Ibid.*

39. Hutton, *Royalist War Effort*, pp. 116–17.

40. Figures based on Ryder, *English Army*, p. 36, and Dore, 'Sea Approaches', *passim*. Malcolm, *Caesar's Due*, p. 116, gives much larger numbers, but these are based partly on Parliamentarian newsletters and other second-hand sources, and are grossly inflated.

41. Quoted in S.R. Gardiner, *History of the Great Civil War*, 4 vols, London, 1886, Vol. I, p. 296.

42. Carte, *Ormonde*, Vol. VI, pp. 30–1.

43. *Ibid.*, p. 53.

44. Notably Malcolm, *Caesar's Due*, pp. 114–16.

45. See Dore, 'Sea Approaches', p. 141.

46. See John Barratt, 'Lord Byron's Foot', in *English Civil War Notes and Queries*, No. 18.

47. See Morris and Lawson, *Siege of Chester*, p. 43.

48. The nature of the evidence makes an accurate estimate impossible. The Parliamentarians had reason to exaggerate the total, and the Royalists to minimise it.

49. Malcolm, *Caesar's Due*, p. 16.

50. See Dore, *Letterbooks*, Vol. II, App. XI, *passim*.

51. *Ibid.*

52. See John Barratt, *Cannon on the Mersey*, Birkenhead, 1996, p. 41.

53. *Ibid.* Ironically, most of Lord Byron's men arrived in Dublin to fall

into the hands of Colonel Thomas Napier, who shipped them back to Chester and the far from tender mercies of their commander. Several were hanged for treachery in betraying Liverpool.

54. Dore, *Letterbooks, Vol. II*.
55. Malcolm, *Caesar's Due, passim*.

14. A Meteor in the North

1. George Wishart, Montrose's chaplain, wrote a panegyric account of his life (*Memoirs of James Graham, Marquis of Montrose 1639–50*, translated by Revd G. Murdoch, London, 1893) which profoundly influenced future biographers. See John Buchan, *Montrose*, London, 1928, and C.V. Wedgwood, *Montrose*, London, 1952. For a somewhat more critical view try Ronald Williams, *Montrose: Cavalier in Mourning*, London, 1975 and E.J. Cowan, *Montrose: For Covenant and King*, London, 1977.
2. See Jane Ohlmeyer, *Civil War and Restoration in the Three Kingdoms: the Career of Randal MacDonnell, Earl of Antrim*, Cambridge, 1993.
3. John Spalding, *History of the Trubles in Scotland*, 2 vols, Edinburgh, 1850–1, Vol. II, p. 385.
4. Stuart Reid, *Campaigns of Montrose*, Edinburgh, 1993, p. 48.
5. *Ibid.*, p. 70; David Stevenson, *Alaistair McColla and the Highland Problem in the 17th Century*, Edinburgh, 1980, pp. 134–7.
6. Reid, *Montrose*, pp. 53–4; Stuart Reid, *Scots Armies of the 17th Century, 3: The Royalist Armies, 1639–45*, Southend-on-Sea, 1989, pp. 54–6.
7. Reid, *Royalist Armies*, pp. 23, 28.
8. Spalding, *Trubles*, Vol. II, p. 349.
9. For the 'Highland Charge' and the impact of Highlanders in general, see Reid, *Royalist Armies*, pp. 42–53.
10. *Ibid.*, p. 27.
11. The best and fullest account is in Reid, *Montrose*.
12. Quoted in Mark Napier, *Memorials of Montrose*, 2 vols, Edinburgh, 1848, Vol. II, pp. 178–9.
13. In October 1645 the remains of the Northern Horse under Digby and Langdale were despatched north but got no further than the Solway Firth.
14. See David Stevenson, *Revolution and Counter Revolution in Scotland, 1644–51*, London, 1977, Chap. 1.

15. Langdale's Ride

1. See Chap. 12 of the present work, p. 121.
2. See Robinson, *Discourse*, pp. 56–7.

3. *Prince Rupert's Diary* (WCRO).

4. Sir John Meldrum to Committee of Both Kingdoms, CSPD, 1644, p. 382.

5. See Chap. 11 of the present work, p. 111.

6. It has been convincingly suggested that Colonel John Fenwick, of the Northern cavalry, was actually wearing a sixteenth-century sallet-type helmet when he was killed at Marston Moor (see *English Civil War Notes and Queries*, No. 6, p. 18).

7. Newman, *Old Service*, p. 221.

8. Lloyd, *Memoirs of the Lives*, p. 550.

9. Slingsby, *Diary*, p. 145.

10. Monckton, for example, had several horses shot from under him both at Marston Moor and Naseby, and was described by Clarendon as 'mad', while Blakiston was also noted for his outstanding bravery in action.

11. Robinson, *Discourse*, p. 58.

12. Bodleian Library, Firth MS C7, ff. 178–9.

13. Quoted in Warburton, *Memoirs*, Vol. III, p. 71.

14. This organisation, suggested by Brigadier Peter Young, seems probable, at least in broad outline. See Young, *Naseby*, pp. 59–64.

15. Warburton, *Memoirs*, Vol. III.

16. Cruso, *Militairie Instructions*, p. 57.

17. *Ibid.*

18. *Ibid.*, p. 60.

19. H.G. Tibbutt (ed.), *Letterbooks of Sir Samuel Luke*, London, 1963, p. 165.

20. Sir Gameliel Dudley's 'Account', *Mercurius Aulicus*, 7 March 1645, pp. 1,401–7.

21. Tibbutt, *Letterbooks*, p. 175.

22. *Ibid.*, pp. 204–5.

23. *Ibid.*, p. 175.

24. Dudley, 'Account'.

25. *Ibid.* The Latin translates as 'At last we see a challenge to match our courage'.

26. Vernon, *Young Horseman*, pp. 85–6.

27. *Ibid.*

28. Dudley, 'Account'.

29. *Ibid.* See also George Fox, *Three Sieges of Pontefract Castle*, Leeds, 1887, pp. 37–46; Nathan Drake, *Sieges of Pontefract Castle*, edited by Richard Holmes, Leeds, 1887, pp. 29–30.

30. Quoted in Dudley, 'Account'.

31. HMC, Portland MSS, I, 1894, pp. 476–7.

16. Siege

1. Young, *Naseby*, pp. 1–17.
2. Carlton, *Going to the Wars*, pp. 150–1.
3. A.M. Johnson, 'Politics in Chester during the Civil War and Interregnum, 1640–1662', in P. Clark and P. Slack (eds), *Crisis and Order in English Towns, 1500–1700*, London, 1972.
4. Dore, *Letterbooks, Vol. II*, pp. 592–3.
5. Morris and Lawson, *Siege of Chester*, pp. 25–32.
6. See John Barratt, *For Chester and King Charles*, Birkenhead, 1995, *passim*.
7. Simon Ward, *Excavations at Chester: the Civil War Siegeworks, 1642–46*, Chester, 1987, pp. 4–11.
8. Quoted in Morris and Lawson, *Siege of Chester*, p. 39.
9. Clarendon, *Great Rebellion*, Vol. IV, p. 102.
10. See Chap. 11 of the present work, p. 111.
11. Letter from Byron to Lord Digby, 26 April 1645, quoted in Morris and Lawson, *Siege of Chester*, pp. 78–9.
12. Byron, 'Account of the Siege of Chester', p. 3.
13. *Ibid.*, p. 4.
14. *Ibid.*
15. BL, Harleian MS 2155, reprinted in Morris and Lawson, *Siege of Chester*, pp. 224–5.
16. Byron, 'Account of the Siege of Chester', p. 6.
17. *Ibid.*
18. See BL, Harleian MS 2155, reprinted in Morris and Lawson, *Siege of Chester*, pp. 225–6; Byron, 'Account of the Siege of Chester', pp. 6–7.
19. Monck, *Observations*, p. 132.
20. Byron, 'Account of the Siege of Chester', p. 9.
21. Morris and Lawson, *Siege of Chester*, p. 127.
22. Byron, 'Account of the Siege of Chester', p. 11.
23. *Ibid.*
24. Morris and Lawson, *Siege of Chester*, p. 128.
25. Possibly a professional soldier.
26. At one stage, Deputy Governor of Chester and later Royalist commander in Merioneth.
27. See Chap. 2 of the present work, p. 11.
28. Byron, 'Account of the Siege of Chester', pp. 11–12.
29. BL, Harleian MS 2155, reprinted in Morris and Lawson, *Siege of Chester*, p. 228.
30. Byron, 'Account of the Siege of Chester', p. 12.
31. *Ibid.*

32. BL, Harleian MS 2155, reprinted in Morris and Lawson, *Siege of Chester*, pp. 228–9.
33. Dore, *Letterbooks, Vol. II*, item 684.
34. *Ibid.*, item 681.
35. Byron, 'Account of the Siege of Chester', p. 13.
36. Dore, *Letterbooks, Vol. II*, item 806.
37. *Ibid.*, item 781.
38. Byron, 'Account of the Siege of Chester', p. 15.
39. Dore, *Letterbooks, Vol. II*, item 905.
40. *Ibid.*, item 928.
41. BL, Harleian MS 2155, reprinted in Morris and Lawson, *Siege of Chester*, p. 234.
42. Dore, *Letterbooks, Vol. II*, item 1,018.
43. *Ibid.*, item 1,091.
44. *Ibid.*, item 1,103.
45. Morris and Lawson, *Siege of Chester*, p. 173.
46. Byron, 'Account of the Siege of Chester', p. 20.
47. Dore, *Letterbooks, Vol. II*, item 1,215.
48. BL, Harleian MS 2135, partially reprinted in Morris and Lawson, *Siege of Chester*, pp. 238–42.
49. CCRO, William Cowper, *Account of the Siege of Chester*, 1764 (DCC 26).
50. Byron, 'Account of the Siege of Chester', p. 21.
51. *Ibid.*
52. *Ibid.*
53. *Ibid.*
54. Annette Kennett (ed.), *Loyal Chester*, Chester, 1984, Section V.

17. Royalist Women at War

1. For a fuller account of these leading figures see Alison Plowden, *Women All On Fire: The Women of the English Civil War*, Stroud, 1998, and Antonia Fraser, *The Weaker Vessel: Woman's Lot in Seventeenth-Century England*, London, 1974.
2. Not the 'Crown Jewels' as sometimes stated.
3. See Chap. 6 of the present work, p. 57.
4. See Chap. 8 of the present work, p. 79.
5. See Colin Pilkington, *To Play the Man*, Preston, 1991.
6. See Plowden, *Women*, pp. 41–7.
7. Dore, *Letterbooks, Vol. II*, items 417 and 458.
8. Quoted in Plowden, *Women*, p. 74.
9. Margaret Toynbee and Peter Young, *Strangers in Oxford*, Chichester, 1973, p. 40.

10. *Ibid.*, pp. 212–13.
11. BL, Harleian MS 6851, f. 45.
12. Robinson, *Discourse*, p. 94.
13. Whitelocke, *Memorials*, p. 127.
14. Information supplied by Alan Turton.
15. *Civil War Tracts of Cheshire*, Chetham Society, Vol. 65, NS, 1909, pp. 110–11.
16. See Foard, *Naseby*, pp. 288–9.
17. For example, C.V. Wedgwood, *King's War*, pp. 457–8.
18. BL, Harleian MS 2155, reprinted in Morris and Lawson, *Siege of Chester*, p. 227.
19. *Ibid.*, p. 229.
20. *Ibid.*, p. 232.
21. Quoted in Carlton, *Going to the Wars*, p. 221.
22. *Ibid.*, p. 308.
23. *English Civil War Notes and Queries*, No. 17, p. 8.

18. The Scourge of War

1. Carlton, *Going to the Wars*, pp. 18–19.
2. Geoffrey Parker (ed.), *The Thirty Years War*, 2nd edn, London, 1997, esp. pp. 186–92.
3. Ian Gentles, 'The Civil Wars in England', in Kenyon and Ohlmeyer, *The Civil Wars*, p. 112. See also B. Donagan, 'Atrocity, War Crime and Treason in the English Civil War', in *American Historical Review*, 1994, p. 1,146.
4. See Chap. 7 of the present work, p. 70.
5. Warburton, *Memoirs*, Vol. II., pp. 393–4.
6. Anon., *Prince Rupert's Burning Love for England*, London, 1643, pp. 25, 29.
7. *Ibid.*
8. R.E. Sherwood, *Civil Strife in the Midlands*, Chichester, 1974, pp. 58–61.
9. Warburton, *Memoirs*, Vol. II, p. 106.
10. F. Larkin (ed.), *Stuart Royal Proclamations*, 2 vols, Oxford, 1983, Vol. II, p. 320.
11. Young, *Edgehill*, p. 272.
12. Derived from an alleged reference to Vaughan in the 'prayer of a Puritan Lady', in *Mercurius Aulicus*, 1 February 1645 , p. 1,364.
13. Young, *Naseby*, pp. 47–8.
14. Newman, *Biographical Dictionary*, item 414.
15. Young, *Naseby*, p. 49.
16. *Ibid.*, pp. 70–2.

17. *Ibid.*, p. 51.
18. J.W. and T.W. Webb, *Memorials of the Civil War as it affected Herefordshire and the Neighbouring Counties*, 2 vols, London, 1879, Vol. II, p. 265.
19. Young, *Naseby*, p. 50.
20. Carlton, *Going to the Wars*, pp. 178–9.
21. For Sandford see Barratt, *Happy Victory*, and Peter F. Wemyss, *My Firelocks Use Not to Parley*, Newtown, 1995.
22. Malbon, *Memorials*, p. 72.
23. BL, T.T.E. 30.1.1, *Mercurius Civicus . . .*, 21 January 1643 [44].
24. See Barratt, *Happy Victory*, and John Lowe, 'Irish-Royalist Army', pp. 49–76.
25. Newman, *Biographical Dictionary*, item 317.
26. See anonymous article, 'Barthomley', in *Cromwelliana*, 1994, pp. 66–70.
27. Amos C. Miller, *Sir Richard Grenville of the Civil War*, Chichester, 1979, pp. 34–6.
28. HMC, Bath MSS, I, p. 29.
29. *Ibid.*, p. 40.
30. Barratt, *Siege of Liverpool*, p. 10.
31. Ormerod, *Lancashire Civil War Tracts*, p. 191.
32. Barratt, *Siege of Liverpool*, p. 10.
33. *Ibid.*
34. Bodleian Library, Carte MS X, f. 664.
35. When present in person, King Charles usually ordered prisoners to be treated leniently.
36. See Miller, *Sir Richard Grenville*, pp. 95–7. The Royalist sack of Leicester in May 1645, though involving looting on a massive scale, does not seem to have been accompanied by systematic destruction of property or killing of unarmed civilians.

19. *The Last Battle*

1. Clarendon, *Great Rebellion*, Vol. IX, p. 161.
2. Walker, *Historical Discourses*, p. 145.
3. *Ibid.*
4. Fissel, *The Bishops' Wars, passim.*
5. David Appleby, *Our Fall Our Fame: the Life and Times of Sir Charles Lucas*, Newtown, 1995, p. 131.
6. Most of these units were greatly understrength. On 14 January the 300-strong remnant of Gerrard's force included 100 men of his Lifeguard and elements of five other regiments (Symonds, *Diary*, p. 80).

7. Quoted in J.W. Willis-Bund, *Civil War in Worcestershire*, Worcester 1905, p. 173.

8. Quoted in Morris and Lawson, *Siege of Chester*, p. 190.

9. Dore, *Letterbooks, Vol. II*, item 983.

10. *Ibid.*, item 977.

11. See Atkin, *Civil War in Worcestershire*, Chap. 8.

12. Hutton, *Royalist War Effort*, pp. 193–4.

13. Clarendon, *Great Rebellion*, Vol. IX, p. 163.

14. Hutton, *Royalist War Effort*, p. 196.

15. Walker, *Historical Discourses*, p. 146.

16. The units in Astley's army may be identified from prisoners listed in Anon., *A True and Fuller Relation of the Batttell Fought at Stow in the Wold, March 21 1646*, London, 1646, and Symonds, *Diary*, pp. 72–80.

17. Anon., *True and Fuller Relation*. This account, by an officer serving with Brereton, endeavours to show his commander's actions in their most favourable light.

18. Account of the battle based on Anon., *True and Fuller Relation*, F.A. Hyett, 'The Last Battle of the First Civil War', in *Transactions of the Bristol and Gloucestershire Archaelogical Society*, 1898; J.W. and T.W. Webb (eds), *Military Memoirs of Colonel John Birch*, Camden Society, NS, Vol. VII, 1873; Willis-Bund, *Civil War in Worcestershire*. Unfortunately, no detailed Royalist account appears to have survived.

20. Aftermath

1. Joshua Sprigge, *Anglia Rediviva*, London, 1647, pp. 221–2, 262.

2. See Stephen Porter, *Destruction in the English Civil Wars*, Stroud, 1994, esp. Chap. Four.

3. Whitelocke, *Memorials*, Vol. II, p. 138.

4. Wedgwood, *King's War*, pp. 532–3.

5. Peter Newman, 'The 1663 list of indigent Royalist Officers considered as a primary source for the study of the Royalist Army', in *Historical Journal* 30, 1987, pp. 84–91.

6. See Stephen Bull and Mike Seed, *Preston, Bloody Preston*, Preston, 1998.

7. David Appleby, *Our Fall Our Fame*, pp. 155–62.

8. See John Barratt, 'King Charles' Forgotten Army', in *Military Illustrated*, No. 110, July 1997, pp. 42–7.

9. *Mercurius Politicus*, 6–23 April 1657, p. 7,737.

10. Barratt, 'Forgotten Army', pp. 45–6.

11. C.H. Firth, 'Royalist and Cromwellian Armies in Flanders', in

Transactions of the Royal Historical Society, 1902, p. 101. On its return to England it became one of the three troops of the Lifeguard of Horse.

12. John Gwynn, *Military Memoirs of the Civil War, being the Military Memoirs of John Gwynn*, Edinburgh, 1822, p. 127.
13. CSPD, 1660–61, p. 332.
14. Gwynn, *Military Memoirs*, pp. 132–3.
15. HMC, Popham MSS, p. 189.
16. CSPD, 1661–2, p. 287.
17. *Ibid.*, pp. 553, 573, 607.
18. See John Childs, *The Army of Charles II*, London, 1976, *passim*.
19. Young, *Edgehill*, pp. 152–3.
20. *Ibid.*
21. Childs, *Army of Charles II*, p. 31.
22. *Ibid.*, p. 118.
23. Young, *Edgehill*, p. 160.
24. 14 Car.II c8. *Statutes of the Realm*, London, 1819, V, pp. 380–4.
25. Newman, 'The 1663 list', pp. 86–7, and Childs, *Army of Charles II*, p. 265n, take differing views.
26. *List of the Officers Claiming to the Sixty Thousand Pounds etc granted by his Sacred Majesty for the Relief of his Truely-Loyal and Indigent Party*, London, 1663.
27. CSPD, 1663–4, p. 31.
28. Peter Young and Wilf Embleton, *The Cavalier Army*, London, 1974, pp. 167–8.
29. 14 Car.II c9. *Statutes of the Realm*, V, pp.189–90.
30. David Underdown, *Revel, Riot and Rebellion*, Oxford, 1985, pp. 192–3.
31. CCRO, QSR, 1/645, ff. 14, 120, 122, 140.
32. WCRO, QSR, quoted in Young, *Edgehill*, p. 229.
33. Young, *Edgehill*, p. 154.

BIBLIOGRAPHY

MANUSCRIPT SOURCES

Bodleian Library

Carte MSS (papers of 1st Duke of Ormonde)
Clarendon MSS 23, 1738, 1834–8 (Civil War papers of 1st Earl of
    Clarendon)
Firth MSS (transcripts mainly of Prince Rupert's correspondence,
    collected by C.H. Firth)
Tanner MSS (miscellaneous Royalist correspondence)

British Library (BL)

Additional MSS 18980–93, 20,778, 28,273 (letters to Prince Rupert; some
    are transcribed, not always fully or accurately, in Eliot Warburton,
    Memoirs of Prince Rupert and the Cavaliers, London, 1849)
Harleian MSS 986 (notebook of Richard Symons); 2125 (material
    relating to Chester in the Civil War); 6802, 6804, 6851–2 (papers
    of Sir Edward Walker, including drafts of entries for the Minute
    Books of the Royalist Council of War, which were presumably
    destroyed prior to the surrender of Oxford in 1646)
T.T.E. 10.3.2, *True Proceedings of the Severall Counties of Yorke, Coventery,
    Portsmouth, Cornewall . . .*, London, 1642
T.T.E. 11.6, *Special Passages*, No. 5, 13 September 1642
T.T.E. 12.2.5, *A Full Relation of our Good Successe*, 1642
T.T.E. 30.1.1, *Mercurius Civicus . . .*, 21 January 1643 [44]
T.T.E. 89.3, *The Welsh-Mans Postures*, London, 1642
T.T.E. 93.6, *True Intelligence from Cornwall . . .*, London, 1642

Cheshire County Record Office (CCRO)

Quarter Sessions Records (QSR)
DCC 26 William Cowper, *Account of the Siege of Chester*, 1764

BIBLIOGRAPHY

Historical Manuscripts Commission (HMC)

Bath MSS, I
12th Report, Beaufort Papers
15th Report
Popham MSS
Portland MSS, I

National Library of Wales (NLW)

Gwydir Papers (Gwydir MSS)

Somerset Record Office (Som. RO)

Phelips MSS (DD/PH/27)

Staffordshire Record Office (Staffs. RO)

Denbigh Letterbooks, CR2017/C9, f. 126

Wiltshire County Record Office (WCRO)

Prince Rupert's Diary
Quarter Sessions Records

PRINTED SOURCES

Primary Sources

Abbott, W.C. (ed.), *Writings and Speeches of Oliver Cromwell*, 4 vols, Cambridge, Massachusetts, 1937–47

Anon. [Bernard de Gomme?], *His Highnesse Prince Rupert's Late Beating up of the Rebels' Quarters . . . and his Victory at Chalgrove Field*, Oxford, 1643

Anon., *Orders and Institutions of War*, London, 1642

Anon., *Prince Rupert's Burning Love for England*, London, 1643

Anon., *A True and Fuller Relation of the Batttell Fought at Stow in the Wold, March 21 1646*, London, 1646

Atkyns, Richard, 'The Vindication of Richard Atkyns', in Peter Young (ed.), *Military Memoirs: the Civil War*, London, 1967

Barratt, John (ed.), 'A Royalist Account of the Relief of Pontefract', in *Journal of the Society for Army Historical Research*, Vol. XLVI, 1973

Barriffe, William, *Militarie Discipline: or the younge artillerieman*, London, 1635

Benfield, F. (ed.), *A Royalist's Notebook: the Commonplace Book of Sir John Oglander*, New York, 1971

Bulstrode, Sir Richard, *Memoirs*, London, 1721

Byron, Lord John, 'Account of the Siege of Chester', in *Cheshire Sheaf*, 4th series, No. 6, 1971

Calendar of State Papers: Domestic, 1641–7

Carlyle, Thomas, *Letters and Speeches of Oliver Cromwell*, London, 1904

Carte, Thomas, *History of the Life of James, First Duke of Ormonde*, 6 vols, Oxford, 1853

——, *Original Letters*, 2 vols, London, 1739

Carter, Matthew, *A True Relation of that Unfortunate as Gallant Expedition of Kent and Colchester, 1648*, 2nd edn, London, 1759

Cholmley, Sir Hugh, *Memoirs*, edited by C.H. Firth in *English Historical Review*, V, 1890

Clarendon, Edward, Earl of, *History of the Great Rebellion*, edited by W.D. Macray, 6 vols, Oxford, 1888

Corbet, John, *Military Government of Gloucester*, London, 1647

Cruso, John, *Militarie Instructions for the Cavall'rie*, London, 1632

Dore, R.N. (ed.), *The Letterbooks of Sir William Brereton*, 2 vols, Record Society of Lancashire and Cheshire, Vols 123 and 128, 1983–4 and 1990

Drake, Nathan, *Sieges of Pontefract*, edited by Richard Holmes, Leeds, 1887

Ellis, Sir Henry (ed.), *Letters Illustrative of English History*, 3rd series, 4 vols, London, 1819

Elton, Richard, *Compleat Body of the Art Militarie*, London, 1650

Fairfax, Sir Thomas, *A Brief Memorial of the Northern Actions in which I was Engaged*, London, 1985 edn

Firth, C.H. (ed.), *Life of William Cavendish, Duke of Newcastle* [1886] by Margaret, Duchess of Newcastle, London, nd

Godwin, G.N., *The Civil War in Hampshire*, London, 1904

Gough, Richard, *The History of Myddle*, London, 1981

Granville, Roger, *History of the Granville Family*, Exeter, 1895

——, *The King's General in the West: the Life of Sir Richard Granville*, London, 1908

Green, M.A.E. (ed.), *Letters of Queen Henrietta Maria*, London, 1857

Gwynn, John, *Military Memoirs of the Civil War, being the Military Memoirs of John Gwynn*, Edinburgh, 1822

Hopton, Lord Ralph, *Bellum Civile*, edited by C.E.H. Chadwyck-Healey, *Transactions of the Somerset Record Society*, Vol. 18, 1902

Larkin, F. (ed.), *Stuart Royal Proclamations*, 2 vols, Oxford, 1983

Lewis, John, (ed.), *Fire and Sword along the Marches*, Newtown, 1996 (diaries of William Maurice and Francis Sandford)

——, *May It Please Your Highness*, Newtown, 1996 (letters to Prince Rupert, mainly of 1644)

Lilly, William, *His Life and Times*, London, 1826

List of the Officers Claiming to the Sixty Thousand Pounds etc granted by his Sacred Majesty for the Relief of his Truely-Loyal and Indigent Party, London, 1663

Lloyd, David, *Memoirs of the Lives, Actions etc of those Excellent Personages . . .*, London, 1668

Malbon, Thomas, *Memorials of the Civil War in Cheshire*, edited by James Hall in Record Society of Lancashire and Cheshire, Vol. 19, 1889

Markham, Gervase, *The Souldier's Accidence*, London, 1625

Mercurius Academicus, 1645–6

Mercurius Aulicus, 1643–5

Mercurius Politicus, 1644

Miller, Amos (ed.), 'Joseph Jane's Account of Cornwall during the Civil War', in *English Historical Review*, Vol. 90, 1975

Monck, George, *Observations upon Military and Political Affairs*, London, 1671

Ormerod, George (ed.), *Military Proceedings in Lancashire*, Chetham Society, II, Manchester, 1844

Reid, Stuart, (ed.) *Declaration of the Earl of Newcastle* [1642], Southend-on-Sea, 1983

Robinson, Edward, *Discourse of the Warr in Lancashire*, edited by Beaumont, William, Chetham Society, Vol. LXII, 1864

Rohan, Duc de, *Complete Captain*, London, 1631

Roy, Ian (ed.), *The Royalist Ordnance Papers*, Parts I and II, Oxfordshire Record Society, 1964 and 1974

Rushworth, John, *Historical Collections*, 8 vols, London, 1688–1701

Slingsby, Sir Henry, *Diary*, edited by D. Parsons, Edinburgh, 1836

Spalding, John, *History of the Trubles of Scotland*, 2 vols, Edinburgh, 1850–1

Sprigge, Joshua, *Anglia Rediviva*, London, 1647

Symonds, Richard, *Diary of the Marches of the Royal Army*, edited by C.E. Long, Camden Society, 1859

Tibbutt, H.G. (ed.), *Letterbooks of Sir Samuel Luke*, London, 1963

Toynbee, Margaret (ed.), *Papers of Henry Stevens*, Oxfordshire Record Society, Vol. XLII, 1962

Tucker, Norman (ed.), *Military Memoirs: The Civil War: Memoirs of John Gwynn*, London, 1967

Turner, Sir James, *Memoirs*, edited by J.Thomson, Edinburgh, 1829

——, *Pallas Armata: Militarie Essayes of the Ancient Grecian, Roman and Modern Art of War*, London, 1683.

Vernon, John, *The Young Horseman*, London, 1644

Walker, Sir Edward, *Historical Discourses upon Several Occasions*, London, 1705

Warburton, Eliot, *Memoirs of Prince Rupert and the Cavaliers*, 3 vols, London, 1849

Ward, Robert, *Animadiversions of War*, London, 1635

Warwick, Sir Phillip, *Memoirs of the Reign of Charles I*, Edinburgh, 1825

Webb, J.W. and T.W., *Memorials of the Civil War . . . as it affected Herefordshire and Adjacent Counties*, 2 vols, London, 1879

——, (eds), *Military Memoirs of Colonel John Birch*, Camden Society, NS, Vol. VII, 1873

Whitelocke, Bulstrode, *Memorials of English Affairs*, London, 1682.

Willis-Bund, J.W. (ed.), *Diaries of Henry Townshend of Elmley Lovett, 1640–1663*, 3 vols, Worcestershire Historical Society, 1915–20

Wishart, George, *Memoirs of James Graham, Marquis of Montrose 1639–50*, translated by Revd G. Murdoch, London, 1893

Young, Peter (ed.), 'Sir John Byron's Relation of the Last Western Action between the Lord Wilmot and Sir William Waller', in *Journal of the Society for Army Historical Research*, Vol. XXXI, 1953

Secondary Sources

Abrahams, Andrew, *The Battle of Montgomery, 1644*, Bristol, 1994

Adair, John, *Roundhead General*, 2nd edn, Stroud, 1997

Appleby, David, *Our Fall Our Fame: the Life and Times of Sir Charles Lucas*, Newtown, 1995

Atkin, Malcolm, *The Civil War in Worcestershire*, Stroud, 1995

Barratt, John, 'The Battle for Oswestry', in *English Civil War Times*, No. 53, nd

——, *The Battle of Langport, 1645*, Bristol, 1995

——, *The Battle of Rowton Heath, 1645*, Bristol, 1995

——, 'Lord Byron's Foot', in *English Civil War Notes and Queries*, No. 18

——, *Cannon on the Mersey*, Birkenhead, 1996

——, *Civil War Stronghold: Beeston Castle at War, 1642–45*, Birkenhead, 1995

——, *For Chester and King Charles: Francis Gamull's Regiment and the Defence of Chester 1643–46*, Birkenhead, 1995

——, *For Duty Alone: Hopton's Account of the Last Campaign in the West*, Birkenhead, 1995

——, *A Happy Victory: the Siege and Battle of Nantwich, 1644*, Birkenhead, 1996

——, 'King Charles' Forgotten Army', in *Military Illustrated*, No. 110, July 1997

——, 'The King's Lifeguard of Foot', in *Military Illustrated*, No. 54, November 1992

——, *The Last Blow in the Business: Royalist Strategy in the Naseby Campaign*, Southend-on-Sea, 1995

——, *The Siege of Liverpool and Prince Rupert's Campaign in Lancashire, 1644*, Bristol, 1994

——, 'What Sandford's Firelocks Did Next', in *English Civil War Notes and Queries*, No. 50

Blackmore, David, *Arms and Armour of the English Civil Wars*, London, 1990

Binns, Jack, *'A Place of Great Importance': Scarborough in the Civil War*, Preston, 1996

Brezezinski, Richard, and Hook, Richard, *The Army of Gustavus Adolphus: Cavalry*, London, 1993

——, *The Army of Gustavus Adolphus: Infantry*, London, 1991

Buchan, John, *Montrose*, London, 1928

Bull, Stephen, and Seed, Mike, *Preston, Bloody Preston*, Preston, 1998

Burne, A.H. and Young, Peter, *The Great Civil War: a Military History*, London, 1959

Carlton, Charles E., *Going to the Wars: the Experience of the British Civil Wars 1638–1651*, London, 1994

Childs, John, *The Army of Charles II*, London, 1976

Chippendale, Neil, *Brentford 1642*, Southend-on-Sea, 1992

Clayton, Howard, *Loyal and Ancient City*, Lichfield, nd

Coate, Mary, *Cornwall in the Great Civil War and Interregnum*, Oxford, 1933

——, 'The Duchy of Cornwall: its History and Administration 1640–60', in *Transactions of the Royal Historical Society*, 4th series, Vol. 10, 1927

Conrad, Sir Thomas, *Richard Wiseman*, London, 1891

Cooke, Dave, *The Forgotten Battle*, Heckmondwyke, 1996

Cowan, E.J., *Montrose: For Covenant and King*, London, 1977

Darman, Pete, 'Prince Rupert and the "Swordsmen" ', in *English Civil War Notes and Queries*, Nos 31 and 32

Davis, Andy, 'The Action at Gainsborough', in *English Civil War Times*, No. 51

Dodd, A.H., *Studies in Stuart Wales*, Cardiff, 1971

Donagan, B., 'Atrocity, War Crime and Treason in the English Civil War', in *American Historical Review*, 1994, p. 1,146

Dore, R.N., 'The Sea Approaches: the Importance of the Dee and the

Mersey in the Civil War in the North-West', in *Transactions of the Historic Society of Lancashire and Cheshire*, Vol. 138, 1986

Eddishaw, David, *Civil War in Oxfordshire*, Stroud and Oxford, 1995

Edgar, F.T.R., *Sir Ralph Hopton: The King's Man in the West, 1642–52*, Oxford, 1968

Eliot-Wright, Philipp, *The English Civil War*, London, 1997

——, 'Firelock Forces', in *Military Illustrated*, No. 75, August 1994

——, 'The Royalist Firelocks', in *English Civil War Notes and Queries*, Nos 49 and 50

Engberg, J., 'Royalist Finances during the English Civil War 1642–1646', in *Scandinavian Ecomomic History Review* 19, 1966

English Civil War Notes and Queries (from No. 51 retitled *English Civil War Times*), various issues

Firth, C.H., *Cromwell's Army*, 4th edn, London, 1962

——, 'Royalist and Cromwellian Armies in Flanders', in *Transactions of the Royal Historical Society*, 1902

Fissel, Mark Charles, *The Bishops' Wars: Charles I's Campaigns against Scotland, 1638–40*, Cambridge, 1994

Foard, Glenn, *Naseby: the Decisive Campaign*, Whitstable, 1995

Fortescue, J.W., *History of the British Army*, 13 vols, London, 1910–13

Fox, George, *Three Sieges of Pontefract*, Leeds, 1887

Fraser, Antonia, *The Weaker Vessel: Woman's Lot in Seventeenth-Century England*, London, 1984

Furgol, Edward M., *A Regimental History of the Covenanting Armies, 1639–51*, Edinburgh, 1990

Gardiner, S.R. *History of the Great Civil War*, 4 vols, London, 1886

Gaunt, Peter, *A Nation under Siege: Wales in the Civil War*, London, 1991

Godwin, G.N., *The Civil War in Hampshire*, London, 1904

Gough, Richard, *The History of Myddle*, London, 1981

Holmes, Clive, *The Eastern Association in the English Civil War*, London, 1974

Hutton, Ronald, *The Royalist War Effort*, London, 1981

——, 'The Structure of the Royalist Party, 1642–46', in *Historical Journal* 24, 1981

Hyett, F.A., 'The Last Battle of the First Civil War', in *Transactions of the Bristol and Gloucestershire Archeological Society*, 1898

Johnson, A.M., 'Politics in Chester during the Civil War and Interregnum, 1642–1662', in P. Clark and P. Slack (eds), *Crisis and Order in English Towns, 1500–1700*, London, 1972

Kennett, Annette (ed.), *Loyal Chester*, Chester, 1984

Kenyon, John and Ohlmeyer, Jane (eds), *The Civil Wars*, Oxford, 1998

Kitson, Frank, *Prince Rupert: Portrait of a Soldier*, London, 1994

Lindley, Keith, 'Impact of the 1641 Rebellion upon England and Wales, 1641–45', in *Irish Historical Studies*, Vol. XVIII, 1972

Lowe, John, 'The Campaign of the Irish-Royalist Army in Cheshire, November 1643–January 1644', in *Transactions of the Historic Society of Lancashire and Cheshire*, Vol. 111, 1959

Lynch, John, *For King and Parliament: Bristol and the Civil War*, Stroud, 1999

Malcolm, Joyce Lee, 'All the King's Men: the Impact of the Crown's Irish Soldiers in the English Civil War', in *Irish Historical Studies*, Vol. XXI, 1975

——, *Caesar's Due: Loyalty and King Charles, 1642–46*, London, 1983.

——, 'A King in Search of Soldiers: King Charles I in 1642', in *Historical Journal* 21, 1978

Miller, Amos C., *Sir Richard Grenville of the Civil War*, Chichester, 1979

Morrah, Patrick, *Prince Rupert of the Rhine*, London, 1976

Morris, R.H., and Lawson, P.H., *The Siege of Chester*, Chester, 1923

Napier, Mark, *Memorials of Montrose*, 2 vols, Edinburgh, 1848

Newman, Peter, *The Battle of Marston Moor*, London, 1981

——, *Biographical Dictionary of Royalist Officers in England and Wales, 1642–1660*, New York, 1981

——, *The Old Service: Royalist Regimental Colonels and the Civil War, 1642–46*, Manchester, 1993

——, 'The Royalist Armies in the North of England', PhD thesis, University of York, 1978

——, 'The Royalist Officer Corps, 1642–46: army command as a reflection of the social structure', in *Historical Journal* 26, 1983

——, 'The 1663 list of indigent Royalist Officers considered as a primary source for the study of the Royalist Army', in *Historical Journal* 30, 1987

Ohlmeyer, Jane, *Civil War and Restoration in the Three Stuart Kingdoms: the Career of Randal MacDonnell, earl of Antrim*, Cambridge, 1993

Parker, Geoffrey (ed.), *The Thirty Years' War*, 2nd edn, London, 1997

Peachey, Stuart, *The Battle of Modbury, 1643*, Bristol, 1993

——, *The Battle of Powick Bridge, 1642*, Bristol, 1994

——, and Prince, Les, *ECW Flags and Colours: English Foot*, Southend-on-Sea, 1991

——, and Turton, Alan, *The Chief Strength of the Army*, Southend-on-Sea, 1991

——, *The Fall of the West*, 5 vols, Bristol, 1992

——, *Old Robin's Foot*, Southend-on-Sea, 1987

Phillips, John Rowland, *Memoirs of the Civil War in Wales and the Marches*, 2 vols, London, 1874

Pilkington, Colin, *To Play the Man*, Preston, 1991

Plowden, Alison, *Women All On Fire: the Women of the English Civil War*, Stroud, 1998

Porter, Stephen, *Destruction in the English Civil Wars*, Stroud, 1994

Reckitt, Basil, *Charles I and Hull*, London, 1951

Reid, Stuart, *All the King's Armies: a Military History of the English Civil War 1642–1651*, Staplehurst, 1998

——, *Campaigns of Montrose*, Edinburgh, 1993

——, *Gunpowder Triumphant*, 2nd edn, Southend-on-Sea, 1989

——, *Officers and Regiments of the Royalist Army*, Southend-on-Sea, nd

——, *Scots Armies of the 17th Century: 1. The Army of the Covenant*, Southend-on-sea, 1988

——, *Scots Armies of the 17th Century: 3. The Royalist Armies, 1639–45*, Southend-on-Sea, 1989

Ridsdell-Smith, *Geoffrey, Leaders of the Civil Wars*, Kineton, 1967

Roberts, Keith, 'Battle Plans', *in English Civil War Times*, No. 51

——, *Soldiers of the English Civil War: 1. Infantry*, London, 1986

Roy, Ian, 'England Turned Germany? The Aftermath of the Civil War in its European Context', in *Transactions of the Royal Historical Society*, 4th series, 1978

——, 'The Royalist Army in the First Civil War', MA thesis, University of Oxford, 1963

——, 'The Royalist Council of War, 1642–46', in *Bulletin of the Institute of Historical Research* 35, 1962

Ryder, Ian, *An English Army for Ireland*, Southend-on-Sea, 1987

Sherwood, Roy E., *Civil Strife in the Midlands*, Chichester, 1974

Stevenson, David, *Alaistair McColla and the Highland Problem in the 17th Century*, Edinburgh, 1980

——, *Revolution and Counter Revolution in Scotland, 1644–51*, London, 1977

Stoyle, Mark, 'Last Refuge of a Scoundrel: Sir Richard Grenville and Cornish Particularism', in *Historical Research* 71, No. 144, 1998

——, 'Sir Richard Grenville's Creatures: the New Cornish Tertia, 1644–46', in *Cornish Studies* 4, 1996

Stucley, John, *Sir Bevill Grenvile and his Times*, Chichester, 1983

Tincey, John, *Soldiers of the English Civil War: 2. Cavalry*, London, 1990

Toynbee, Margaret, and Young, Peter, *Cropredy Bridge, 1644*, Kineton, 1970

——, *Strangers in Oxford*, Chichester, 1973

Tucker, Norman, *Denbighshire Officers of the Civil War*, Colwyn Bay, nd

——, *North Wales in the Civil War*, Colwyn Bay, 1957

——, *Royalist Officers of North Wales*, Denbigh, 1961

Underdown, David, *Revel, Riot and Rebellion*, Oxford, 1985

——, *Royalist Conspiracy in England, 1649–1660*, New Haven, 1960

Varley, Frederick John, *The Siege of Oxford*, London, 1932

Wanklyn, M.D.G., 'Royalist Strategy in Southern England', in *Southern History*, V, 1985,
pp. 45–64

——, and Young, Peter, 'A King in Search of Soldiers: a Rejoinder', in *Historical Journal* 24, 1981

Ward, Simon, *Excavations at Chester: the Civil War Siegeworks, 1642–46*, Chester, 1987

Wedgwood, C.V., *The King's Peace*, London, 1955

——, *The King's War*, London, 1958

——, *Montrose*, London, 1952

Wemyss, Peter F., *My Firelocks Use Not to Parley*, Newtown, 1995

——, 'The Shropshire Dragoons', in *Intelligencer*, Vol. 1, No. 1, August 1993

Williams, Glanmor, *Renewal and Reformation in Wales*, Oxford, 1987

Williams, Ronald, *Montrose: Cavalier in Mourning*, London, 1975

Willis-Bund, J.W., *Civil War in Worcestershire*, Worcester, 1905

Young, Peter, *Edgehill, 1642*, Kineton, 1967

——, *Marston Moor, 1644*, Kineton, 1970

——, (ed.), *Military Memoirs: the Civil War*, London, 1967

——, *Naseby, 1645*, London, 1985

——, 'The Northern Horse at Naseby', in *Journal of the Society for Army Historical Research*,
Vol. XIV, 1964

——, 'The Royalist Army at the Relief of Newark', in *Journal of the Society for Army Historical Research*, Vol. XXX, 1952

——, and Embleton, Wilf, *The Cavalier Army*, London, 1974

——, and Holmes, Richard, *The English Civil War: A Military History of the Three Civil Wars 1642–1651*, London, 1974

INDEX